**Portrait of Oliver Cromwell, attributed to Robert Walker**
(copyright The Cromwell Museum, Huntingdon)

*Related titles from Palgrave Macmillan*

John Adamson (ed.), *The English Civil War: Politics, Religion and Conflict, 1640–49*

# Oliver Cromwell

## New Perspectives

*Edited by*

PATRICK LITTLE

First published 2009 by
PALGRAVE MACMILLAN

Palgrave Macmillan in the UK is an imprint of Macmillan Publishers Limited,
registered in England, company number 785998, of Houndmills, Basingstoke,
Hampshire RG21 6XS.

Palgrave Macmillan in the US is a division of St Martin's Press LLC,
175 Fifth Avenue, New York, NY 10010.

Palgrave Macmillan is the global academic imprint of the above companies
and has companies and representatives throughout the world.

Palgrave® and Macmillan® are registered trademarks in the United States,
the United Kingdom, Europe and other countries.

ISBN 978-0-230-57420-5 hardback

ISBN 978-0-230-57421-2      ISBN 978-1-137-01885-4 (eBook)
DOI 10.1007/978-1-137-01885-4

This book is printed on paper suitable for recycling and made from fully
managed and sustained forest sources. Logging, pulping and manufacturing
processes are expected to conform to the environmental regulations of the
country of origin.

A catalogue record for this book is available from the British Library.

Library of Congress Cataloging-in-Publication Data
Oliver Cromwell : new perspectives / edited by Patrick Little.
    p.   cm.
Includes bibliographical references and index.
ISBN 978-0-230-57420-5 (alk. paper) —
ISBN 978-0-230-57421-2 (pbk. : alk. paper)
1. Cromwell, Oliver, 1599–1658.  2. Great Britain—History—Puritan
Revolution, 1642–1660.  3. Great Britain—History—Commonwealth
and Protectorate, 1649–1660.  4. Great Britain—Politics and
government—1642–1660.  5. Great Britain—History—Puritan Revolution,
1642–1660—Historiography.  I. Little, Patrick, 1969–
DA428.1.O45 2009
941.06′4092—dc22
   [B]                                                    2008038419

10  9  8  7  6  5  4  3  2  1
18  17  16  15  14  13  12  11  10  09

# Contents

# List of Illustrations

# List of Maps

# Notes on Contributors

**Philip Baker** is a Senior Research Officer at the Centre of Metropolitan History, University of London. He is the author of a number of articles on army–civilian relations in the 1640s, the editor of *The Levellers: The Putney Debates* (2007) and the co-editor of a forthcoming collection of essays on the *Agreements of the people*.

**Andrew Barclay** is a Senior Research Fellow with the 1640–1660 Section of the History of Parliament Trust. His work on Cromwell's court combines his two principal research interests, namely the British courts of the latter half of the seventeenth century and the life of Oliver Cromwell. His study of Cromwell's career in the late 1630s and early 1640s, *Oliver Cromwell: The Unknown Politician*, is forthcoming.

**Lloyd Bowen** is Lecturer in Early Modern and Welsh History at Cardiff University. He has published a number of articles on early modern Wales, a monograph, *The Politics of the Principality: Wales c.1603–42* (2007), and an edition of household accounts, *Family and Society in Early Stuart Glamorgan* (2006). He is currently working on popular royalism in the civil wars, with an essay on royalist sedition in the Interregnum to be published shortly.

**Simon Healy** is a Senior Research Fellow in the 1604–1629 Section of the History of Parliament. His publications include an edition of early Jacobean parliamentary diaries, and articles on recusancy and war finance. He is also completing a PhD thesis on 'State Formation and the Political Nation in Early Stuart England' at Birkbeck College, University of London.

**Patrick Little** is a Senior Research Fellow in the 1640–1660 Section of the History of Parliament. His recent books include an edited collection, *The Cromwellian Protectorate* (Woodbridge, 2007) and (with David L. Smith) a monograph, *Parliaments and Politics during the Cromwellian Protectorate* (Cambridge, 2007).

**Kirsteen MacKenzie** has recently been awarded a PhD by the University of Aberdeen, for a thesis entitled 'Presbyterian Church

Government and the "Covenanted Interest" in the Three Kingdoms 1649–1660'. She has given numerous conference papers in the United Kingdom and Ireland and has been a member of the Cromwell Association for 15 years.

**Jason Peacey** is Lecturer in History at University College London. He is the editor of *The Regicides and the Execution of Charles I* (2001), co-editor of *Parliament at Work* (2002), editor of *The Print Culture of Parliament, 1600–1800* (2007), and author of *Politicians and Pamphleteers. Propaganda in the Civil Wars and Interregnum* (2004).

**Stephen K. Roberts** is editor of the House of Commons 1640–1660 Section at the History of Parliament Trust. He is joint editor of the journal *Midland History* and general editor of the Worcestershire Historical Society. He has published extensively on the political, social, administrative, and regional history of England and Wales, and has contributed over 35 articles to the *Oxford Dictionary of National Biography*.

**S. L. Sadler** was formerly a part-time Lecturer in History for Anglia Ruskin University, principally at Huntingdon Regional College. Dr Sadler has published articles on aspects of the civil war and Cambridgeshire, was a contributor for the *Oxford Dictionary of National Biography*, and most recently wrote '*Doddington and the First Civil War: The Impact of War in an East Anglian Parish, 1642–1646*' which will be published on the Cromwell Museum website (www.cambridgeshire. gov.uk/cromwell).

# Abbreviations

| | |
|---|---|
| *A&O* | C. H. Firth and R. S. Rait (eds), *The Acts and Ordinances of the Interregnum, 1642–1660* (3 vols., Oxford, 1911) |
| Abbott | W. C. Abbott (ed.), *The Writings and Speeches of Oliver Cromwell* (4 vols., Harvard, 1937–47). |
| Add. | Additional |
| BL | British Library, London |
| Bodl. | Bodleian Library, Oxford |
| *Burton Diary* | J. T. Rutt (ed.), *The Diary of Thomas Burton Esq* (4 vols., 1828) |
| *CCAM* | M. A. E. Green (ed.), *Calendar of the Proceedings of the Committee for the Advance of Money, 1642–56* (3 vols., 1888) |
| *CCC* | M. A. E. Green (ed.), *Calendar of the Proceedings of the Committee for Compounding, 1643–1660* (5 vols., 1889–92) |
| *CCSP* | O. Ogle, W. H. Bliss and F. J. Routledge (eds), *Calendar of Clarendon State Papers* (5 vols., Oxford, 1869–1932) |
| *CJ* | *Journal of the House of Commons* |
| Clarendon, *Rebellion* | Edward, Earl of Clarendon, *The History of the Rebellion and Civil Wars in England*, ed. W. D. Macray (6 vols., Oxford, 1888). |
| *Clarke Papers* | C. H. Firth and F. Henderson (eds), *The Clarke Papers* (5 vols., 1891, 1894, 1899, 1901, 2005) |
| Coward, *Cromwell* | Barry Coward, *Oliver Cromwell* (Harlow, 1991) |
| *CSPD* | *Calendar of State Papers, Domestic* |
| *CSPI* | *Calendar of State Papers, Ireland* |
| *CSPV* | *Calendar of State papers, Venetian* |
| CUL | Cambridge University Library |

| | |
|---|---|
| Davis, *Cromwell* | J. C. Davis, *Oliver Cromwell* (2001) |
| Eg. | Egerton (BL) |
| *EHR* | *English Historical Review* |
| Firth, *Cromwell* | C. H. Firth, *Oliver Cromwell and the Rule of the Puritans in England* (1900) |
| Gardiner, *Constitutional Documents* | S. R. Gardiner, *Constitutional Documents of the Puritan Revolution, 1625–1660* (3rd edn. Oxford, 1906) |
| Gaunt, *Cromwell* | Peter Gaunt, *Oliver Cromwell* (Oxford, 1996) |
| Harl. | Harleian (BL) |
| *HJ* | *Historical Journal* |
| *HMC* | *Historical Manuscripts Commission* |
| *LJ* | *Journal of the House of Lords* |
| Lomas-Carlyle | S. C. Lomas (ed.), *The Letters and Speeches of Oliver Cromwell, with Elucidations by Thomas Carlyle* (3 vols., 1904) |
| NAS | National Archives of Scotland |
| *Nicholas Papers* | G. F. Warner (ed.), *The Nicholas Papers* (4 vols., 1886, 1893, 1897, 1920). |
| NLS | National Library of Scotland |
| NLW | National Library of Wales |
| *ODNB* | *Oxford Dictionary of National Biography* |
| *Old DNB* | *Dictionary of National Biography* |
| *PJ* | W. H. Coates, Anne Steele Young and Vernon F. Snow (eds), *The Private Journals of the Long Parliament* (3 vols., Yale, 1982–92) |
| *Procs. LP* | Maija Jansson (ed.), *Proceedings in the Opening Session of the Long Parliament* (7 vols., Rochester NY, 2000–2007) |
| RO | Record Office |
| *TNA* | The National Archives of the United Kingdom, Kew |
| *TSP* | Thomas Birch (ed.), *A Collection of the State Papers of John Thurloe, Esq* (7 vols., 1742) |
| *Whitelocke Diary* | Ruth Spalding (ed.), *The Diary of Bulstrode Whitelocke, 1605–1675* (Oxford, 1990) |

Note:

Unless otherwise stated, all places of publication are London. Spelling has been modernised, and dates are old style, but with the year beginning on 1 January.

# Acknowledgements

This book is very much a collaborative effort. In the spring of 2007 the contributors met to outline their plans and discuss how the chapters might fit together to form a more-or-less coherent whole, and that discussion continued over dinner, and, over the following months, by telephone and email. Aside from fellow-contributors, a number of other academics have read and commented on one or more of the following chapters, notably Barry Coward, Robert Armstrong, Paul Seaward, Elliot Vernon, and Vivienne Larminie (who translated the French quotations in Chapter 9), and they all deserve thanks. Thanks are also due to the director and trustees of the History of Parliament Trust for permission to use its draft biographies in Chapters 2 and 8, the Cromwell Museum for permission to use the portrait of Oliver Cromwell attributed to Robert Walker, and Peter Furtado, editor of *History Today*, for allowing the re-use (in Chapter 9) of material that originally appeared as 'Offering the Crown to Cromwell' (*History Today*, 57 (2007)). Finally, I would like to thank Kate Haines and the team at Palgrave Macmillan for their help and advice in the preparation of this book.

# Introduction

Patrick Little

Another book on Oliver Cromwell—and especially one that claims to provide 'new perspectives'—perhaps requires a certain amount of justification. Famously, Dr Johnson abandoned his plan to write a 'Life of Oliver Cromwell... on discovering that all that can be told of him is already in print', and, more than two centuries on, it is easy to agree with him.[1] John Morrill, in his study of Cromwell in the *Oxford Dictionary of National Biography*, calculates that since the protector's death in 1658 'more than 160 full-length biographies have appeared, and more than 1000 separate publications bear his name'.[2] These works vary in quality and interpretation, of course, and it can be argued that each age has created its own image of Cromwell, from the Machiavellian villain of the Restoration and the non-conformist hero of the nineteenth century to the great dictator of the 1930s and 1940s and the betrayer of revolution of the 1970s.[3] The most recent interpretation, which emerged during the 1980s and continued into the early years of the twenty-first century, emphasises Cromwell's religious motivation as the key to understanding the man and his career. This can be traced back to the ground-breaking research of Blair Worden, seconded by the work of John Morrill and Colin Davis, who explored Cromwell's deeply held belief in God's providential intervention in the world, his intense engagement with the Bible, and the fundamental importance to him of 'liberty of conscience' among the Protestant sects.[4] Another strand of Cromwellian studies that developed at the same time originated with the work of Peter Gaunt on the protectorate, who argued that the council was a more important part of the protectoral regime than had previously been realised, and that Cromwell's hands were tied by the need to maintain collective responsibility.[5] Combined with the increased emphasis on Cromwell's religion, the result was to make the protector seem a somewhat other-worldly figure, semi-detached from power and

1

obsessed with the working of Providence. These two theories have proved useful to historians eager to attribute Cromwell's rise to something other than naked ambition. Furthermore, instead of overseeing a 'retreat from revolution' in the 1650s, Cromwell is seen as having retreated from the world, leaving the compromises and contradictions of the later period to be blamed on others.

The generally sympathetic biographies of the 1990s and early 2000s have been strongly influenced by both these ideas—although not all historians have accepted them uncritically—but the latest research on the protectorate has begun to question the validity of this approach.[6] For example, Blair Worden has questioned the strength of the council, arguing that Cromwell was very much in charge of the government in the 1650s, and that part of his political skill throughout his career was an ability to distance himself from unpopular or provocative decisions.[7] Cromwell's otherworldliness has also been challenged by new work on the protectoral court. Paul Hunneyball, in particular, has demonstrated that Cromwell was a driving force behind the increasing grandeur of the court, and that the quasi-regal tone was not something thrust upon him.[8] Such ideas undermine the accepted view of Cromwell as a distant, godly head of state, and they also have implications for our attitude to him during his earlier career. Another important development is the appearance in recent years of a number of scholarly biographies of those around Cromwell, including John Lambert, Henry Ireton, Sir Thomas Fairfax and Lord Broghill, as well as new research on Richard Cromwell.[9] There is no longer any excuse for seeing Cromwell in isolation, exaggerating his military or political abilities and playing up the uniqueness of his religious or ideological commitment. Together, these new developments suggest that the tectonic plates of Cromwellian studies are on the move once again; and it is within this context that this new volume should be read.

But why 'new perspectives'? The underlying problem with existing studies of Oliver Cromwell is their reliance on two collected editions: Thomas Carlyle's *Letters and Speeches of Oliver Cromwell* (as edited and updated by S. C. Lomas in the early twentieth century) and W. C. Abbott's *Writings and Speeches of Oliver Cromwell*, published in America in the 1930s and 1940s. The words of John Morrill, written apparently without irony, demonstrate the mesmeric effect of these collections:

> All the serious biographers have drawn on very similar bodies of evidence. And although the judgement of the vast majority of his peers is harsh in its

assessment of his honesty, integrity, and credibility, historians have opted to take him much more at his own valuation, finding in his words an openness and striving that usually appeals and just sometimes appals.[10]

In this volume, the contributors have been careful not to take Cromwell's word for it. Both collected editions are used extensively in what follows—it would be perverse to do otherwise—but none of the chapters *relies* on either. Instead of seeing the world through Cromwell's eyes, the aim is to balance his own account with the view from without. The new 'perspectives' thus include views of Cromwell from Scotland and Wales, East Anglia and the backbenches at Westminster; from those who were intimate with him, such as his Steward relations, the Levellers, the members of the protectoral household and individuals such as John Thurloe and Richard Cromwell; and from unusual angles, whether looking at his interaction with Ireland before 1649, his relations with the Levellers in the same period or the 'pre-history' of the kingship debates of 1657. Gaps in the coverage are inevitable, but it is hoped that the overall effect will be to present something different, against which Cromwell's own writings and speeches can be compared, and his career reconsidered. The remainder of this introduction will consider the chapters individually, and then see how, taken together, they might provide new insights into Cromwell's career and character.

## I

Cromwell's rise from East Anglian obscurity to political importance has always fascinated historians. John Morrill's influential article on the 'making of Oliver Cromwell' demonstrates what can be done—although, as it turns out, his article is far from being the last word on the subject. Equally, there has been much interest in Cromwell's activities in the early years of the Long Parliament. His involvement in the first civil war has also attracted attention, as the period witnessed a crucial stage of his 'rise', from provincial to national importance. The first three chapters of this book revisit the problem of Cromwell's rise to power, but approach it from very different viewpoints from those usually adopted by historians.

In the first chapter, Simon Healy concentrates on one aspect of Cromwell's early life that has puzzled scholars: the background to his inheritance of the Ely leases from his maternal uncle, Sir Thomas Steward, in 1636. These leases, worth perhaps £300 per annum,

secured Cromwell's position as a gentleman—a position that had been
in doubt since he had sold up his lands at Huntingdon and become a
farmer in St Ives in 1631—and his relative prosperity allowed him to
begin his political career as MP for Cambridge in 1640. Yet, as Healy
has discovered, the Steward inheritance may have been of more than
merely economic significance. Cromwell, impatient for the money
coming to him, tried to have his uncle declared a lunatic; and when
this ploy failed, the uncle retaliated by changing his will, saddling
Cromwell with the repayment of all his debts. On the uncle's death,
legal suits ensued, and it was only in October 1638 that Cromwell
finally enjoyed the income that he so badly needed. In the same
month he wrote the famous letter to his cousin, Mrs St John, pro-
claiming his assurance of salvation and his repentance of his past life.
Healy links the two events, arguing that the letter was 'a semi-public
*mea culpa*', acknowledging that Cromwell had committed 'a genuinely
damning sin, for which he faced public humiliation as a greedy charlatan; but nevertheless, God elected to save him from disgrace'. This
curious mixture of religion and money will become a common theme
in many of the chapters that follow. The other important point that
Healy makes is that Cromwell should not be studied in isolation.
Indeed, 'the key question to be asked about Cromwell's early life is,
what marked him out from his cohort'. Cromwell was hardly alone
in being the son of a younger son, acutely aware that his own children might slip from the charmed circle of the gentry altogether;
nor was he exceptional in being saved (financially, at least) by the
death of a wealthy relative. What is striking is Cromwell's behaviour,
which was far from ordinary. His sale of the Huntingdon lands in
1631 was eccentric indeed, and can only be explained by his hopes
of 'greater expectations elsewhere'; yet instead of playing his cards
carefully, Cromwell took a huge risk in trying to have Sir Thomas
Steward declared a lunatic; furthermore, having got hold of the Ely
leases, he did not keep them but, in October 1640, sold them back to
the cathedral authorities. In these early years, Cromwell was already
demonstrating 'a penchant for taking risks of a magnitude which
would have staggered most of his contemporaries'.

Stephen Roberts, in his examination of Cromwell's career as an
ordinary MP in the first two years of the Long Parliament, also com-
pares him with his contemporaries. There is a danger in any study
of Cromwell of singling him out from the mass of gentlemen and
MPs, emphasising his lowliness as a backbencher and backwoodsman,
while searching for signs of the greatness to come. In returning to the

bread and butter sources of the parliamentary historian—principally the *Journals* and the various diaries—Roberts takes a more measured and less anachronistic approach. Cromwell's activity in the Commons was often humdrum and unexceptional; like many other MPs he enjoyed 'a matrix of relations and other acquaintances in the House'; indeed, 'far from being an awkward loner . . . he was an animal that usually hunted with the pack'. Yet this picture of Cromwell as a team player, as a small cog in some 'opposition' machine, must be offset by a definite eccentricity in his approach. Cromwell is notable for his 'self-discipline in following things through', and 'once a topic had captured his attention, he was likely to stick with it'. This made him useful to outside petitioners and to the leaders in the Commons itself. His energy is also obvious—'seizing the initiative came naturally to Cromwell'—while his 'iconoclastic streak' and willingness to upset and provoke made him 'one to watch'. He leaped at new opportunities, especially after the recess in the autumn of 1641, when 'the deepening political crisis impelled him to decisive political activity'. Thus, although basically a team player, working not only with his East Anglian allies but also with other godly critics of the regime (notably Sir Robert Harley, Sir Henry Vane the younger and Denzil Holles), Cromwell can also be seen as a maverick in the House, whose apparent gaffes and blunders 'can be read as deliberate provocations of the staid, the complacent and smooth-mannered'. He was certainly no 'backbencher', being 'too busy, too controversial, too noticed by the diarists, too much in the thick of things'.

Cromwell may have spent 1640–1642 moving 'from being an outsider to being an insider' (in Roberts's words), but the radical streak that had characterised his behaviour in the 1630s clearly remained. In Chapter 3, Sue Sadler explores how that radicalism developed further, within the local, East Anglian, context, during the early years of the first civil war. In August 1642 Cromwell suddenly left the Commons and rushed back to Cambridge, where he raised a troop of horse and masterminded the interception of the college plate, which was being taken in convoys to the king's army at Nottingham. Thereafter he served with the earl of Essex at Edgehill, before returning to the fens to organise a desperate resistance against the royalists in the north, who might use the routes through from Lincolnshire to strike at the parliamentarian stronghold of East Anglia. This was the time of Cromwell's first military victories, at Crowland, Burghley House, Gainsborough and Winceby—the actions that brought him to public notice, and established him as a 'heroic and valiant' figure, a paladin of parliament. It was also the period that made him controversial as a religious radical and (in the eyes of his enemies at least) a social revolutionary, and which led to his bitter row with his commander, the earl of Manchester, in November 1644. Sadler's perspective is that of a regional historian, and she seeks to put Cromwell into his local context by evaluating the claims of an anonymous 'opponent' who supplied Manchester with information about Cromwell's misdeeds in the fens. This 'opponent' (who can be identified as another parliamentarian soldier, William Dodson) claimed that Cromwell 'gloried in his command and promoted religious factionalism', taking credit for the work of others and deliberately playing up his role in victories to his own advantage. An analysis of the 'opponent's' claims suggests that there was more than a grain of truth in them. There is little doubt that Cromwell became skilled at propaganda during this period, or that he was capable of putting a 'spin' on events, to his own advantage. His victories, moreover, were not always strategically important, and his advancement of Independents and other religious radicals was deeply divisive. His status as a hero was not so obvious to those who had to work with him in the fens around Ely.

## II

Cromwell's increasingly strong attachment to Independency is key to understanding why he became such a controversial figure by the autumn of 1644. This militant brand of religion, with its emphasis on individual conscience rather than rigid rules imposed by a ministerial hierarchy, appealed to Cromwell the outsider; and it is not difficult to see why the more conservative parliamentarians in East Anglia saw this as not only religiously heterodox but also socially subversive. Such views bound Cromwell to a particular section of the army, and with the reorganisation that led to the creation of the New Model Army in the spring of 1645, that section came to the fore. The victory at Naseby in June of that year, the successes that followed and the eventual defeat of the royalists in the spring of 1646, were taken as a sign of divine pleasure in the New Model, and by extension, in the Independents that now dominated it.[11] Chapter 4 looks at a related subject: Cromwell's relationship with the Levellers, that loose group of radicals, inside the army and out, which called for religious reform to go hand-in-hand with political and social change. As Philip Baker emphasises, Cromwell had much in common with the Leveller leaders—they were 'natural allies rather than mortal enemies'—and his personal connections with John Lilburne dated from the very beginning of the Long Parliament (a point dealt with in detail by Stephen Roberts in Chapter 2). It was Cromwell who secured Lilburne's commission in the Eastern Association army, and both men attacked the earl of Manchester in 1644. Lilburne refused to join the New Model (as he would not take the Covenant) and his relationship with Cromwell declined thereafter; but other Levellers, notably William Walwyn, remained on intimate terms with Cromwell at least until the summer of 1647. There are, in fact, good reasons for seeing the Putney debates in October 1647 as a forum for discussion between groups that agreed on broad principles, and disagreed only on details. In later months Cromwell and his son-in-law, Henry Ireton, did not oppose the Levellers on principle but for political reasons, especially when it became clear that their former allies were fomenting mutiny in the army. This is an important point, and one that fits well with the earlier chapters. From the Leveller perspective Cromwell remained a radical, even as his methods became more reactionary, and his refusal to compromise ever more pronounced.

**III**

The relationship of Cromwell and the Levellers is of course but one strand of the complicated history of the later 1640s. The period saw the rise of the New Model as a political force; the great rift between the political Independents and Presbyterians at Westminster in 1647; the repeated attempts to negotiate with the king; the signing of the Engagement with the Scots; the second civil war and the purge of the Commons, led by Colonel Pride, in December 1648; the trial and execution of the king in January 1649: all have been studied and restudied in the last 30 years, and Cromwell's part in them is well known.[12] Less obvious is the role of Ireland and Scotland and Wales in shaping Cromwell's reaction to these events; and the next three chapters deal with this period as well as looking forward to the very different political landscape of the 1650s.

Chapter 5 examines the 'pre-history' of the Cromwellian invasion of Ireland in 1649 by reviewing Cromwell's sometimes complex relationship with the island in earlier years. In doing so, it challenges the idea that when he arrived in Dublin in August 1649 Cromwell was ignorant of Irish affairs and guided merely by religious bigotry and hatred of Catholicism. In fact, Cromwell was very knowledgeable, at least about earlier English attempts to address the Irish question, as he had been involved in plans to send expeditionary forces in 1642, 1645–1646, 1647 and 1648. When he went to Ireland as lord lieutenant in the summer of 1649 he was guided by these earlier experiences, both in planning his strategy and in relying on Irish Protestants as advisers and agents. Underlying this was Cromwell's investment in Ireland, which was both financial and religious in nature. Despite his precarious financial position, he had put a significant amount of his money into the Irish 'adventure' scheme in 1642, and he also looked to Ireland to provide him with a continuing military command—and salary—as the first civil war came to an end. Yet Cromwell's commitment went beyond that of a speculator. In 1642 his investment was 'a huge gamble' for a man in his unsettled financial position, and in 1646 and again in 1648 his promises to give up much-needed monetary awards to fund Irish expeditions were reckless by any standard. From Cromwell's point of view, however, these offers may have been intended 'as a sign of his selfless commitment to the cause and his trust in Providence', and also as a way of 'putting his financial survival into the hands of God'. There was nothing inherently hypocritical about this mixing of money and religion, as it was generally believed that God's favour would lead to success in the world as well as entry to the next. Certainly a belief in Providence was central to Cromwell's overriding ambition to reconquer Ireland, but it was not something that he first experienced in 1649. As his military ideas and understanding of the political situation matured, so did his religious conviction that 'God had brought him to Ireland, after humbling him by eight years of false-starts and missed opportunities'. It is this hard-won certainty that provides the background for Cromwell's terrible single-mindedness at the siege of Drogheda in the autumn of 1649.

Cromwell's relationship with Ireland was straightforward compared with his tense, complicated interaction with Scotland. The Scots had been allies of the godly in England in the early 1640s, and it was hoped that they might become so again, despite their refusal to accept what Cromwell and his friends knew to be right. Cromwell's military interventions in Scotland, in 1648 and 1650–1651, were not conducted with anger but with sorrow; instead of the zeal with which he faced the invasion of Ireland, Cromwell looked for allies among the Scots. He debated with them, pleaded with them to compromise, begged them to 'think it possible you may be mistaken'.[13] Cromwell's frustration with the Scots is well known, but Kirsteen MacKenzie, in

Chapter 6, considers the other side of the equation: the reaction of the Scottish covenanters to the rise to power of Cromwell. Tensions were apparent even before the Solemn League and Covenant, uniting the two nations in a religious and civil bond, was signed in September 1643, and Cromwell's record of cooperation with Scottish commanders during the first civil war was not a good one. The victory at Marston Moor in July 1644 was considered by Cromwell to be 'God's victory' and he believed that he himself was the 'instrument' of that victory; but the Scots had good reasons for seeing it as a joint effort—a victory of the 'covenanting interest'. Cromwell's attack on the Presbyterian earl of Manchester and the exclusion of Scots from the New Model Army confirmed opinions that Cromwell was an 'enemy of the Covenant'. Between 1648 and 1651 Scottish views of Cromwell changed as the political situation changed. His defeat of the 'engagers', the royalist supporters of the duke of Hamilton, was celebrated by the kirk faction, which saw Cromwell as a tool of Providence; but the execution of Charles I again turned the Scots against Cromwell. From then on his role was a negative one, as a 'severe instrument of punishment for all their sins'—most notably at Dunbar in September 1650. In this the covenanters were almost in agreement with Cromwell himself. The victory was a sign of God's judgement. For Cromwell it showed that he was right; for the Scots, God had ruled against them. The religious language used by both sides was strangely similar, and this serves to underline the parallels between them, and the oddity of their relationship. The foundation of the protectorate in 1653, MacKenzie tells us, was neither celebrated by the Scots, nor resisted, and the regime received support only from a minority, as it was clear that 'military force, not covenanted authority, was the root of the protector's power in Scotland'.

Compared with Scotland and Ireland, Cromwell's relationship with Wales was deeply ambiguous. As Lloyd Bowen argues in Chapter 7, although there was no 'intense "special relationship" between Cromwell and the principality', bonds between the two were pronounced. Cromwell had been involved in religious reform in Wales in 1642 and returned to the cause in 1650, with the creation of the commission for the propagation of the gospel there; he acquired substantial estates in south Wales in the late 1640s; and he enjoyed Welsh ancestry (as Oliver Cromwell *alias* Williams) which 'remained significant throughout his life', reappearing in the iconography of the 1650s, and encouraging supplicants to emphasise that they too were Welshmen. There was a personal element in Cromwell's involvement in Wales that was different from his zealous attitude towards Ireland or his coldness with the Scottish covenanters; but, Bowen warns us, this connection between Cromwell and Wales should not be pushed too far. There are parallels between Wales and Ireland that might be teased out, especially as both involved the unstable mixture of religion and money. When it came to Ireland, Cromwell made apparently rash investments to demonstrate his commitment to the cause, and in later years his lands in south Wales became 'a base from which earlier impulses of puritanism could be sustained'. Just as he had come to value the opinion of a tight circle of Irish Protestants, so Cromwell sought advice on Welsh policy from a small group of godly Welshmen, notably Philip Jones and Walter Cradock. Having said that, it is clear that Cromwell considered that the Welsh were ultimately redeemable, and in this they were perhaps closer in his eyes to the Catholic Irish. As Bowen says, the Welsh were not irreconcilable to the Cromwellian regime, but were rather seen as 'wayward brethren to be brought back into the fold', despite their lingering royalist sympathies. Like the Scots, however, they were not willing to meet Cromwell half-way, and his reliance on a small clique of the godly hampered attempts to broaden support as the 1650s continued. In this, the experience of Wales can also be seen as running in parallel to that of the English localities, governed by the notorious major-generals. Any attempt to suggest that Ireland, Scotland, Wales and the English regions shared a common experience during the Cromwellian protectorate would be decidedly premature. But the general failure of the regime to win 'hearts and minds' across all four nations leads us back to a suitably Cromwellian paradox: that in his 'golden years',[14] as lord protector of England and Wales, Scotland and Ireland (1653–1658), he did not once leave London and its immediate surroundings.[15]

## IV

The protectorate has only recently experienced a resurgence of interest after many years as the poor relation of Cromwellian studies (and, for that matter, of the civil war and interregnum era as a whole).[16] Instead of simplistic portrayals of the protectorate as the retreat from revolution, the forerunner of the Restoration, or as a period of conservative military rule, historians have now begun to cast their nets more widely. A recent collection of essays included such varied fare as a study of civic culture in towns, the response to the regime from the literati in Wales and the role of art and architecture in fashioning the Cromwellian court.[17] The complexities of politics under the protectorate, and the difficulties faced by Cromwell in dealing with his parliaments, have also received their first comprehensive analysis in recent years.[18] The final three chapters in the present book take this new interest in the protectorate one stage further.

Andrew Barclay's chapter explores rather different aspects of Cromwell's court than those discussed elsewhere: not its outward show but its internal structures and procedures as a department of state; and the personal connection between the protector and his household servants. In fact, the two protectoral palaces at Whitehall and Hampton Court were used in a very similar way as under the monarchy, and, as Barclay puts it, 'the echo of the more traditional royal structure can only have been deliberate'. There were also close parallels between the personnel of the Cromwellian court and the former royal establishment. When these household officials are examined in detail, they prove to be a mixture of extended family and recent clients, with a smattering of more important politicians. Two groups are notable for their absence: those with a local connection with Cromwell before 1645 and the army officers who had been so close to him during the civil wars and remained among the most powerful men on the council. The exclusion of the latter group is most striking, as is the conclusion that 'the protectoral household was overwhelmingly staffed by civilians'—and there is even the likelihood that this was a deliberate policy as Cromwell 'may have hoped to use his court appointments to distance himself from the army'.

My own chapter on the prehistory of the offer of the crown to Cromwell also explores his apparent tensions with the army, through his relationship with another valued servant, the secretary of state (and head of intelligence), John Thurloe. Thurloe was behind a concerted attempt to prepare the ground for kingship in the early months of 1657, using as a pretext the failed plot to kill the protector, led by Miles Sindercombe. Thurloe's tactic was to use his control of foreign intelligence and the domestic newsbooks to create a climate of unrest, warning MPs that the government needed to be put on a more settled, civilian footing, while heightening fears among the military that a foreign invasion was imminent in order to head off any potential rebellion against the planned changes at the centre. It is suggested that Thurloe was thereby 'mounting an elaborate confidence trick with the army as the main target', and in this he was apparently aided and abetted by Cromwell himself. Overall, the fact that 'historians agree that Thurloe and Cromwell acted as one' in other matters reinforces the suspicion that the protector was happy to dupe the army into obedience, and that he initially sought the crown—despite his famous rejection of it a few weeks later.

In the final chapter, Jason Peacey continues his systematic revision of our understanding of the career of Oliver's son and successor, Richard Cromwell, by looking at the relationship between the two men.[19] There was nothing strange about Richard's undistinguished early career: he was at first merely the younger son of a minor gentleman turned soldier, and only after the death of his two elder brothers and his father's rise to prominence in the later 1640s was he brought out from the shadows. It was only when Oliver was made protector in 1653 that Richard assumed a more public role, and not until 1657 that he became a national figure. According to this thesis, Oliver's 'plans for his son changed in entirely logical and understandable ways during this period' and in the end he was 'perfectly happy to prepare Richard for life on the highest stage'. It was the move to make the protectorate hereditary—an ambition that ran in parallel with the possibility of Oliver taking the crown—that made the big difference as the 1650s wore on, and Peacey identifies a 'fairly clear correlation between the growing willingness to make the protectorate hereditary and the more or less conscious enhancement of his [Richard's] status'.

The chapters on the protectorate dovetail together. Larger themes can easily be identified. First, these chapters reinforce the idea that Cromwell was the dominant force in his own government. He chose his own court officials and household servants, apparently keeping the army officers at arm's length; he seems to have encouraged Thurloe to push for the initial offer of the crown in February 1657; and he was actively grooming his son, Richard, to succeed him. These elements fit neatly with the current historiographical trend to reinstate Cromwell at the very centre of the protectorate, whether in council or through the grandeur of the court. The second theme that emerges is the increasing importance of the civilian interest as a serious rival to the army. This was a central argument in the recent book on the protectoral parliaments, and it reappears, and is endorsed, here. The civilians had unrivalled access to the protector through the court, and their cause was championed by both John Thurloe and Richard Cromwell. What is new here is the close identification of Oliver Cromwell himself with this particular faction. This is only half the story, however. Cromwell's cultivation of civilians had its limits. He rejected the crown in the end, when he realised that the risk of incurring God's wrath outweighed the advantages of a return to the 'ancient constitution', and in doing so he not only upset the 'kinglings' but also mystified them. Thurloe was left in limbo as his 'confidence, so obvious in March [1657] suddenly evaporated in April'. Thereafter there were other signs that the civilians could not rely on Cromwell's unequivocal support. The council remained the stronghold of the army, and only John Lambert was sacked—leaving such powerful figures as Charles Fleetwood and John Disbrowe still in office. The new upper chamber of parliament, the 'Other House' personally appointed by Cromwell in the last days of 1657, had a strong military flavour. Far from giving the civilians *carte blanche*, it could be argued that Cromwell was intent on creating a balance of interests, which would ensure that he (and his successors) would continue to exercise the ultimate authority in the three nations.

## V

The ten chapters of this book provide a more or less chronological account of Oliver Cromwell's career, from the obscurity of the 1630s to his death, as head of state, in 1658. Certain overarching themes can be traced through many of the chapters, and as these provide interesting insights into Cromwell's character as well as his career, they are worth further discussion. The first concerns money. As Stephen Roberts has pointed out elsewhere, 'it is interesting that little work seems to have been done on his personal finances', and there is more than a suspicion that biographers have deliberately avoided this 'mundane, not to say grubby, topic'.[20] Here the question of Cromwell's finances resurfaces with surprising regularity: his greediness over the Steward inheritance; the way in which his involvement in Ireland was complicated by his concern to secure his investments and his military salary; the impact of the large land grants in south Wales on his relations with that country; and his particular closeness to (in Andrew Barclay's words) 'those who had... been looking after his money' during the protectorate. It would be wrong to extrapolate from this that Cromwell was entirely venal and self-serving, however. In three of the four cases listed, Cromwell's financial motives are less than straightforward. In the 1630s Healy is surely right to emphasise that Cromwell's financial crisis was thoroughly mixed up with his religious conversion. Giving way to greed had brought him to the lowest of moral ebbs, and yet even the 'chief of sinners' had found mercy at the hand of God. Cromwell's subsequent decision to sell up the Ely leases may have had a religious and political angle, and this can also be seen in his reinvestment of much of the money into extremely unwise, yet religiously unimpeachable, schemes such as the Irish adventure. Indeed, Cromwell's willingness to offer up his newly secured land grants and much-needed arrears payments in 1646 and 1648 appears to have been motivated by a desire to show commitment to the cause and his unlimited trust in Providence. Equally, Cromwell's Welsh lands were treated not so much as a source of income or of worldly pride (he rarely visited them), but as a resource for the godly, as a base from which to establish radical religion in the land of his fathers. It might almost be said that for Cromwell money was not an end in itself: more often than not it was a tool for the advancement of godly reformation. To dismiss the topic as 'mundane' or 'grubby' is to miss a very revealing area of Cromwell's character, and one that 'earths' his godliness in the real world.

Another, connected, theme is the sheer radicalism of Cromwell compared with many of his contemporaries, not only in his attitude to religion (which is invariably emphasised by modern biographers) but also his willingness to take risks. In his early career, this is most obvious in his astonishing decision to try to have the (evidently perfectly sane) Sir Thomas Steward declared a lunatic, but the sale of the Huntingdon lands in 1631 and the Ely leases in 1640 were scarcely less momentous gambles. In the first years of the Long Parliament, Cromwell may have learned to hunt with the parliamentary pack, but one suspects that he was chiefly useful for his 'iconoclastic streak', and his willingness to take on difficult cases. His pre-emptive strike against the Cambridge colleges in the summer of 1642, before the civil war had started in earnest, was also a big risk, and although his impetuosity would pay dividends on the battlefield, his political attack on his commanding officer, the earl of Manchester, could easily have seen him cashiered, or worse. This 'all or nothing' approach can also be seen in his support for the self-denying ordinance in 1645—a move that should have ended his own military career as well as that of his factional enemies. Against this background, Phil Baker is surely right to see Cromwell as having much in common with the radical Levellers; and that he turned against them, rather than their ideas, in the autumn of 1647. In a different way, Cromwell's radicalism also emerges from the fanatical determination—and willingness to take personal and financial risks—with which he approached Ireland both before and after August 1649.

Cromwell's reckless radicalism links into another aspect of his personality that can be seen in almost all the chapters of this book: a restlessness which verged on rootlessness. Again, we should be aware of just how unusual Cromwell was in comparison with his contemporaries. The gentry defined themselves in terms of lineage and of land—family tombs, ancestral seats and patrimonial estates were as important to them as family trees and kinship ties.[21] Cromwell, by contrast, insisted on moving on. The uprooting of his family from the patrimonial lands in Huntingdon and the sale of the Ely leases long held by his mother's family were eccentric, as they disassociated him from areas with which he had strong historical links, and in later years he seemed intent on kicking over the traces altogether. During the 1640s Cromwell's commitment to Independency superseded any loyalty he may have had to his wider kinship group, or to East Anglia as a whole. Local Presbyterians such as the 'opponent'/William Dodson saw Cromwell not only as religiously and politically dangerous, but as a man who had turned his back on his roots, who no longer put the people of the fens before his own selfish ends. Cromwell's abrupt departure from East Anglia in 1644, to pursue a national agenda, merely confirmed this. Independency transcended locality as well as existing family or religious ties, and it was no coincidence that by the mid-1640s Cromwell had also dropped many of his closest political associates from the early months of the Long Parliament. His new radical friends were not to remain in favour for long, however. Cromwell's falling out of love with the Levellers began in 1645–1646, even if the process was not complete until the autumn of 1647. The years after the execution of the king saw Cromwell drop his republican allies one by one as his contempt for the Rump Parliament grew. Even the army—God's instrument in the wars of the 1640s—was not immune. By the mid-1650s Cromwell, by now lord protector, appears to have made a conscious effort to publicly distance himself from the army. His household was staffed by civilians not soldiers; his closest advisers were no longer senior officers; and it might be argued that by 1657 he had come to see the army as an obstacle, not only to 'healing and settling' but also to his own ambitions to be king. Yet in these final years, Cromwell's restlessness seems to have diminished. The footloose Cromwell was now settling himself and his family into the former royal palaces, carefully arranging for his son to succeed him, and rediscovering a Welsh genealogy that was more glorious—and more spurious—than anything East Anglia could offer. Was this the final re-invention? Had the 'restless Cromwell' finally come to rest?[22]

This brings us to the final point. When considering these themes—whether money, risk-taking or restlessness—it soon becomes apparent that they are much more obvious in Cromwell's life before 1653 than afterwards. Historians have tended to look for consistency across the career—not least, one suspects, because the speeches of the protectorate appear to be such rich sources for Cromwell's innermost thoughts—but that is not so obvious from the chapters in this book.[23] The three chapters on the protectorate could almost be describing a completely different person, as the restless, reckless radical gave way to the London-based, conservative head of state. This is perhaps the familiar story of the revolutionary-turned-ruler, as Peter Gaunt argues:

> As head of state, Cromwell did many things which seem to contradict his earlier calls for justice and liberty... To draw a modern parallel, it is always easier for an MP in opposition or on the back-benches to be idealistic and to retain pure principles; once in government, cold, harsh necessities often lead to messy compromise and unwelcome entanglements.[24]

It might be added that the evidence from this volume, alongside some of the most recent research, suggests that Cromwell actively welcomed the changes that came with his promotion with apparent alacrity, and that he enjoyed the trappings of power just a little too much. His exclusion of the army from the household or his efforts to keep them in check when kingship was proposed; his cultivation of the young and fashionable, the beautifying of his palaces; his estrangement from old friends such as the Independent divine, John Owen, and his embracement of less principled cronies such as Philip Jones and John Thurloe; above all his promotion of Richard as heir: these were not forced on him by others, or by his position as head of state, but were free choices of a man whose priorities seemed to have shifted.

There is plenty of ammunition here for those who see (or saw) Cromwell as the arch-dissembler, the godly fraud, guided by his over-vaulting ambition; or those who shake their heads at the sad truism that power corrupts. But whatever the contrasts between Cromwell's career before and after 1653, such harsh interpretations do not quite ring true. As we have seen, there is a strong case for seeing Cromwell's protectorate not as a conservative reaction, a 'selling out', but as a conscious attempt to balance elements within an unstable regime: the army and the civilians, the council and the court, the various religious groupings, the political factions and interest groups within parliament. In all this Cromwell comes across as an honest broker, not a megalomaniac, despite the claims of his enemies. John Morrill is surely right to compare Cromwell favourably with another successful potentate, Cardinal Wolsey:

> unlike Wolsey, that achievement was not vitiated by any of the greed or the agglomeration of wealth and pomp that Wolsey insatiably craved. What other self-made ruler with the world at his feet has ever taken less for himself and his family of what the world has to offer in goods and services?[25]

Cromwell's enjoyment of the fruits of success never tipped over into excess; his court was a far cry from the hedonistic debauchery of Charles II's reign. He may have moved away from the more radical elements of the army or the sectaries, but he did not (or could not?) cut the traces completely. He remained, at heart, the godly hero of the 1640s. To take but the most obvious example, it can be argued that Cromwell actively sought the crown, probably in the hope of securing legitimacy and longevity to his regime; but when challenged by the godly brethren and by his own conscience he drew back, refusing to repeat the sin of the biblical Achan and refusing to accept the crown he could so easily have taken. Contemporaries recognised that this was a true test of the man—that 'the contempt of a crown . . . can not proceed but from an extraordinary virtue'.[26] It is certainly apparent that, for all Cromwell's compromises and connivances as head of state, by the time of his death the corruption of power had not yet reached his core.

## Notes

1. Quoted in Gaunt, *Cromwell*, 7; see also Davis, *Cromwell*, 1.
2. *ODNB*, 'Oliver Cromwell'.
3. For a survey, see Davis, *Cromwell*, ch. 3.
4. B. Worden, 'Oliver Cromwell and the Sin of Achan', in D. Beales and G. Best (eds), *History, Society and the Churches* (Cambridge, 1985); B. Worden, 'Providence and Politics in Cromwellian England', *Past and Present*, 109 (1985); B. Worden, 'Toleration and the Cromwellian Protectorate', in W. Sheils (ed.), *Persecution and Toleration: Studies in Church History XXI* (Cambridge, 1984); Davis, *Cromwell*, ch. 6; Davis, 'Cromwell's Religion' in J. Morrill (ed.), *Oliver Cromwell and the*

*English Revolution* (Harlow, 1990); J. Morrill, 'Introduction', in his *Oliver Cromwell and the English Revolution*; *ODNB*, 'Oliver Cromwell'.

5. P. Gaunt, 'The Councils of the Protectorate, from December 1653 to September 1658' (University of Exeter PhD thesis, 1983); P. Gaunt, ' "The Single Person's Confidants and Dependants"? Oliver Cromwell and his Protectoral Councillors', *HJ*, 32 (1989); see also Gaunt, *Cromwell*, ch. 6.

6. For good recent biographies, see those by Barry Coward, Colin Davis and Peter Gaunt (all entitled *Oliver Cromwell*), and also John Morrill's shorter study in *ODNB*, now republished as a separate volume (Oxford, 2007).

7. B. Worden, 'Oliver Cromwell and the Council', in P. Little (ed.), *The Cromwellian Protectorate* (Woodbridge, 2007).

8. P. Hunneyball, 'Cromwellian Style: The Architectural Trappings of the Protectorate Regime', in P. Little (ed.), *Cromwellian Protectorate*; see also P. Little, 'Music at the Court of King Oliver', *The Court Historian*, 12 (2007).

9. D. Farr, *John Lambert, Parliamentary Soldier and Cromwellian Major-General, 1619–1684* (Woodbridge, 2003); D. Farr, *Henry Ireton and the English Revolution* (Woodbridge, 2006); A. Hopper, *'Black Tom': Sir Thomas Fairfax and the English Revolution* (Manchester, 2007); P. Little, *Lord Broghill and the Cromwellian Union with Ireland and Scotland* (Woodbridge, 2004); J. Peacey, 'The Protector Humbled: Richard Cromwell and the Constitution', in P. Little (ed.), *Cromwellian Protectorate*; P. Little and D. L. Smith, *Parliaments and Politics during the Cromwellian Protectorate* (Cambridge, 2007), ch. 7.

10. *ODNB*, 'Oliver Cromwell'.

11. See I. Gentles, *The New Model Army in England, Ireland and Scotland, 1645–1653* (Oxford, 1992).

12. See D. Underdown, *Pride's Purge: Politics in the Puritan Revolution* (Oxford, 1971); M. Kishlansky, *The Rise of the New Model Army* (Cambridge, 1979); A. Woolrych, *Soldiers and Statesmen: The General Council of the Army and its Debates, 1647–1648* (Oxford, 1987); J. Peacey (ed.), *The Regicides and the Execution of Charles I* (Basingstoke, 2001).

13. Abbott, ii. 303.

14. A. Marvell, 'A Poem upon the Death of His Late Highness the Lord Protector', line 4.

15. For Cromwell's itinerary, see P. Gaunt, *The Cromwellian Gazetteer: An Illustrated Guide to Britain in the Civil War and Commonwealth* (Stroud, 1987), 224–7.

16. For an overview, see B. Coward, *The Cromwellian Protectorate* (Manchester, 2002).

17. See P. Little (ed.), *Cromwellian Protectorate*, especially chs 4, 8 and 9.

18. Little and Smith, *Parliaments and Politics*.

19. See also J. Peacey, 'The Protector Humbled', in Little (ed.), *Cromwellian Protectorate*.
20. S. K. Roberts, 'The Wealth of Oliver Cromwell', in P. Gaunt (ed.), *Cromwell 400* (Brentwood, 1999), 85.
21. See F. Heal and C. Holmes, *The Gentry in England and Wales, 1500–1700* (Basingstoke, 1994).
22. The quotation is from Marvell's 'Horatian Ode upon Cromwell's Return from Ireland', line 9.
23. They have not necessarily found it. See Coward, *Cromwell*, 4, 161, 164–5; Gaunt, *Cromwell*, 22; Morrill, 'Introduction', 2; Davis, *Cromwell*, 199.
24. Gaunt, *Cromwell*, 204.
25. Morrill, 'Introduction', in his *Oliver Cromwell and the English Revolution*, 2.
26. TNA, SP 78/113, fo. 155r: Sir William Lockhart to Richard Cromwell, 11/21 April 1657. For the full quotation, see Chapter 9 below.

# 1

# 1636: The Unmaking of Oliver Cromwell?

Simon Healy

Three hundred and fifty years after his death, Oliver Cromwell remains an enigmatic figure: a man of action, but prone to moments of indecision; fiercely loyal, but prepared to abandon his allies when it suited him. Students of Cromwell's early years must also confront an evidential problem, as the sources for the first two-thirds of his life comprise only a handful of letters and a smattering of information about his birth, education, marriage, some of his contacts and interests.[1] Few statesmen leave a copious archive of their youth, but while Cromwell's origins clearly had a significant impact on his later life—his regiment of 'ironsides' and the protectoral court were populated by a fair number of his relations and early acquaintances—he was remarkably sparing with personal reminiscences about his formative years. One wonders whether Cromwell's reticence over the obscurer parts of his life suggests that he had something to hide.

In the absence of concrete information about Cromwell's early years, James Heath, Sir William Dugdale and other royalist detractors rushed to fill the void with tittle-tattle, much of which is unprovable, and some of which may have been outright lies. John Morrill's study of Cromwell's origins discards such reminiscences out of hand, but it is perhaps fairer to treat such tales with caution unless they are corroborated by other sources.[2] For example, Lord Treasurer Juxon's secretary, Sir Philip Warwick, recalled his first encounter with Cromwell in the opening weeks of the Long Parliament, describing him as a grubby individual who nevertheless swayed the House with his passion:

> I came into the House well clad and perceived a gentleman speaking (whom I knew not) very ordinary apparelled, for it was a plain cloth suit, which seemed to have been made by an ill country tailor. His linen was plain, and not very clean, and I remember a speck or two of blood upon his little band, which was not much larger than his collar. His hat was without a hatband, his stature was of a good size, his sword stuck close to his side, his countenance swollen and reddish, his voice sharp and untuneable, and his eloquence full of fervour.[3]

This recollection may have been fabricated or distorted, but others testify to Cromwell's inelegant appearance at the time (his wife had not accompanied him to Westminster), while the point of Warwick's tale—that MPs were inclined to underestimate Cromwell in November 1640—was palpably true.

Cromwell's adversaries often painted him as an ordinary man floundering out of his depth, but he was astute enough to realise that a reputation as an ignorant backwoodsman could be turned to political advantage. At the opening of the 1654 parliament, he portrayed his relatively humble origins as an apprenticeship in civic and religious virtues:

> I was by birth a gentleman, living neither in any considerable height, nor yet in obscurity. I have been called to several employments in the nation—to serve in parliaments—and ... I did endeavour to discharge the duty of an honest man in those services, to God and his people's interest, and the commonwealth.[4]

John Morrill's researches suggest that the lord protector's memory was somewhat selective; at the least, his patrimony was barely sufficient to sustain his status as a gentleman, which helps to explain his view during the first civil war that 'I had rather have a plain, russet-coated captain that knows what he fights for, and loves what he knows, than that which you call a gentleman and is nothing else'.[5] As protector, Cromwell was at pains to emphasise his ordinariness: on 17 September 1656 he protested to MPs that 'I am plain and shall use a homely expression'; on 8 April 1657 he told parliament that he would 'speak very clearly and plainly to you'; and on 21 April 1657 he protested to the parliamentary committee that 'I speak not this to evade ... but I say plainly and clearly I hope', adding that he would 'be very ready, freely, and honestly and plainly, to discharge myself' in his dealings with them.[6] In the Cromwellian lexicon, of course, epithets such as 'plain' and 'honest' implied not only candour, but also moral probity and godliness, the best example of the latter being an oft-quoted letter of 13 October 1638 to his cousin Mrs St John:

> My soul is with the congregation of the firstborn, my body rests in hope, and if here I may honour God either by doing or by suffering, I shall be most glad . . . You know what my manner of life hath been. Oh, I lived in and loved darkness, and hated the light. I was a chief, the chief of sinners. This is true; I hated godliness, yet God had mercy on me. O the riches of His mercy![7]

Reproduced at the start of the *Thurloe State Papers*, this is the earliest example of the biblical and evangelical rhetoric which suffuses Cromwell's later correspondence, and is often cited as proof of his acquisition of the mental fortitude necessary to surmount the challenges he subsequently faced as a military and political leader.[8] Yet this puts the cart before the horse. In 1638, Cromwell may have gained personal assurance of God's mercy, but this cannot have come through foreknowledge of what divine Providence held in store for him over the next two decades.

Our perception of Cromwell as a godly gentleman has been substantially altered by the researches of John Morrill, whose study of the youthful Cromwell portrays a man more uncertain about his social and religious status than previous historians allow. By his account, Cromwell had tasted failure at least twice, first as a municipal politician in Huntingdon, then as a tenant farmer in St Ives. Moreover, while Cromwell clearly enjoyed many contacts among the godly in his early years, Morrill suggests that he was no cradle puritan, but experienced an evangelical awakening only in the aftermath of his humiliating confrontation with the Huntingdon corporation in 1630.[9] What more can be said? The most significant point is that his biographers tend to view the Great Man in isolation. His later career obviously justifies such an approach, as it was quite exceptional: he was one of a few dozen men who exercised high military command during the civil wars; and the only one who went on to become ruler of the nations. In Morrill's words, 'no man who rises from a working farmer to head of state in twenty years is other than great'.[10] Yet before 1640, he was—as he later claimed—a 'mere' gentleman worth (at best) a few hundred pounds a year, unlikely to become a leader of county society, let alone the nation at large. English local administration was staffed by thousands of that ilk, most of whom progressed little further up the *cursus honorum* of the early modern ruling classes. Therefore, the key question to be asked about Cromwell's early life is, what marked him out from his cohort?

## I

As John Morrill has established, Cromwell was not born with any expectation of a grand inheritance. This was in sharp (and perhaps painful) contrast to his closest relatives, the Cromwells of Hinching-brooke House. Descended from the sister of Henry VIII's minister Thomas Cromwell, the family acquired Ramsey Abbey, Hinch-ingbrooke Nunnery and a vast estate of around 60,000 acres in Huntingdonshire following the dissolution of the monasteries, making them one of the great gentry families of Elizabethan England. Sir Henry Cromwell was considered for a peerage in 1588, as was his eldest son Sir Oliver in 1604, and the latter became an intimate of King James I.[11] However, when old Sir Henry died in January 1604, he bequeathed each of his five younger sons, including Oliver's father Robert Cromwell, no more than a house, a few acres of land and the income from an impropriate rectory. Under the circumstances, Robert did reasonably well for himself: he married into a well-established family from the Isle of Ely, served as MP for Hunt-ingdon in 1593 and as a JP for his county later in life.[12] However, he did little to improve his family's economic fortunes. A relative, Captain Henry Cromwell, who died at Robert's house in December 1601, left him all his goods, but the main part of this bequest was the right to recover a loan of £300 to Richard Whalley (a cousin by marriage). A protracted legal dispute ensued, and the debt seems never to have been repaid.[13] Robert Cromwell's only known attempt to improve his son's inheritance lay in an ingenious act of administrative cunning. As he lay dying in 1617, he granted his wife a 21-year lease of his freehold lands, in order to allow the 18-year-old Oliver to escape the clutches of the court of wards (which would otherwise take control of the estate, on behalf of the crown, until the heir came of age). The ploy was initially accepted by the court of wards, but in July 1619 Cromwell's wardship was nevertheless sold for £150. Payment was undertaken by the exchequer auditor, Thomas Hutton, and Sir Lionel Cranfield's servant, Nicholas Harman, who were perhaps acting on behalf of Cromwell's mother.[14]

The controversy over his wardship presumably explains why Cromwell was not married until August 1620, shortly after he came of age, at which time it was agreed that his main property, Hartford rectory (which lay just outside Huntingdon), was to be settled on his wife as a jointure estate. The bride's father, Sir James Bourchier, was essentially a Londoner, although he had also purchased an estate at Little Stambridge, Essex, making him a neighbour of the earl of Warwick, one of the leading godly peers of England. As Bourchier had sons to inherit his lands, his daughter must have been promised a cash dowry (the sum given to the groom by the bride's family); and the fact that Cromwell undertook to assign his largest estate as the jointure lands (assigned to the bride in return for the dowry payment) suggests that it was reasonably substantial. However, there is no indication that he invested any dowry money in freehold lands, so (if it was paid) it seems likely that he either bought leases of 'copyhold' lands (the sales of which are difficult to trace), loaned the cash out at interest, or used it to settle accumulated debts.[15]

The most significant financial transaction in which the young Cromwell participated was the sale of his Huntingdon estate. In May 1631 he passed his house (Austin Friars), most of his lands and the Hartford rectory to Richard Oakeley of Westminster and Richard Owen of Middlesex for £1800. At the time, arable land usually sold for around 20 times its annual rental value, but the tithes which comprised the main income of any rectory fetched a little less, so the sale price values Cromwell's patrimony at around £100 *per annum*. His mother, whose jointure interest was included in the sale, seems to have remained in Austin Friars as a tenant, but nothing is mentioned of his wife's interest in Hartford rectory. This suggests that he had failed to make a jointure settlement, despite having given a bond to do so at his marriage, and raises some doubt as to whether he ever received a dowry from his father-in-law.[16] Equally interesting is the identity of one of the purchasers, Richard Oakeley, who was receiver-general of the lands of Westminster Abbey and a secretary to the Bishop John Williams of Lincoln (then resident at the episcopal palace at Buckden, only three miles from Huntingdon).[17] It seems likely that Oakeley and Owen were acting as attorneys for Bishop Williams, as after his death, the latter's niece and her husband, Sir Owen Wynn, claimed the inheritance of lands in Huntingdonshire as part of a longstanding dispute arising from the bishop's failure to provide an adequate dowry at their marriage in 1624. In 1653 Wynn nominated Oakeley, 'whom I have not seen these 22 years and above' as an arbitrator of this dispute, but Oakeley apparently sold the lands back to the Cromwell family before his death in September 1653.[18]

The circumstances of Cromwell's departure from Huntingdon have been closely explored elsewhere. Having probably been a common councillor there since 1624 (when he became a JP for the borough), he was returned as MP in 1628. Thereafter he quarrelled with other members of the corporation over a bequest from Richard Fishbourne, a Huntingdon native who, having made his fortune as a London Mercer, left £2000 to the corporation for the endowment of a weekly sermon. As the town schoolmaster, Dr Thomas Beard, was already engaged to give lectures twice a week, a faction on the corporation led by Thomas Edwards (and probably supported by Cromwell) proposed to divert the money to poor relief. However, others successfully insisted that the original bequest be honoured, and while they failed to get Beard appointed to the new lectureship, he was given £40 to ease the pain of rejection. In the middle of this dispute, the town obtained a new charter appointing a bench of aldermen, from which Edwards and Cromwell were excluded. In such a small town, this omission constituted a public humiliation; and Cromwell and William Kilborne, similarly slighted, railed against their enemies in an outburst for which they were summoned before the privy council and forced to make a public apology.[19]

This local context certainly explains Cromwell's desire to leave Huntingdon, but property was the ultimate form of security in early modern England, and most landowners in his situation—that is to say, not being hotly pursued by their creditors—would simply have leased their estate and used the rental income to establish themselves elsewhere. So why did he sell up? It is often said that alterations in religious practices being promoted by William Laud—soon to be archbishop of Canterbury—and his Arminian allies prompted godly puritans to contemplate resettlement in New England. As we shall see, Cromwell's only recorded speech as an MP in 1629 certainly demonstrates that he was an opponent of the Laudians, and it is interesting that Henry Lawrence, who became Cromwell's landlord at St Ives after he left Huntingdon, was a patentee of the Connecticut company. However, the Plymouth colony was struggling at this time; Boston had been founded less than a year earlier; and Connecticut had only just obtained its charter; so any such interest on Cromwell's part would have been a little premature in 1631. In any case, his early biographer, Mark Noble, connects the story about emigration to the foundation of the Saybrook company in 1635–1636, by which time Cromwell had acquired other interests.[20] The most straightforward answer to the conundrum of the Huntingdon sale in 1631 is, quite simply, that Cromwell had greater expectations elsewhere.

## II

Cromwell's maternal uncle, Sir Thomas Steward, was by any standards a prosperous man. He owned around 60 acres of freehold land in Ely, 50 acres situated some ten miles away at Elme, Cambridgeshire and Emneth, Norfolk, and 200 acres of fen at nearby Upwell. Like many fenland families, he leased further estates from the ecclesiastical authorities, who owned most of the choicest land in the Isle of Ely. He held Paradise Close in Ely, the rectory of Ely St Mary, and Chapman's close and Tilekiln close in the adjacent manor of Wichford from the dean and chapter, and the manor of Ely Barton from the bishop, which comprised at least 100 acres of land and a lucrative tithe income. Finally, Steward may have enjoyed the profits of the manor of Mullicourt House in the parish of Outwell, which was granted to his cousin Edward Fincham in 1626, and later inherited by Cromwell.[21] The Stewards had been major tenants of church lands since the time of Sir Thomas's great uncle Robert Styward, the first post-Reformation dean of Ely, and they generally arranged to keep their estates within the family, so it is important to know when Steward decided to break with tradition and make Cromwell, his sister's son, his main heir.

The first time Cromwell was mentioned in connection with Steward's estates was in October 1610, when he was named as one of the three lives for which Steward's lease of Ely St Mary rectory was to endure. This citation conferred no legal rights upon Cromwell: leases for lives were customarily bestowed upon the children of the tenant in order to gain the maximum term for the lease; and in the absence of any children of his own, Steward chose his wife and two adolescents, Cromwell, and Robert Steward, son of his first cousin Sir Simeon Steward of Stuntney. A year later, in his lease of Paradise Close, Steward selected three different lives, including Robert Fincham, second son of his cousin Edward Fincham of Outwell, and Cromwell's infant sister, Robina.[22] The first formal indication that Cromwell might be under consideration as one of Steward's heirs came in January 1625, when the bishop granted Sir Thomas a 21-year lease of the manor of Ely Barton, which included a covenant preventing Steward from alienating the lease without episcopal permission, 'unless it be to his wife, his children, his sisters or their children'. This clause was not repeated when the lease was renewed in 1629, but the

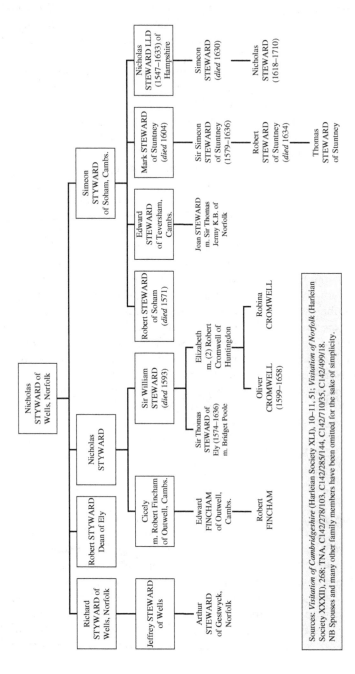

**Oliver Cromwell and the Steward family** (copyright Simon Healy)

Sources: *Visitation of Cambridgeshire* (Harleian Society XLI), 10–11, 51; *Visitation of Norfolk* (Harleian Society XXXII), 268; TNA, C142/278/103, C142/285/144, C142/710/35, C142/499/18.
NB Spouses and many other family members have been omitted for the sake of simplicity.

omission may simply indicate that Steward had by then drafted a will naming Cromwell as the heir to much of his estate.[23] This decision is likely to have been controversial, as it ignored the claims of his second cousins, the Stewards of Stuntney.

Sir Thomas Steward enjoyed an unusual degree of freedom over his inheritance, as neither he nor his father, William, had established an entail on their estates. (Freehold land held under an entail descends *in tail male*, that is, to the sons, brothers, male cousins, and sometimes more distant male relatives of the landowner, effectively excluding female heirs from inheriting.) Gentry families were expected to follow the custom of male primogeniture, under which property reverted to the collateral branches of a family if the head produced no male heirs. This can be seen in the case of William Steward's first cousin Robert Steward of Stuntney, Cambridgeshire, who died childless: in his will of 1570 he entailed the Stuntney estate on each of his six brothers and their heirs male in turn, with reversions to Arthur Steward of Norfolk (a first cousin once removed) and then to William Steward of Ely, before finally conceding a remainder to his female heirs. Such entails were normally made at the marriage of the heir to the estate, or (as in Robert's case) shortly before death, but neither William nor Sir Thomas are known to have made any such settlement. There were, in fact, obligations on another part of Sir Thomas's estate, as a reversion of copyhold lands he held in Ely was assigned to Edward and Sir Mark Steward of Stuntney and their heirs male. There is also evidence of some closeness between the Ely and Stuntney families: Sir Thomas's father died at Teversham, a property owned by his Stuntney cousins; and when Sir Mark's grandson, Robert, died in 1634, Sir Thomas obtained the wardship of his heir, Thomas Steward. However, in the absence of an entail Sir Thomas was under no legal obligation to leave his freehold or leasehold estates to his Stuntney cousins; nor were they in any position to put pressure upon him, particularly after he became guardian to the heir of Stuntney.[24]

In the absence of any draft will or other settlement, we cannot be sure that Cromwell was designated as heir to Steward's estate before 1636, but it seems likely that the decision was made at some time in the late 1620s; and the prospect of a larger inheritance would certainly explain why Cromwell was willing to sell his patrimony at Huntingdon in 1631. What happened next, however, was perhaps unique: in July 1635 an inquiry was ordered into Sir Thomas Steward's mental health. This was not, in itself, a particularly uncommon occurrence: the court of wards routinely dealt with the estates of lunatics such as the father of the regicide Sir John Bourchier. However, wardship was generally the last resort of any family troubled by mental illness, as it greatly complicated routine legal and financial transactions.[25] So why was a writ sued in this case? In a much later account of 1681, the royalist Sir William Dugdale insisted that Cromwell had

> so wasted his patrimony that, having attempted his uncle Steward for a supply of his wants, and finding that on a smooth way of application to him he could not prevail, he endeavoured by colour of law to lay hold of his estate, representing him as a person not able to govern it; but therein he failed.[26]

It is easy to discount Dugdale's claim as a partisan attempt to smear the late lord protector's reputation, but the record verifies the most astonishing aspect of the case: an inquisition taken at Cambridge on 30 September 1635 certified that Steward was *not* a lunatic.[27] Given the profound reluctance of most families to initiate lunacy proceedings, this outcome strongly suggests that some form of foul play was at work, and as one of Steward's closest relatives, Cromwell must fall under suspicion as he stood a good chance of being appointed guardian, perhaps in tandem with Steward's wife, Dame Bridget. Cromwell's role in this enquiry is alluded to in two other pieces of evidence. First, at Oxford during the civil war, John Williams, by then archbishop of York, advised the king that 'your majesty did him [Cromwell] but justice in refusing his petition against Sir Thomas Steward of the Isle of Ely; but he takes them all for his enemies that would not let him undo his best friend'.[28] Secondly, Humphrey Steward, defendant in a lawsuit brought by Cromwell in 1636, recalled 'the disfavour wherein the complainant [Cromwell] stood with the said Sir Thomas not long before his death'.[29] These statements provide no more than circumstantial evidence, but the circumstances are most suggestive, as we shall see.

James Heath, Cromwell's most hostile biographer, claims that Steward was only dissuaded from disinheriting his nephew by the entreaties of puritan clergymen, who convinced him that Cromwell was a truly repentant sinner. Once again, the basic fact is verifiable: in his will of 29 January 1636 Steward left much of his property to Cromwell. However, one does not have to be a royalist to appreciate that Steward must have been incensed by his nephew's behaviour, and it is possible that Dame Bridget was even more upset—it was

only after her demise in December 1635 that Steward came to a settlement with Cromwell, as he himself lay dying.[30] Steward's will is
a complex document which was misinterpreted by the most comprehensive chronicler of his life, W. C. Abbott, whose conclusions
have influenced more recent biographers. Abbott stated, correctly,
that Cromwell was to inherit part of Steward's freehold estate and
most of his leasehold lands, but he overlooked the significance of
the conditions Steward attached to this bequest. First, on the day
before his will was signed, Steward assigned his leaseholds to Daniel
Wigmore, the archdeacon of Ely, and Anthony Page, steward learned
of the dean and chapter estates. Secondly, in his will he assigned these
revenues and those of the freehold lands Cromwell was to inherit to
his executor, Humphrey Steward, until his debts were paid off. Finally,
he left his goods to his executor, and not to Cromwell.[31] The extent of
Steward's generosity to his nephew thus revolved around the scale of
his debts, which Abbott tacitly assumed were relatively modest.[32] He
was wrong.

The contentious nature of Steward's will is demonstrated by the
fact that Cromwell filed a lawsuit against the executor, Humphrey
Steward, within a few months of his uncle's death (the date of
his complaint is not legible, but Steward's answer was filed on 16
May 1636). Cromwell claimed that his uncle had intended that his
goods should be assigned to pay off his debts, but Steward responded
(correctly) that he had been granted Sir Thomas's goods without conditions; moreover, at the time of the lawsuit he had already agreed to
sell these goods back to Cromwell for £2000. Humphrey Steward
also observed that Sir Thomas had appointed him as executor because
since 1633 the two men had been joint executors to Dr Nicholas
Steward, another member of the Stuntney branch of the family, and
that Sir Thomas's inventory included goods worth £1077 12s. 5d.
which actually belonged to the estate of the late Dr Steward. He
was legally entitled to recoup this sum from the deceased's estates,
plus legacies of £200 and the costs of the funeral, all of which sad-
dled the estate with debts of at least £1300.[33] What was Cromwell's
landed inheritance worth? Humphrey Steward valued Sir Thomas's
income at £500–600 *per annum*, but noted that this included copyhold lands which were settled on Thomas Steward, the underage heir
of Stuntney. Much later, in the 1650s, Ely rectory was valued at £344
annual net value; as this was by far the most lucrative estate in the
portfolio, the whole might therefore be valued at around £450 *per
annum*.[34] By this conservative estimate, Sir Thomas Steward had thus

tied his estate up for around three years after his death, which some may have considered a remarkably mild reproach for his nephew's folly.

In highly charged circumstances such as those surrounding the Steward inheritance disputes often dragged on for years, but Cromwell, perhaps with the advice of his legal counsel, Oliver St John, quickly settled out of court.[35] The first indication of a compromise was the grant of a 21-year lease of Ely St Mary rectory to Cromwell by Dr William Fuller, dean of Ely, in October 1636. However, Humphrey Steward held on to the remaining lands for a full two years. The dean and chapter lands were eventually turned over to Cromwell on 29 October 1638, and the episcopal manor of Ely Barton four weeks later, on 24 November. These transactions probably indicate that Cromwell had finally cleared the debts due from his late uncle's estate to Humphrey Steward.[36]

Ironically, Cromwell, having striven so mightily to secure the Steward inheritance, quickly alienated his ecclesiastical estates to the archdeacon of Ely, on 30 October 1640.[37] The cathedral authorities were presumably irritated at having a religious radical as one of their main tenants, and Cromwell was perhaps unhappy with the obligation imposed upon him by the Ely rectory lease to support two curates nominated by the dean and chapter. Nevertheless, it seems likely that the main factor behind the sale was Cromwell's return to the Long Parliament, as MP for Cambridge, three days earlier. If the session went well, financial resources might prove useful; but in the event of an abrupt dissolution, such as that of May 1640, a portable cash reserve could prove invaluable for someone who might suddenly become a fugitive. In short, the sale allowed Cromwell to keep his options open. What price might the archdeacon have paid for his lands? 21-year leases usually commanded an entry fine of 5–7 years' rental value, and with little of the term expired and an annual yield of around £400, Cromwell probably received around £2000. This would explain where he came by the £600 he subscribed to the Irish Adventurers in April 1642, and also the £500 he pledged to Parliament's English army two months later.[38]

## III

What does this excursion into the financial byways of Cromwell's youth tell us about the other key event of his formative years, his spiritual conversion? Most immediately, it puts his letter to Mrs St John

into a profoundly *personal* context. Its date, 13 October 1638, anticipated the final settlement of the dispute over Sir Thomas Steward's
estates by just over two weeks. Thus when Cromwell stated 'you
know what my manner of life hath been', he was assuming that
the wife of his cousin and legal counsel was familiar with the controversy over the Steward bequest. Making no bones about his own
responsibility, he continued, 'I lived in and loved darkness, and hated
the light...I hated godliness, yet God had mercy on me'.[39] Finally,
this was not simply a private letter. The recipient was staying with
Sir William Masham, one of the Essex godly network to whom
Cromwell was connected via his aunt Joan (the widow of Sir Francis
Barrington of Hatfield Broad Oak); and at this time Cromwell's sons
were being raised in the same environment, at Felsted school, also in
Essex.[40] The letter was thus probably destined to be passed among a
wide circle of acquaintances, and therefore his aspiration that 'I may
honour my God either by doing or by suffering' suggests an awareness
that there might be some among his own friends and relations who
still doubted the authenticity of his repentance. If this assumption is
correct, the epithet 'a chief, the chief of sinners' was not merely an
allusion to St Paul's words,[41] but a semi-public *mea culpa*, which may
well explain why this letter was preserved, when most of his early
correspondence has been lost.

In theological terms, the conversion of St Paul had an obvious
appeal to a chastened Cromwell. Saul, assiduous persecutor of the
earliest Christians, had been confronted by his Saviour in a (literally)
blinding moment of revelation on the road to Damascus, following
which he was charged to bear witness of Christ's salvation 'unto all
men'.[42] This analogy undoubtedly suited Cromwell's purposes in the
autumn of 1638, when he needed to demonstrate the humility of
a prodigal son to his godly relations, but it is unlikely that it was
the whole story. Conversion narratives, which abound for the post-
Reformation period, generally record a more gradual process—akin
to that described in St Augustine's *Confessions*—where a growing dis-
quiet over the temptations of worldly existence, often accompanied
by bouts of physical illness or mental anguish, eventually lead to a profound awareness of the immanence of God's saving grace.[43] There is
ample evidence that Cromwell experienced such doubts long before
arriving at an assurance of salvation.

First of all, there is the fact that Cromwell sprang from a godly
milieu, where the quest for evangelical assurance was a commonplace.
The only speech he is recorded to have made in parliament before

1640 places him on the fringes of the anti-Arminian group headed by John Pym and his half-brother Francis Rous. In a debate on 11 February 1629, Christopher Sherland claimed that Bishop Richard Neile of Winchester had been responsible for the procurement of royal pardons for the Arminians John Cosin, Roger Mainwaring and Robert Sibthorpe, all of whom had been investigated by the House of Commons in 1628. Cromwell recalled that Neile, some years earlier, had ordered Dr Thomas Beard not to attack the 'flat popery' preached by the Catholic convert, Dr William Alabaster, at Paul's Cross. This allegation was quickly corroborated by Sir Robert Phelips, Sir John Backhouse and Sir John Jephson, who provided another example of Neile stifling anti-Catholic preaching, and proceedings concluded with a vote to summon witnesses for an investigation which clearly had the potential to grow into an impeachment.[44]

Beyond this, there is evidence that the young Cromwell was a hypochondriac, and that his affliction included a spiritual dimension. The source most frequently quoted is the notebook of the royal physician Sir Theodore de Mayerne, who, following a consultation with a 'Monsieur Cromwell' in September 1628, disgnosed *'valde melancholicus corpus ad modum sici opsius, habere dolorum ventric' periodicum'*. This is sometimes stated to have been a case of depression (*melancholicus*), but Mayerne actually identified a genuinely physical complaint, a severe affliction of the melancholic humour (black bile) producing periodic stomach pains—perhaps a stomach ulcer. There is an additional problem with this source. The patient is usually assumed to have been the future lord protector, but it could have been his cousin Henry Cromwell, who had every reason to be suffering from either real or stress-induced illness following his father's sale of Hinchingbrooke House and a large slice of his inheritance.[45]

There are, however, several other quasi-medical tales specifically linked to Oliver. Cromwell's biographer, Mark Noble, recalled a story, still circulating in Georgian times, that as a tenant farmer, Cromwell was habitually seen around St Ives with 'a piece of red flannel around his neck, as he was subject to an inflammation of the throat'.[46] His personal neuroses were also noted by his local physician, Dr John Symcotts. In 1642, Symcotts recalled that, years before, Cromwell 'taking abundance of Mithridate to avoid the infection of the plague, cured his pimpled face'. Mithridate was the contemporary equivalent of snake-oil, and Symcotts was thus suggesting that Cromwell had been somewhat credulous. Later still, the courtier Sir Philip Warwick recalled discussing Cromwell with Symcotts while visiting the widow

of Sir Capell Bedell at Hamerton, Huntingdonshire in 1646. The
doctor recalled his erstwhile patient as

> a most splenetic man, and had fancies about the cross in that town [Hunt-
> ingdon], and that he [Symcotts] had been called up to him at midnight
> and such unseasonable hours very many times, upon a strong fancy which
> made him believe he was then dying; and there went a story of him that
> in the daytime, lying melancholy in his bed, he believed that a spirit
> appeared to him and told him that he should be the greatest man (not
> mentioning the word king) in the kingdom, which his uncle Sir Thomas
> Steward, who left him all the little estate Cromwell had, told him was
> traitorous to relate.[47]

While Warwick obviously imparted a royalist spin to this tale, there
is no intrinsic reason to doubt its authenticity. Symcotts clearly dined
out regularly on tales of the eccentricities of his celebrated patient, and
nothing about this story seems unusual in the context of an evangelical
struggling to find spiritual assurance.

## IV

This account of Cromwell's formative years has important consequences for our view of his later career. First, the closet of his early
life did contain at least one obvious skeleton: the mendacity, or—to
express it more delicately—the connivance he exhibited in trying to
deprive Sir Thomas Steward of his estates. Far more than a figment
of royalist imagination, this incident shows Cromwell in a thoroughly
unsavoury light, although paradoxically, it was ultimately the making of him. Having fretted for years about the perils his soul faced
from the trivia of everyday existence, he eventually committed a genuinely damning sin, for which he faced public humiliation as a greedy
charlatan; but nevertheless, God elected to save him from disgrace.
As he himself said of this deliverance, 'truly no poor creature hath
more cause to put forth himself in the cause of his God than I'. In
other words, God had destroyed the unregenerate Cromwell—as with
Saul—in order to create an apostle fit to bear witness to the gentiles
of Caroline England.

Of course, this is to view the unmaking of Oliver Cromwell
through his own eyes. One does not have to be a complete cynic
to see that his personal epiphany involved a good deal of what a post-
modernist might politely term 'self-fashioning'. Yet this is not quite

fair. The facility with which he persuaded others of his evangelical certainty over the years certainly suggests a capacity to convince
himself of the rectitude of his arguments: to put a 'spin' upon his
motives. Moreover, he was born with a penchant for taking risks of a
magnitude which would have staggered most of his contemporaries.
In particular, the decision to sell up at Huntingdon, or to pursue
the incredibly rash course of having his uncle declared insane, suggests a man with an instinct to act rather than reflect. This was to
serve him well on the battlefield, and also helps to explain why he
staged more *coups d'état* than any other figure in English history. Yet
the memory of the near-fiasco over the Steward inheritance may also
help to explain the intermittent bouts of political indecision, as he
weighed up the pros and cons of purging parliaments, executing the
king or refusing the crown for himself. In short, the peculiar dispute
over the Steward inheritance suggests that Cromwell's personality was
not forged in the crucible of war and revolutionary politics, but was
already there, fully formed, with all its inherent contradictions, in
1636–1638.

## Notes

1. Most of the factual information about his life before 1640 is recorded in
   Abbott, i. 10–107.
2. J. Morrill, 'The Making of Oliver Cromwell' in Morrill (ed.), *Oliver
   Cromwell and the English Revolution* (Harlow, 1999), 20n.
3. Sir Philip Warwick, *Memoirs of the Reign of Charles I* (1813), 247–8.
4. I. Roots (ed.), *The Speeches of Oliver Cromwell* (1989), 42.
5. Morrill, 'Making', 19–22; Abbott, i. 256; Gaunt, *Cromwell*, 48–51.
6. Roots (ed.), *Speeches of Oliver Cromwell*, 92, 119, 163.
7. Abbott, i. 97; also printed in *TSP*, i. 1.
8. R. S. Paul, *The Lord Protector*, (1955), 34–42.
9. Morrill, 'Making', 19–36.
10. *ODNB*, 'Oliver Cromwell'.
11. BL, Lansdowne MS 104, fo. 52v; *HMC Hastings*, iv. 1.
12. TNA, C142/283/106; TNA, C142/361/140; P. W. Hasler (ed.), *History
    of Parliament Trust, House of Commons, 1558–1603* (1976), i. 682; TNA,
    SP14/33, fo. 32v.
13. M. Noble, *Memoirs of the Protectoral-House of Cromwell* (1787) 37, 77;
    TNA, PROB 11/99, fo. 309; TNA, C2/Jas.I/W2/52.
14. TNA, PROB 11/130, fo. 115; TNA, WARD 9/93, fos. 145v-6; Abbot,
    i. 31; TNA, WARD 9/162, fo. 311v.

15. Abbott, i. 35–6; TNA, C2/Jas.I/B17/63. TNA, LC4/199, fo. 220v gives the date of the marriage bond as 21 August 1620, not 25 August. This would make more sense, as it was the day *before* Cromwell's marriage.

16. Abbott, i. 71–2.

17. John Williams was both dean of Westminster and bishop of Lincoln; while until his sacking by Charles I in November 1625, he had also been lord keeper of the great seal.

18. C. S. Knighton (ed.), *Acts of the Dean and Chapter of Westminster* (Woodbridge, 2006), 93, 100; NLW, 468E/1999, 2003, 2005, 2014, 2018; Abbott, i. 72; J. Gwynfor Jones, *The Wynn Family of Gwydir* (Aberystwyth, 1995), 98–100; W. G. D. Fletcher, 'Sequestration Papers of Richard Oakeley of Oakeley', *Transactions of the Shropshire Archaeological Society* (4th series), ii. 196–9.

19. Paul, *Protector*, 44; Morrill, 'Making', 26–33; *Acts of the Privy Council, 1630–1631*, 128, 140.

20. Paul, *Protector*, 44; Abbott, i. 73; *ODNB*, 'Oliver Cromwell'; Noble, *Protectoral-House*, i. 108.

21. TNA, C142/710/35; CUL, EDC 2/4/1, fos. 241, 284–6, 289; CUL, EDC 2/4/2, fos. 48–9; CUL, EDR, CC95553, 59–62.

22. CUL, EDC 2/4/1, fos. 284, 289; J. W. Clay (ed.), *Visitations of Cambridgeshire, 1575 and 1619* (Harleian Society xli, 1897), 10–11, 51; Noble, *Protectoral-House*, 90.

23. CUL, EDR, CC95553, 59–62; CUL, EDR, CC95554/7. Steward's will of January 1636 begins by revoking all former wills: TNA, PROB 11/170, fo. 72.

24. TNA, C142/285/144; TNA, C142/278/103; TNA, PROB 11/170, fos. 73v-4; *Visitations of Cambridgeshire*, 10–11; W. Rye (ed.), *Visitations of Norfolk, 1563, 1589 and 1613* (Harleian Society xxxii, 1891), 268.

25. *HMC Hatfield*, xi. 233; H. E. Bell, *Introduction to the History and Records of the Court of Wards & Liveries* (Cambridge, 1953), 128–32.

26. Dugdale's account in *A Short View of the Late Troubles* (1681) is reprinted in Abbott, i. 81–2.

27. TNA, C142/727/157.

28. J. Hacket, *Scrinia Reserata* (1693), ii. 212 (cited in Abbott, i. 82).

29. TNA, C2/Chas.I/C92/53.

30. Abbott, i. 82; TNA, C3/399/163.

31. CUL, EDC 2/4/2, fo. 79; TNA, PROB 11/170, fos. 72–4.

32. Abbott, i. 82–3.

33. TNA, C3/399/163; TNA, C2/Chas.I/C92/53; TNA, PROB 11/170, fo. 74. Humphrey Steward valued Sir Thomas's goods at £2000, with jewels worth £176 and £38 in cash.

34. CUL, EDC 8A/1/8, fo. 1v; Lambeth Palace Library, Comm. XIIa/7, fos. 164–6. I owe these references to Andrew Barclay.

35. The Lincoln's Inn lawyers, John Glanvill, Oliver St John and John Fountayne, signed Cromwell's complaint in TNA, C3/399/163. Of these three, only St John continued to give Cromwell (his cousin by marriage) legal advice in subsequent years; this early evidence of a professional connection between the two men has hitherto been overlooked.
36. CUL, EDC 2/4/2, fos. 94v-6, 100v-1, 103v-4 (printed in Abbott, i. 85–8, 97–9, 100–1, respectively). Abbott overlooked the new lease of Ely Barton in CUL, EDR CC95554/34.
37. Lambeth Palace Library, Comm. XIIa/7, fos. 167–8. I owe this information to Andrew Barclay, who is exploring the wider circumstances of this sale in his forthcoming book, *Oliver Cromwell: The Unknown Politician*.
38. *CSPI (Adventurers) 1642–59*, 319–20; *PJ*, iii. 472. These figures were subsequently verified by Cromwell in a letter to St John: Abbott, i. 258–9.
39. Abbott, i. 97.
40. Noble, *Protectoral-House*, 36, 132–4, 158–9; Abbott, i. 85, 107; Morrill, 'Making', 23, 42–3.
41. 1 Timothy 1:15 '... Christ Jesus came into the world to save sinners; of whom I am chief'. For a fuller analysis of the biblical allusions in this letter, see Paul, *Protector*, 399–400.
42. Acts 22:6–16.
43. See, for example, M. C. Questier, *Conversion, Politics and Religion in England, 1580–1625* (Cambridge, 1996), 12–75; M. P. Winship, *Making Heretics* (Princeton, NJ, 2002), 12–27.
44. W. Notestein and R. H. Relf (eds), *Commons' Debates 1629* (Minneapolis, MN, 1921), 58–60, 139, 192–3; H. F. Snapp, 'The Impeachment of Roger Maynwaring', *Huntington Library Quarterly*, xxx (1966–1967), 217–32. Because of the early dissolution, nothing came of the Neile investigation. This interpretation differs from that offered in Morrill, 'Making', 25–6.
45. BL, Sloane MS 2069, fo. 92v; Huntingdonshire RO, D/DM50/1, 7; BL, Eg. MS 2644, fo. 246. Among many others, Hugh Trevor-Roper assumes Mayerne's patient to have been Oliver Cromwell: *Europe's Physician: The Various Life of Sir Theodore de Mayerne* (New Haven, CT, 2006), 8. I owe the medical analysis to Carole Rawcliffe.
46. Noble, *Protectoral-House*, i. 105n.
47. F. N. L. Poynter and W. J. Bishop (eds), *A Seventeenth Century Doctor and His Patients* (Bedfordshire Historical Record Society xxxi, 1951), 76; Warwick, *Memoirs*, 275–6.

# 2

# 'One that Would Sit Well at the Mark': The Early Parliamentary Career of Oliver Cromwell, 1640–1642

Stephen K. Roberts

Informal parliamentary activity in the mid-seventeenth century is a huge, ill-defined and badly documented subject. Much went on outside the personal gaze of the Speaker, and its importance is obvious because key indicators of it survive, such as the crowds in Westminster Hall, the invention of printing for parliament from 1641 and the scale of petitioning in 1641–1642, which must have been accompanied by massive personal lobbying. The daily experience of any rank-and-file parliament-man in the early phase of the Long Parliament is often hard to re-create, that of a rank-and-file member who during the life of that same parliament achieved fame and notoriety in equal measure, and whose later reputation has been fashioned by centuries of contestation, harder still. Although Oliver Cromwell had played a part in two previous parliaments, the assembly that gathered in November 1640 was the first in which he was visibly active in a number of roles. Inevitably, students of this period in Cromwell's life have pored over his conduct in search of signs of future greatness, or hallmarks of his character and career, good or ill. Among these might be listed his commitment to godly Protestantism, his impatience with the hesitant or uncommitted, his predilection for 'networking' and his social marginalisation. The first two of these attributes can be measured by Cromwell's own pronouncements and by the official record, but a judgement on the latter two must hang upon an assessment of parliamentary behaviour as a whole.

Two approaches to parliamentary history dominate the landscape of recent research. One is comparable to the geologist's study of the drift and higher strata of the solid, through studies of individual parliaments as a whole. The other is through the study of the public lives of the parliament-men, which might be compared to the vertical sampling of cores of the solid geology. In any study of the proceedings of the first 20 months of the Long Parliament, Cromwell will merit an occasional mention, although were it possible rigorously to exclude hindsight, it should be perfectly feasible to write the parliamentary history of that time without mentioning him at all. The pre-eminent project working on the biographies of MPs is that of the History of Parliament Trust, and this essay follows the methodology of the History in prioritising the systematic study of the parliamentary sources.[1] Both method and format permit a focus on Cromwell's parliamentary career that is a challenge for any whole-life biographer to encapsulate without reference to the entire trajectory of Cromwell's public and private life.

The ambivalence in Cromwell's relations with parliaments is apparent to any student of his life. Recent biographers of the man who sat as an MP, called parliaments into being, nurtured them, but also broke them by force, identify a number of themes visible in 1640–1642. These are the question of Oliver's social standing and the related question of where he fitted into the hierarchy of parliamentary seniority; the issue of how far his kinsmen by their own presence in the lower House underwrote whatever status he enjoyed; the patterns visible in the parliamentary topics that absorbed his time and commitment; and of course the overarching theme of Cromwell's motivation. A spectrum of opinion on each of these topics can be found in the recent biographies. Most authorities treat Cromwell's time in parliament before the outbreak of civil war in August 1642 as a single entity, although one commentator sees May 1641 as marking a downgrading in Cromwell's standing in the House.[2] As much for the sake of managing the narrative as for marking any contemporary political milestone, this study will consider initially the so-called first session of the parliament, from November 1640 to September 1641, and then the period from October 1641 to August 1642 when Cromwell left London to organise armed resistance in Cambridgeshire to the king. Within these two spans of time, the focus will be on Cromwell's parliamentary tasks and skills.


# I

Cromwell's first recorded appearance in the Long Parliament was in connection with a petition, so we can make a start by looking at his record in responding to petitions. It was very early in the life of the assembly, portending the day when, in Ivan Roots's memorable phrase, 'the prison gates creaked open' to release the victims of Laudian authoritarianism.[3] On 9 November, in somewhat confused circumstances, the petitions of a number of sufferers were read. It seems that first a petition from the wife of the puritan lawyer, William Prynne, was presented. Then, that of Alexander Leighton, the Scots puritan minister and physician, who had endured corporal punishment and repeated mutilation during his long incarceration, was read. Unusually, suggesting a deliberate staging, that petition was read a second time, in order to satisfy those members who were absent from the chamber on a message to the House of Lords. Immediately after the second reading, Cromwell was named to the investigative committee. After another committee was appointed to investigate papists in London, a petition on behalf of Prynne himself was read. William Strode spoke against procedure in the court of Star Chamber and then Cromwell rose to deliver a petition on behalf of John Lilburne.[4] An observer remembered how Cromwell's fervour would have been appropriate in one revealing a dire threat to the state.[5] It is generally reckoned that Sir Philip Warwick was thinking of Lilburne when recalling Cromwell speaking up for a servant of Prynne's, because there is no evidence that Lilburne was ever in Prynne's service.[6] But a servant of Prynne's did deliver the petition on behalf of his master, and Warwick recalled the offence as having been a libel against the queen, a charge associated with Prynne and not Lilburne. The petitions that day were probably linked, and Cromwell probably spoke up not only for Lilburne.

If the conjectural order of business recently compiled for the day's proceedings is accurate, the petitions for Leighton, Prynne's wife, Prynne himself and finally Lilburne were orchestrated and shepherded by a group of MPs. Among them was Cromwell himself but also including William Strode and Sir Robert Harley, who tried to follow Cromwell's alleged histrionics with a speech, missed by most of the diarists, on some local incident involving irregularity in legal

procedure. Barry Coward considers that only Cromwell's 'family connections and religious and political views' can explain his involvement
with Lilburne.[7] There is certainly no evidence to suggest that the two
men knew each other before Cromwell's speech. Cromwell delivered
Lilburne's petition, the senior puritan parliament-man Francis Rous
presented Prynne's, but no MP sponsor is recorded for Leighton.
It would be entirely in line with what we know of parliamentary
social relations if what we are observing is a hierarchy of sponsorship at work. Leighton's case was so notorious and long-standing—a
decade spent in prison—that no individual sponsor was necessary;
the landed gentleman Prynne attracted the attention of the grave and
pious Rous; while the rough-hewn Lilburne secured the proxy voice
of a member whose fervour and commitment amply compensated for
his inexperience. Furthermore, Cromwell's intervention on Lilburne's
behalf on 9 November was not opportunistic. Two days earlier, on 7
November, the House had given permission to Leighton, Peter Smart,
George Walker and Lilburne to have their cases presented at the bar.[8]

The Lilburne petition illustrates a theme of orchestration and max-
imising verbal fire-power which recurs in Cromwell's political conduct in these months. It is also an early example of his self-discipline
in following things through, since he spoke again on Leighton's case
and sat on the committee for critical scrutiny of Star Chamber.[9] His
intervention on 21 April 1641 in the Leighton affair was probably
the occasion that one who was in the House on that day—probably
Giles Strangways—recalled Cromwell speaking passionately until he
'dropped tears down with his words'.[10] Petitions have been described
as 'the first source of pressure on MPs', and Cromwell responded well
to petitions that came to his attention.[11] Before July 1642, Cromwell
preferred ten other petitions in the House, and was named to committees formed in response to another 12.[12] Cromwell was evidently
a persuasive advocate, but the petitioners who drew upon his talents were typically individuals whose problems chimed with his own
known interests. Before the recess in September 1641, he spoke to
petitions about conditions in two London gaols and about the excesses
of the court of Star Chamber.[13] In May 1642, he brought in a petition
from the inhabitants of Cottenham, Suffolk, against their minister;
their charge against him, of not preaching, was of course a coded
statement of their own Puritanism.[14] In this case, Cromwell was acting as an MP with local knowledge, and in other examples of petitions
arising from London or from Ulster, his physical proximity or special
expertise account for his involvement.

The petitions from South Wales of February and May 1642, discussed by Lloyd Bowen in Chapter 7 of this volume, are exceptional, in that they originated far from Cromwell's home territory and they seem naturally to have emerged under the aegis of Sir Robert Harley, a long-standing patron of godly causes in eastern Wales. Edward Hollister was identified by the diarist, John Moore, as a moving spirit behind the February petition. There were two family groupings of some substance of that name. One was concentrated around Westerleigh, Gloucestershire, and produced the Bristol sectary and 1653 MP, Denis Hollister.[15] The other group was settled in various parishes in Monmouthshire, and is obviously more likely to have been active in the 1642 petition from that county. Edward Hollister was probably the propertied individual from Shirenewton whose heirs in the 1650s held burgages in the earl of Pembroke's town of Caerleon.[16] It is suggested by Bowen that the embattled godly Welsh petitioners refocused their hopes away from Harley and on to the more radical Cromwell. An alternative line of explanation is that the Welsh petitioners had lobbied the Long Parliament regularly and energetically from its opening: indeed, on the day that Cromwell spoke for Lilburne, John Whistler, a member for Oxford, produced evidence of privileges unlawfully enjoyed by Catholics in Llantarnam, in the heart of Monmouthshire.[17] On this reading, Cromwell could be viewed as another friend in the House used by the determined and astute Welsh lobbyists, rather than as successor to the somehow flagging (or moderate) Harley; the latter, after all, was full of vigour in chairing important committees and had used his brief vacation break in September 1641 not to rest but to visit Leintwardine and Wigmore churches with a sledge-hammer.[18]

Cromwell's immediately noticeable quality of persistence doubtless recommended him to lobbyists, and is also evident in another area of Cromwell's activity in the House, which we must now address: moving items of business. The House rewarded men who could effectively frame a question, as Bulstrode Whitelocke smugly recorded in regard to himself, with early recognition when they stood up to speak.[19] Cromwell was successful in catching the Speaker's eye, and once a topic had captured his attention, he was likely to stick with it. His interest in the case of the Thynne brothers is an example. Sir James Thynne, MP for Wiltshire and 'one of the wealthiest members of the House', sued his brother, Henry Frederick Thynne, a Shropshire landowner who had sought a seat unsuccessfully in both parliaments of 1640.[20] They disputed their patrimonial inheritance. In February

1641, Cromwell was named to a committee on breaches of parliamentary privilege in general, but on 22 May along came an opportunity to pursue a concrete example. He moved an irregularity by Sir James, who when an order had been brought against him by his brother had claimed parliamentary privilege. Sir James's own petition then went to the Lords. It was Cromwell again who moved on the 31st that Sir James Thynne should attend the House to account for himself, and in July and August had himself included in committees on the Thynne dispute and for a bill to allow disafforesting of the Thynne estate.[21] The case was kept warm throughout the summer, and on 20 July there was a division in the Commons in which Sir James Thynne was given support by the courtiers Edward Hyde and Lord Falkland, against his critics, who included Bulstrode Whitelocke and John Maynard.[22] The final judgment in the case was that Thynne had indeed breached privilege. Here was an upholding of parliamentary privilege, a beleaguered principle, but here also was one, said in one recent account to have been 'the least wealthy man returned to both the Short and the Long Parliaments', clipping the wings of one of the most wealthy.[23]

In parliamentary affairs, seizing the initiative came naturally to Cromwell. The Thynne case was by no means the only business in the first session of the parliament to be moved by him, but his advocacy was not always rewarded. On 30 December 1640, it was he who moved the second reading of the bill for annual parliaments, which had been brought in by William Strode on the 24th. After the second reading, it went to committee and under the supervision of Edmund Prideaux emerged as a very different bill on 19 January. There seems to be no record of Cromwell's further participation in the process that led the bill to mutate into an act for triennial parliaments.[24] On 10 April 1641 in a House preoccupied by the trial of Charles I's chief minister, the earl of Strafford, Cromwell moved that Sabbath observance should be improved by strengthening the existing good laws, and stimulated a debate that focused on reported breaches of the Sabbath in London. As a magistrate of significant experience, albeit punctuated by a lengthy exclusion from office during most of the 1630s, Cromwell could speak credibly of the topic, but the outcome was an order to the metropolitan authorities to tighten up on enforcement, rather than concrete proposals for enhanced legislation.[25] On 4 June, Cromwell moved the first business of the day, consideration of a clerk's office in exchequer. Presumably, it was this matter that led Christopher Hill to attribute to Cromwell a leading part in exchequer reform, but this cannot be supported by the evidence.[26] Cromwell called for investigation of the clerkship of the parcels, an office that was considered superfluous even in Queen Elizabeth's time. It was no more than an archaic minor imposition, which though a function of the exchequer, was closely associated with the court of wards.[27] This association with a discredited law court, the target of remedial legislation, exposed the clerk of the parcels to attack from reformers, and the office was in the gift of the lord chief baron, whose occupant in 1641, Sir Humphrey Davenport, was facing impeachment. Cromwell's attack on this obscure clerkship was no drive for wide-ranging exchequer reform but rather a minor tying up of loose ends, or an opportunistic hunt for some fresh clauses for the impeachment bill. A committee was formed, but nothing more was heard of the clerk of the parcels, and the impeachment of Davenport was dropped.

He was on firmer ground in the case of the Huntingdonshire enclosures. These were of lands centred on Somersham, near St Ives, allotted to the queen as part of her marriage settlement. They had been enclosed and subsequently sold to the earl of Manchester and his son, Lord Mandeville. The interests of a number of groups were allegedly prejudiced by the enclosure: not only the titled tenants and poorer inhabitants of the lands in question, but also inhabitants of other manors who had lost common rights.[28] A bill to confirm the jointure element of the royal marriage settlement had been given a first reading in the Commons on 12 December 1640, having originated in the Lords.[29] In February, dressing his motion as a reciprocal compliment after the king had approved bills for the subsidy and for triennial parliaments, Denzil Holles moved the second reading.[30] Subsequently, Cromwell was named to the bill's committee, which took on the petition of the Somersham inhabitants.[31] The jointure committee now became a vehicle for pursuing the affair of the enclosures. On 22 May, the day that he moved a breach of parliamentary privilege by Sir James Thynne, Cromwell turned the business of the queen's jointure into another matter of privilege. Holles had presented the petition of Lord Mandeville against rioters who had thrown down enclosures even while their own petition was pending in the Commons. Mandeville sought an order to grant him possession until the inhabitants' petition was determined, but Cromwell attributed the violence, 'which he did not approve nor desire to justify', to Mandeville's interference, which he claimed was a breach of Commons' privilege.[32] He resumed the attack on 1 June, speaking again in lurid terms of petitions from ten towns (did the diarist who recorded it mean townships or settlements?) against the jointure bill, of the populace assembling to destroy enclosures and of peers ready to send in the militia.[33] On the 9th, he moved for a committee to consider the claim that the earl of Manchester had issued 60 writs against the poor of Huntingdonshire for pulling down enclosures, and successfully demanded that it should be a revived jointure committee, which had by then evidently run out of steam on its original subject of the royal marriage settlement.[34]

The names of Holles and Cromwell appear too often together in the unfolding enclosures affair for them not to have been working together. It was during committee hearings on this matter that Sir Edward Hyde clashed with Cromwell, who orchestrated the tactics at the committee of the dispossessed inhabitants, 'a very rude kind of people', according to Hyde. Cromwell, 'in great fury', objected to Hyde's attempts to impose order on the proceedings.[35] The support shown by the committee towards its chairman when he appealed for their help 'enflamed' Cromwell further, to the extent that Hyde threatened a suspension of the committee and a report to the full House. Hyde was convinced that Cromwell pursued a lifelong vendetta against him as a result, but the matter never went beyond the committee chamber, so should not be included among the failures and gaffes which historians have attributed to Cromwell. It was in connection with this clash that John Hampden, whose death in 1643 makes him useful to us as a commentator unclouded by later prejudice, described Cromwell as 'one that would sit well at the mark'. My attempts to elucidate this phrase, which seems a mix of horsemanship and archery, have not been fruitful; but I believe it is an attempt to convey Cromwell's habit of taking things to limits, 'to the wire', as we might say.[36]

Cromwell seems to have been in confident mood in the enclosures affair, and was effective in representing fellow East Anglians. He was not always so successful. On 9 August, his suggestion that the godly Lords Bedford and Saye and Sele should be added to the less reliable marquis of Hertford as guardians of the prince of Wales fell on deaf ears. This has been characterised as a failure by Cromwell to find a seconder, but it is unclear whether he deliberately and formally moved his proposal or whether it was an impulsive suggestion thrown into debate.[37] Just before the recess, he secured a significant success in moving that parishioners should be encouraged to fund lecturers in parishes where there was no preaching, including on weekdays. This order was later printed.[38] But in introducing petitions and moving orders to the Commons before the six-week recess, Cromwell had been busy rather than overwhelmingly successful. The energy, the passion and the sheer memorableness of his interventions—Sir Simonds D'Ewes, in particular, seems to have become something of a Cromwell-watcher—have to be set against the committees that went nowhere, unsuccessful attempts to blow fire into what were sometimes pretty dull embers, and the emphasis in the issues he sponsored on the particular, not to say the parochial, as opposed to the great and general.

Away from the particular causes for which he was the leading spokesman, Cromwell was also active in playing a significant part, albeit a contributory one, in the great issues of the day, and here his achievement was consistent and impressive. On 28 November 1640, he was named to the strategically important committee on religion at the universities, a sub-committee of the grand committee of religion with potential for shaping the theological orientation of the clergy. On 11 December, the London petition on religion, the 'root and branch' petition, was presented to parliament, and a week later Cromwell was named to another sub-committee of the grand committee on religion, this time to examine petitions in favour of preaching (i.e. puritan) ministers.[39] Bishops were in Cromwell's sights from December, when he was named to a committee to impeach Matthew Wren of Ely.[40] It was during a debate on the root and branch petition in February 1641 that Sir John Strangways asserted that bishops were the third estate of the realm, goading Cromwell into a sharp contradiction that provoked calls for him to be brought to the bar.[41] Cromwell was 'reprimanded by the House' in a recent summary of this incident, but this is too strong.[42] Some MPs, doubtless opponents of root and branch, wanted him brought to the bar, but the Speaker did not intervene, Cromwell was never brought to the bar, and after not only Pym and Holles but also D'Ewes (no natural ally of Oliver's) spoke in support of him, he resumed his trenchant attack on the wealth of the bishops. Hardly a 'counter-productive' gaffe or a blunder, but a failed (and counter-productive) attempt by his opponents to silence him.

Three months later, on 11 May, in a debate on how £400,000 might be raised to supply the government, Cromwell spoke in support of the burgess for Barnstaple, George Peard, who suggested that the estates of the deans of cathedrals would supply a plentiful fund.[43] On the 21st, Cromwell and Sir Henry Vane junior handed a bill for the abolition of episcopacy to Sir Arthur Hesilrige, who in turn passed it to Sir Edward Dering to put before the House, and Cromwell was able to sustain the momentum of his anti-episcopal zeal in committees for the impeachment of the bishop of Bath and Wells.[44] The icono-clastic streak was visible also in the weeks before the recess, when as well as securing liberty for founding lectureships (a significant blow against the church's disciplinary machinery) he spoke against the Book of Common Prayer persuasively enough to provoke a division in the House.[45] Cromwell's speech in favour of an 'oath of association', on the day that the Protestation was adopted by the Commons (3 May 1641), chimed perfectly with this religious outlook. The Protestation was an affirmation by the members of the House of Commons in support of the 'true reformed Protestant religion' against innovations in the church, of the king's person and of the privileges of parlia-ment. A near-contemporary view that this had been first mooted by opposition peers, but was bounced into the Commons in a pre-cipitate speech by Henry Marten finds cautious support in a recent detailed narrative of the high politics of 1640–1641.[46] If this were the case, then Cromwell's speech was another strategic intervention rather than a general oration of approval. The oath of association had been an Elizabethan state security device, but the Protestation of 1641 was a vow rather than an oath. If Cromwell did indeed use the words 'oath of association', it suggests that his frame of mind was at this point more in tune with Tudor precedent than with contemporary puritan sensibilities, which scrupled, not to say stumbled, over the principle and practice of oath-taking.[47]

When the exhausted members adjourned themselves on 9 September for a short recess, a less self-critical soul than Cromwell would have been justified in considering his performance in this parliament so far generally a success. He had been named to 22 committees, had moved nine items of business, had brought in six petitions, had in the first month found a place on the important committee on the universities and had made speeches that impressed contemporary observers, even if we discount the later memoirs of politicians compiled in the knowledge of Cromwell's greatness or notoriety. This has not been the view taken by historians, who have seen his performance as energetic but marred by 'gaffes'[48] or 'a string of blunders'.[49] The examples of his maladroitness presented above—and others might be cited to the same effect—involve his bluntness or even violence of speech and his willingness to flout convention or social niceties. Politicians of any age might consider the less than positive image that Cromwell was creating in the minds of some in parliament a reasonable price to pay for being noted as one to watch. In his separately-published *Oxford Dictionary of National Biography* study of Cromwell, John Morrill has seen May 1641 as something of a turning-point in Cromwell's early parliamentary career. Because he was 'a man on the margins socially and not entirely at ease with himself... he was dropped from the opposition front bench speaker's panel after May 1641'. He 'remained a useful man on committees', but spoke less in the House.[50] This is misleading. May 1641 certainly was a busy month for Cromwell as it was for other parliament-men who opposed the government; but I would argue that it was no particular watershed and that it was rather the brief interval between the sessions that marked a significant shift in the pattern of Cromwell's parliamentary career.

## II

Between 20 October 1641, when parliament resumed its sittings, and 6 September 1642, when Cromwell was called to his last committee, he was nominated to 39 committees, an average of three a month as against two a month in the earlier period. This evidence of a quickening pace of activity is visible in the number of motions which Cromwell initiated in the same period: 33, as against nine before the recess. The number of petitions he sponsored remained about the same, by contrast, providing the impression that Cromwell's experience of parliament in the first session was qualitatively different from his experience in the second. He now also added new skills to his portfolio of parliamentary experience. He became a regular intermediary between the two Houses. His first visit to the Lords followed his own motion for a conference, on 24 August 1641, on the topic of financing the disbanding of the English and Scots armies. He went up successfully to request the conference, but not until March 1642 did he again walk on a mission through the court of requests and the Painted Chamber to the peers' chamber, as a spokesman for his own House.[51] Professor Crawford has discussed the variety and significance of contacts between the Houses. Conferences could be proposed by either House, with Commons men acting as reporters from those initiated by the Lords or as managers of those suggested by the lower House. The task of a reporter was to bring back a clear summary of the Lords' arguments, while a manager had to present arguments that had usually been constructed in a Commons committee. At a free conference, both tasks were harder, as the whole issue was thrashed out in debate. Some of Cromwell's increased involvement is explained by the increasing number of conferences as a medium for contact between the Houses: there were only five in November 1640, but in August 1641 a high water mark was reached when 46 conferences were held.[52] The range of tasks associated with inter-cameral co-operation was rather wider than simply reporting or managing, of course. A parliament-man could also go to the Lords to request a conference, take a message, bring an answer back (not necessarily having taken a message), take a bill to the Lords, join a committee to prepare for a conference with them or be part of the conference itself. Professor Crawford suggests that the simple carrying of messages to the Lords called for some skill but was 'mainly a ceremonial duty'.[53] This may be to understate the level of diplomatic and social skills required, not only because the messenger usually hoped for a satisfactory answer and thus had to frame it appropriately, but also because of the social gulf between peers and parliament-men which the intermediaries had successfully bridged with a code of etiquette. It was possible for even the most experienced to make a hash of it on either score. Sir Robert Harley once forgot one of the messages he had come with, and only rescued his mission after some urgent and unseemly whispering by one of his colleagues.[54]

In support of those who argue for his lack of polish, it must be noted that after his visit to the Lords in August 1641, Cromwell never again went there specifically to request another conference. But he was occupied instead in tasks that were probably more important. He brought answers back on six occasions, and a report back once; took a message to the Lords on six occasions and took up a bill, some orders, votes, lists and a letter on seven separate visits. He was a member of five inter-House committees, managed two conferences and reported one. Almost every one of these endeavours was associated with the military build-up prior to the outbreak of the civil war. They included orders in support of Sir John Hotham after he had closed the gates of Hull in the face of the king;[55] various orders and plans for the expeditionary force to quell the rebellion in Ireland;[56] and a number of instruments on the implementation of the militia ordinance.[57] This degree of specialisation of purpose by Cromwell is striking, and is in contrast with the performance of Sir Robert Harley in the same period. Harley's inter-cameral work was greater in volume, but was across a wider range of topics. Harley took 16 messages to the Lords in this period, as against Cromwell's six, and managed four conferences compared with Cromwell's two. Sir Peter Wentworth was another radical whose 13 appearances in conferences with the Lords easily outstripped Cromwell's five. For carrying of messages, none of these men could apparently match John Pym, who carried 18 messages in the first session and 20 in the second, but caution needs to be exercised when defining the 'carrying of messages'.[58]

Adding another new string to his bow as a parliamentarian, Cromwell acted as a teller in four divisions in the second session. In the context of the total number of divisions in the first two whole years of the Long Parliament—54 in 1641, remarkably also 54 in 1642—his contribution in this area seems scarcely worthy of mention. But in the context of divisions in the entirety of this parliament down to December 1648, it was to be a significant start, since Cromwell comes seventh in the list of first-named tellers, performing this task on 17 occasions. Among tellers as a whole (either first-named or second-named), he is still in the top 20, with 31 tellerships in total.[59] Harley, by contrast, was a teller on 14 occasions, while at the top of the tree of opposition leaders there was a wild variation in the statistics, with Holles being a teller in 162 divisions, and Pym in none.[60] It is as yet unclear as to what recommended parliament-men to their colleagues as tellers, and even more so why some men should usually have taken first or second place in this particular activity, but Cromwell's four tellerships provide some insight into his thinking in 1642. It was perhaps natural that he should support the Independent minister, Thomas Coleman, in his aspirations to be lecturer in a London parish, but in March led those in favour of Coleman's appointment to defeat in a division by ten votes.[61] On the 17th, London merchants supported a proposal that double customs duty should be imposed on imports of sugar, with relief for cargoes from the colonies and from Portugal. The move anticipated the navigation act of 1651, but it may have been the gesture towards Portugal, newly liberated from Spanish rule, that provoked the objection from Cromwell, as it did from D'Ewes.[62] The division was a draw, but on 4 April Cromwell was again on the losing side when the Houses divided on taxes to be paid by foreign merchants.[63] None of these was a matter of first or even second importance, but the division on 11 June certainly was, when Cromwell teamed with Holles in support of a motion that the departure for the king's camp in York of nine peers was 'a high affront and contempt of both Houses'. This time Cromwell caught the mood well. With a count of 100 votes to 55, the yeas outnumbered the noes by nearly 100 per cent.[64]

Cromwell was busier in the second session because the deepening political crisis impelled him to decisive political activity, but the same was not true of every member of the Long Parliament. When the

House re-assembled after the recess, Cromwell was immediately evident in the attack on the bishops as a political bloc in the Lords,
supporting the younger Sir Henry Vane in preparing reasons to
present to the Lords why 13 bishops should lose their votes in the
upper House. Vane asserted that bishops had in the canons of 1640
bound themselves never to assent to laws that would remove their
votes, and Cromwell proposed presenting to the peers a line of argument that seemed like an attempt to fudge the significance of the
move, a suggestion that the suspension of the bishops' votes was but
a temporary makeshift. D'Ewes spoke to expose the folly of suggesting such a pretence to the Lords. The two men clashed again
soon after, when D'Ewes defended a candidate for an episcopal see
as pro-reform, but Cromwell continued ever the root-and-brancher,
and helped win a division which secured the halting of any further admissions to the episcopal bench.[65] Although he is not known
to have played a part in drafting the Grand Remonstrance, he was
keenly in support of it, in the teeth of government managers who
thought it 'unseasonable' after the king's many concessions. In mid-
November came the famous exchange between Cromwell and Lord
Falkland, in which Cromwell assured the member for Newport, Isle
of Wight (Lucius Carey, who enjoyed the courtesy title of Lord
Falkland) that the Remonstrance commanded such support that it
needed no debate. On 22 November, the argument raged from nine
in the morning until two the following morning, and when it was
over Falkland dryly asked Cromwell whether there had after all been a
debate. Cromwell promised to accept Carey's predictions in future but
then whispered urgently that 'if the Remonstrance had been rejected
he would have sold all he had the following morning and never have
seen England more'.[66]

There seems little doubt that the urgency visible in Cromwell's
political conduct late in 1641 was stimulated by the Irish rebellion, which intensified his anti-popish outlook. On 4 November, he
reported further details of the army plot of the previous summer, and
on the 6th moved that the earl of Essex should be asked to command the militia south of the Trent. While one historian has recently
presented this as Cromwell acting as a 'cat's paw' of the opposition
leadership in both Houses, in the context of Cromwell's parliamentary performance since November 1640 the idea of his being anyone's
stooge is scarcely convincing. It must however be conceded that he
was indeed playing an essentially supportive role in this debate, behind
Holles, Hotham and Sir Henry Vane junior, and doubtless supplying

the passionate advocacy.[67] On 6 December, he involved himself in the disputed election at Arundel, Sussex. His intervention was framed as a call for elections without interference, but here it is hard to avoid the conclusion that his interest had been aroused just as much by the Catholicism of the local proprietor, Thomas Howard, 14th earl of Arundel.[68] In similar vein, on the 28th, Cromwell persisted in an attack on John Digby, earl of Bristol (a privy councillor but not a Catholic), now made opportune by the turn of high politics: among Bristol's crimes was his attempt to convert the king to Catholicism, and to the charge sheet Cromwell added an allegation that the earl had advised Charles to raise an army.[69] Bristol's allies rallied successfully to thwart the attack.

From this point until the outbreak of civil war, Cromwell exhibited many indications of being in the grip of the crisis that seized the country at large. His own sense of alarm was inflamed further by the king's failed attempt on a group of five MPs and one peer early in January, and his subsequent withdrawal to York. Cromwell's interventions became even more pointed. Immediately after his frustrated attack on the earl of Bristol, Cromwell began to try to influence the composition of the officer cadre destined for service in the army being raised for Ireland; instigated the arrest of a Huntingdonshire magistrate for spreading lurid rumours of an impending war between king and parliament; and successfully moved that the apologia published by Sir Edward Dering, erstwhile collaborator with Cromwell in the campaign to abolish episcopacy, should be burnt by the common hangman.[70] On 14 January 1642, after a conference with the Lords, he persuaded the Commons that a committee should be set up to put the country on military alert. The resulting committee was a small group dominated by opposition leaders, but in a consequence unusual after one of Cromwell's successful motions, he himself was not among them. It must have been a put-up job, and given that he played no further known part in the drafting of what became the militia ordinance, the phrase 'leading role' seems not the most apposite description of his involvement.[71]

In February 1642, Cromwell was named a commissioner for Irish affairs, and was an enthusiast of the adventurers' act by which cash was raised for the punitive expedition in return for land grants. He acted in support of Sir John Clotworthy in this scheme, but was unable to persuade the House to allow the reluctant Clotworthy a delay in taking up his commission in Ireland.[72] By April and through the summer, Cromwell was among the most assiduous attenders at the committee for Irish affairs.[73] When on 3 May he sought to put this committee in charge of ejecting Catholics from Dublin, other counsels prevailed, and his motion was laid aside as 'impertinent and useless'.[74] But Cromwell was not daunted, appearing in May on other committees for Ireland, requesting the Lords to prioritise the raising of the expeditionary force and taking other initiatives on Ireland in the Commons.[75] He was very active in promoting the additional 'sea adventure' to Ireland, and must have been party to the appointment to a command in the army of John Humfrey, former sergeant-major-general of Massachusetts and a client or friend of Lord Brooke (the newly-appointed commander) and Lord Saye and Sele, Sir Henry Vane junior, John Winthrop and Hugh Peter: enthusiasts of the 'New England Way' of Independency, and veterans of Providence Island and other godly colonial schemes in the Americas.[76] On 24 June, Cromwell helped ensure that the earl of Clanricarde's unauthorised concessions to Catholics in Galway were referred to the commissioners for Irish affairs, and the following day was able, this time successfully, to suggest once more that the commissioners should consider how to deal with the Catholic hordes in Dublin.[77] For reasons discussed elsewhere in this volume (Chapter 5), the plans for Ireland drawn up in 1642 were not a success, despite the best efforts of Cromwell and other equally committed individuals, and after June, his attention switched to the military build-up and the preparations for civil war that led him to quit parliament for East Anglia by early August.

## III

Finally, consideration needs to be given to the questions of Cromwell's social standing in the Commons and his allies. The prevailing tendency of modern biographers is to accept rather uncritically the picture of the rustic, clumsily-shaven unknown Cromwell painted by Sir Philip Warwick, a view that finds a resounding echo in the remarks by the earl of Clarendon and others. These were either wholly or partly social sneers, however, and need to be offset by consideration of Cromwell's extensive matrix of relations and other acquaintances in the House. The adventitious roots of Cromwell's kinship in parliament were exposed and dissected in Victorian times.[78] John Hampden and Sir Thomas Barrington of Hatfield Broad Oak were two prominent MPs who were his cousins, but if relatives by marriage are taken

into account, Cromwell and Hampden between them could identify between them 17 relatives of one kind or another who were
parliament-men.[79] As for Cromwell's wealth, John Morrill in a glorious hostage to fortune tells us that 'Cromwell must have been the least
wealthy man returned to both the Short and the Long Parliaments'.[80]
Even before the evidence of Cromwell's liquidating his estates in 1640
to make himself cash-rich is taken into account, this seems a doubtful assertion.[81] Could he, for example, have been poorer than Ralph
Goodwin, servant of the earls of Northampton, on an annuity of £50
a year, or William Chadwell, burgess for Mitchell in Cornwall, the
son of a yeoman? Both these were men-of-business or agents, so perhaps we should be asking whether Cromwell was the least wealthy
independent man returned to both these parliaments, for no-one has
yet argued that Cromwell was directly beholden to a great patron. But
as Barry Coward suggests, kinship in itself is no guarantee of political
alliances, and it is difficult to be certain how close Cromwell was to
opposition leaders in either House. The best evidence may be found
in the 56 committees where Cromwell was named with others: who
were his associates?

Caveats need immediately to be entered before analysing the
committee lists of the Commons. Chris Kyle has cautioned against
assuming too much of the lists of committee members, which had
grown hugely in number under James I and Charles I. It is particularly hazardous to take name order as a measure of seniority on a given
committee.[82] It cannot even be taken for granted that parliament-men
turned up at the committees to which they were nominated. In a
sample six months of 1644, D'Ewes averaged a committee a month
that he ignored.[83] Also there were plenty of other places in parliament where men might work constructively or destructively, socialise
and gossip. Nevertheless, the evidence of the 56 committees provides
some basis for useful generalisations about who Cromwell's colleagues
were. These individuals may not have liked Cromwell; they may not
even necessarily have interacted with him, any more than individuals who travel on the same train every day or drink in the same pub
like or interact with each other. What follows is simply a guide to
associations in the period November 1640–August 1642, but association is a perfectly respectable and statistically valid line of enquiry,
the sample is actually quite substantial, and the caveats should not be
allowed to impede use of what remains our most plentiful, if most
obvious and well-known, source, the *Commons Journal* committee
lists.

Among these associates were men known to Cromwell before 1640. William Spurstowe, a London mercer, worked with Cromwell on the lectureship in Huntingdon in the 1630s, and we find that he served on some five committees with him in 1640–1642. But this is a quite a low level of association, and indeed suggests that no enduring contacts between the men persisted beyond their work on the lecture.[84] Spurstowe was a merchant, and generally speaking the London merchants, forming a bloc with each other, were not to be found frequently appearing with Cromwell. Samuel Vassall, a very prominent opposition figure in a wide range of committees on trade and especially the navy and related matters, was another merchant who like Spurstowe cannot be considered an associate of Cromwell's (they sat on a mere six committees together), and others from the London business and civic community could be added to the list. Isaac Penington is probably the best known of all these men, and he also sat with Cromwell on only six committees. Cromwell was in fact not to be found on the great committees involving the directly linked topics of trade, the navy and the customs: it was an area he rarely strayed into.

Of course, it was perfectly possible for men who shared Cromwell's outlook on religious and political affairs not to serve on many committees with him, because of their own comparatively low level of activity in this particular aspect of parliamentary life. Sir Nathaniel Barnardiston, knight of the shire for Suffolk, is a good example. He served on only three committees with Cromwell, but his overall profile in committees was modest, with a total of 10 committee nominations. There were also those, like Bulstrode Whitelocke, who sat on eight committees with Cromwell, but did not include him among the seven or eight men he considered his political associates at this time.[85] Of those whose names coincided more often with Cromwell's on the committee lists, there is a significant cluster around the double-figure mark. Among these are Harbottle Grimston, famous for his denunciation of Archbishop Laud as the 'sty of all pestilent filth' (eight committees);[86] Sir Arthur Hesilrige and William Strode, two of the five Commons men sought by Charles in January 1642 (11 committees each); Sir Samuel Rolle, knight of the shire for Devon and a vigorous anti-papist and anti-episcopal campaigner (10 committees) and Thomas Pury, whose speech against deans and chapters of cathedrals was published in 1641 (11). All of these figures were fellow-travellers with Cromwell, but the example of Sir John Culpeper (10) is an illustration of how sheer ubiquity in the Commons (Culpeper sat

on around 130 committees in the first session alone) could ensure that
Cromwell would inevitably rub shoulders with people with a different
outlook from his. Although Culpeper was strongly in favour of reform
and is said to have been significant in the drafting of the Protestation, he drew the line at the attack on bishops, and became a leading
supporter of the king. It is not the case, however, that Cromwell
was named routinely with men who became prominent in the king's
counsels. Sir Edward Hyde sat only on 6 committees with him, so the
two may well have had little contact with each other before their spat
at the committee on the fenland enclosures.

When we examine who sat on more than a dozen committees
with Cromwell in this period, we encounter some familiar faces.
Miles Corbett (12), an East Anglian lawyer with, in political terms, a
similar profile to Cromwell's, is there, as are the important legislator
from Worcestershire, Serjeant John Wylde (13) and the Welsh-born
London lawyer, John Glynn (14). The three others of the 'five members' group come into this category: Pym (14), Cromwell's cousin,
Hampden (15) and Denzil Holles (15), as do, less famously, William
Wheeler, MP for Westbury (15), an associate of Sir Robert Pye (12),
both men being anti-episcopalians. A number of Cromwell's relatives
can be found in this list of associates: we have mentioned Hampden
and Pye, and among others there were Sir William Masham (13) and
Oliver St John (13). Even when these associations are traced, however,
kinship with Cromwell remained no guarantee that a parliament-man
would be galvanised by his dynamism: Valentine Walton sat only on
5 committees with Cromwell and Edmund Dunch, 2.

Three names stand out as being called to serve by the Commons
clerks most frequently in conjunction with Cromwell's, and therefore did indeed probably turn up with him in the chambers around
the palace of Westminster. Two of these were his relatives, Sir Gilbert
Gerard (19) and above all, his most frequent accomplice, Sir Thomas
Barrington, who was named to 21 committees with him. Barrington
was Cromwell's first cousin and Barrington's sister married Sir Gilbert.
Barrington was senior to Cromwell both in age and political experience. He had been a member of the Providence Island company
with opposition peers like Lord Brooke and Lord Saye and Sele and
with Commons men like Pym, and it was through Barrington that
Cromwell came within the orbit of what has been called the 'junto'
of reformers working in both Houses. Like Cromwell, Barrington
was actively anti-episcopalian and anti-papist, but unlike him worked
on drafts of important parliamentary documents such as the militia

ordinance and the Grand Remonstrance. Barrington was named to the recess committee of September 1641 and the committee of safety of January 1642, two bodies that guaranteed the continuity and integrity of the Commons' programme when normal sittings were suspended, marking him as of considerably greater importance than his cousin, the member for Cambridge. Barrington, in other words, must have been Cromwell's parliamentary mentor. Gerard was named to around 180 committees before August 1642, and like Barrington had been a Providence Island company member. Both he and his brother-in-law Barrington had been active in managing the trial of Strafford, another area in which his cousin by marriage had contributed nothing, so he has to be considered another figure senior to Cromwell.[87]

The third outstanding associate of Cromwell was Sir Robert Harley: the two men sat on 19 committees together. Harley was outside the typical East Anglia and kinship matrix in which we find Cromwell habitually situated politically, and no convincing evidence has been assembled to associate him with the Providence Island bicameral 'junto'. Like Barrington and Gerard, though, he was Cromwell's senior by age and political experience, and was as much in the grip of perfervid anti-popery as any of them. Harley and Cromwell worked together throughout the period under review, and in 1642 alone worked on a number of important projects. They joined Hampden and Strode to tackle university regulation and served together as commissioners for Irish affairs.[88] They were both members of a small group of seven added to the committee for innovations;[89] worked together on the bill for the Irish Adventurers;[90] served together on a joint committee with the Lords on the news of the king's activities in York;[91] took responsibility for ensuring that the Tower of London was in safe hands,[92] in June were both at the committee for scandalous ministers to receive a petition from Huntington, which was referred to Cromwell;[93] and in August it was Harley who took to the Lords an ordinance indemnifying Cromwell for his military activities in and around Cambridge.[94]

In June 1642, on a committee formed to receive military intelligence on the king's movements, Cromwell's 15 colleagues served on committees with him on an average of 12 times each, from November 1640 to September 1642.[95] In the interventions by Cromwell that impressed the diarists, he is often seen surrounded by his associates. The committee of 13 that drafted the Protestation, for example, included Pym, Hampden, Barrington, Harley and only two, Fiennes

and Stapilton, were not regularly found in his company.[96] He was
far from being an awkward loner; indeed, by nature and practice,
I would contend, he was an animal that usually hunted with the pack.
Among Cromwell's very last engagements in parliament, before he left
to take up arms full time, was a conference with the Lords on bringing in gold and silver plate for the impending war effort. A group
of four among the eight delegates had worked together many times
before: Harley, Barrington, Pye and Cromwell himself.[97] These were
the 'godly honest men' that Cromwell was comfortable to have about
him in parliament: soon afterwards he would be recruiting the godly
and the honest in the field.[98] And yet it is striking that few of his
close associates of 1641–1642 were still in that relationship to him a
few years later. By 1645, Barrington, Pym and Hampden were dead,
and Gerard and Harley had become aligned with Presbyterianism to
a degree that would help ensure that both were imprisoned when
the New Model army purged parliament in December 1648. Ties of
region, kinship, anti-popery and 'root and branch' opposition to the
church hierarchy may have been the crucial ingredients in Cromwell's
parliamentary debut, but they soon yielded to an identification with
Independency, an ideological vehicle that transcended the politics of
family or region, and which proved infinitely adaptable to changing
political conditions.

## IV

The portrait of Cromwell that emerges from this survey is of a busy
and well-connected parliament-man, who from the opening ceremonial threw himself unstintingly into life at Westminster during the
Long Parliament. He proved himself as an effective and dogged advocate in causes that engaged his energies and commitment. We see him
extending his range across the various tasks and skills of a parliament-
man, starting off as a vocal proxy for interests outside the House but
by degrees acquiring the skill, polish and reputation required of an
agent or servant of the House itself. He moved, in other words, from
being an outsider to being an insider, acting as a teller in divisions and
becoming practised in the various means of communication between
the Houses. He took on his share of committees, tending to con-
centrate on those involving redress of grievances, whether suffered by
individuals or the common weal, or the performance of some exec-
utive action by parliament. His involvement in legislative committees
was markedly more modest, and Cromwell seems to have evinced

little interest in the detail of the landmark orders, ordinances and remonstrances that emerged in this phase of the Long Parliament's history. At no stage, from his first utterances in November 1640, in aid of the martyrs to Laudianism, does the word 'backbencher' convincingly capture Cromwell's profile. He was too busy, too controversial, too noticed by the diarists, too much in the thick of things for that anachronistic word to exercise much purchase. A historian seeking to prove that Cromwell really was obscure has to reckon with the disproportionate amount of surviving unwitting testimony documenting his doings. Nor was this a tale of Oliver in Blunderland. Too many of his 'gaffes' can be read as deliberate provocations of the staid, the complacent and the smooth-mannered in what he would have considered were in fact good causes, for that to be so. Politically, Cromwell was doubtless on the margins of the main opposition grouping spread through the two Houses of parliament, the 'junto', to use the word sometimes used at the time, and now current in scholarly parlance.[99] But as his political behaviour and associations suggest, he was no-one's stool pigeon, and in less than two years built up his own networks of contacts and specific parliamentary skills. This was a parliament in which men could construct special skills, probably the first in which an individual, unmandated member could build sustained expertise as a legislator, an advocate, a teller, a mediator. These technical competences were honed in a highly-charged political climate in which the baser political skills of forging allegiances and identifying enemies were at a premium. John Hampden's summary of Cromwell's habitual near-the-knuckle early conduct in parliament provides us with the title of this essay; by April 1644 Sir Simonds D'Ewes was hearing stories of how Cromwell was packing his regiment with Independents.[100] The Cromwell who returned from the field to parliament for brief periods in 1644 had become a formidable political operator, but we must not under-estimate how much he had learned of the trade of politicking between 1640 and 1642.

## Notes

1. Biographies of all MPs mentioned in this essay will appear in the *History of Parliament: House of Commons 1640–1660* volumes when published on completion.
2. J. Morrill, *Oliver Cromwell* (Oxford, 2007), 12.
3. I. Roots, *The Great Rebellion* (1966), 34.
4. *Procs. LP*, i. 52–3, 58–61, 63–7, 69–72.

5. Sir P. Warwick, *Memoires of the Reign of King Charles I* (1701), 248.
6. Warwick, *Memoires*, 248; *Old DNB*, 'John Lilburne'.
7. Coward, *Cromwell*, 17.
8. BL, Add. MS 70,081, fo. 2.
9. *CJ*, ii. 44.
10. BL, Harl. MS 163, fo. 182; *A Letter from an Ejected Member of the House of Commons* (1648), 6. The initials of 'G. S.', the author of *A Letter from an Ejected Member*, are filled out in *Online English Short Title Catalogue* and *Early English Books Online*, though not in Wing, as George Skutt, the MP for Poole who was secluded at Pride's Purge. But George Thomason acquired his copy of this publication on 14 September 1648, so the ejection took place before the purge. Skutt, in any case, did not enter the House until December 1645, and 'G. S.' was evidently an MP in 1641. Strangways, member for Bridport, was disabled from sitting on 22 January 1644.
11. J. Morrill, 'The Attack on the Church of England in the Long Parliament', in D. Beales and G. Best (eds), *History, Society and the Churches: Essays in Honour of Owen Chadwick* (Cambridge, 1985), 113.
12. BL, Harl. MS 164, fos. 71, 100v, *PJ*, i. 302–3; ii. 275, 368, 401; iii. 8.
13. BL, Harl. MS 164 fos. 71, 100v.
14. *PJ*, ii. 275.
15. History of Parliament Trust, House of Commons 1640–1660, draft biography of Denis Hollister by S. K. Roberts.
16. J. A. Bradney, *A History of Monmouthshire* (4 vols., 1904–1933), iii. 195.
17. *Procs. LP*, i. 67.
18. J. Spraggon, *Puritan Iconoclasm during the English Civil War* (Woodbridge, 2003), 84–5; J. Eales, *Puritans and Roundheads. The Harleys of Brampton Bryan and the Outbreak of the English Civil War* (Cambridge, 1990), 115–6.
19. BL, Add. MS 37,343, fo. 218.
20. M. F. Keeler, *The Long Parliament, 1640–1641* (Philadelphia, 1954), 360; Coventry Record Office, BA/H/Q/A79/190; Shropshire Archives, BB/B/6/4/1/2.
21. BL, Harl. MS 477, fos. 87v, 117; Harl. MS 163, fo. 218; *CJ*, ii. 91, 217 (where 'Lord' Cromwell should be Oliver), 239.
22. *LJ*, iv. 257, 270, 275, 296, 315, 323, 333; *CJ*, ii. 162, 191, 200, 210, 215, 217, 226, 232.
23. Morrill, *Oliver Cromwell*, 11.
24. *Procs. LP*, ii. 63–4, 222, 223, 225, 228, 229; Conrad Russell, *The Fall of the British Monarchies, 1637–1642* (Oxford, 1991), 225. Professor Morrill incorrectly gives the date of Cromwell's moving the bill for annual parliaments as May 1641: Morrill, *Oliver Cromwell*, 12.
25. *Procs. LP*, iii. 496, 500.
26. BL, Harl. MS 163, fo. 263; C. Hill, *God's Englishman* (1970), 61.

27. L. Squibb (ed.), 'A Book of all the Several Offices of the Court of Exchequer', in *Camden Miscellany* 26 (Camden Society 4th ser. xiv, 1975), 117, 126.
28. *The Life of Edward, Earl of Clarendon* (3 vols, Oxford, 1761) i. 78–9.
29. *Procs. LP*, i. 578, 580, 583; ii. 228.
30. *Procs. LP*, ii. 464.
31. Ibid., 486.
32. BL, Harl. MS 163, fos. 222v, 223v, 224.
33. University of Minnesota Library, Z 942.062, fo. 125.
34. BL, Harl.MS 478, fo. 46a; Harl. MS 163, fo. 303v.
35. *Life of Clarendon*, i. 79–80.
36. Warwick, *Memoires*, 251; J. L. Sanford, *Studies and Illustrations of the Great Rebellion* (1858), 372 seems to take it this way, as does Abbott, i. 132.
37. BL, Harl. MS 478, fo. 46; BL, Harl. MS 163, fo. 303v; *Procs. LP*, ii. 469, iv. 322; A. Fletcher, *The Outbreak of the English Civil War* (1981), 59.
38. BL, Harl. MS 164, fo. 101.
39. J. W. Willis Bund (ed.), *Diary of Henry Townshend of Elmley Lovett* (Worcestershire Historical Society, 2 vols., 1915–1920), i. 16; *CJ*, ii. 54.
40. *CJ*, ii. 56.
41. *Procs. LP*, ii. 398–9.
42. Coward, *Cromwell*, 18.
43. BL, Harl. MS 163, fo. 208.
44. Sir E. Dering, *A Collection of Speeches* (1642), 62.
45. BL, Harl. MS 164, fo. 83.
46. J. Adamson, *The Noble Revolt* (2007), 289–90, 642–3 (n. 123).
47. D. Cressy, 'The Protestation Protested, 1641 and 1642', *HJ*, 45 (2002), 254–6; the discussion of the Protestation in E. Vallance, 'Protestation, Vow, Covenant and Engagement: Swearing Allegiance in the English Civil War', *Historical Research*, 75 (2002), 411–5 blurs the distinction between it and an oath that its framers sought to draw.
48. Coward, *Cromwell*, 17.
49. Gaunt, *Cromwell*, 40.
50. Morrill, *Cromwell*, 12.
51. *CJ*, ii. 270; BL, Harl. MS 164, fo. 57v. For the topography of the palace, see P. Hunneyball, 'Conjectural Plan of the Palace of Westminster', in C. R. Kyle and J. Peacey (eds), *Parliament at Work* (Woodbridge, 2002), xii.
52. P. Crawford, *Denzil Holles 1598–1680. A Study of his Political Career* (1979), 53–4.
53. Crawford, *Denzil Holles*, 55.
54. BL, Harl. MS 164, fo. 288v.
55. *CJ*, ii. 555.
56. *CJ*, ii. 588, 590, 606, 607, 627, 629, 680, 685.
57. *CJ*, ii. 583, 591, 609, 625, 641, 647, 648, 680, 754.

58. Harley and Wentworth data from *CJ*, ii.; for Pym see J. Morrill, 'The Unweariableness of Mr Pym: Influence and Eloquence in the Long Parliament', in S. D. Amussen and M. A. Kishlansky (eds), *Political Culture and Cultural Politics in Early Modern England* (Manchester, 1995), 30, 34, 49 n. 81. The references provided in n. 81 show that between 1 November 1641 and 1 March 1643 (not 1642 as printed in the note), Pym's role between the Houses was overwhelmingly that of a reporter.

59. Analysis of data from *CJ* ii–vi.

60. Pym's death in December 1643, at a point not even half-way through the parliament, needs of course to be taken into account when assessing these performances.

61. *CJ*, ii. 470.

62. *PJ*, ii. 51–2; *CJ*, ii. 482.

63. *CJ*, ii. 620.

64. Ibid.

65. W. H. Coates (ed.), *The Journal of Sir Simonds D'Ewes* (Yale, 1942), 40, 52–4; *CJ*, ii. 298; J. S. A. Adamson, 'Parliamentary Management, Men-of-Business and the House of Lords, 1640–49', in C. Jones (ed.), *A Pillar of the Constitution: The House of Lords in British Politics, 1640–1784* (1989), 25–8.

66. Clarendon, *Rebellion*, i. 420.

67. Coates (ed.), *D'Ewes*, 80, 97–8; Adamson, *Noble Revolt*, 428; Fletcher, *Outbreak of the English Civil War*, 142.

68. Coates (ed.), *D'Ewes*, 236, 260; *CJ*, ii. 333a, 337b.

69. Coates (ed.), *D'Ewes*, 357; Adamson, *Noble Revolt*, 479.

70. Coates (ed.), *D'Ewes*, 359, 371; *CJ*, ii. 360, 361, 365, 386; *PJ*, i. 101, 114, 177–8, 180, 257, 264, 255.

71. *PJ*, i. 67; Fletcher, *Outbreak of the English Civil War*, 142.

72. *PJ*, i. 395; Fletcher, *Outbreak of the English Civil War*, 249.

73. *PJ*, ii. 403, 469; iii. 438.

74. *PJ*, ii. 268.

75. *CJ*, ii. 569, 571, 588, 590, 600, 605, 606; *PJ*, ii. 372, 375–6.

76. *CJ*, ii. 607; *PJ*, iii. 14. For Humfrey, see draft biography of his son, also John Humfrey, History of Parliament, House of Commons 1640–1660 Section.

77. *PJ*, iii. 126, 134; *CJ*, ii. 638.

78. S. J. Weyman, 'Oliver Cromwell's Kinfolk', *EHR*, 6 (1891), 48–60.

79. Weyman, 'Cromwell's Kinfolk', 56.

80. Morrill, *Oliver Cromwell*, 11.

81. See chapter one, above.

82. C. R. Kyle, 'Parliamentary Committees in Early Stuart England', in Kyle and Peacey (eds), *Parliament at Work*, 49–50. For a much earlier attempt to analyse the committee lists, M. F. Keeler, ' "There are No Remedies for Many Things but by a Parliament": Some Opposition

Committees, 1640', in A. A. Aiken and B. D. Henning (eds), *Conflict in Stuart England* (1960), 129–146.

83. BL, Harl. MS 483 compared with the *CJ* record.

84. J. Morrill, 'The Making of Oliver Cromwell', in J. Morrill (ed.), *Oliver Cromwell and the English Revolution* (1990), 30, 42–3.

85. BL, Add. MS 37,343, fos. 249, 249v.

86. For the quotation see *Mr Grymstons Speech in Parliament* (1641).

87. Cromwell and Oliver St John witnessed a deed of settlement made by Gerard in September 1640, in which two other figures from the same kinship network, Sir William Masham and John Hampden, were parties (see Centre for Buckinghamshire Studies, D-X 1/72).

88. *CJ*, i. 425.

89. Of that little group, a further three could claim some kind of kinship with Cromwell; viz.: Sir William Masham, Henry Marten (arguably), Humphrey Salwey. *CJ*, i. 465; Weyman, 'Cromwell's Kinfolk', 51, 52, 56; F. Harrison, *Oliver Cromwell* (1890), 47.

90. *CJ*, ii. 569.

91. Ibid. 609.

92. Ibid. 654.

93. College of Arms, Curia Militaris 1631–1642, fo. 273v. I am grateful to Richard Cust for drawing this document to my attention.

94. *CJ*, ii. 729.

95. Ibid. 630.

96. BL, Harl. MS 477, fo. 28v; Russell, *Fall of the British Monarchies*, 294.

97. *CJ*, ii. 754.

98. The phrase of course was Cromwell's, when describing the kind of soldiers he sought to recruit. Abbott, i. 256.

99. Adamson, *Noble Revolt*; D. Scott, *Politics and War in the Three Stuart Kingdoms, 1637–49* (Basingstoke, 2004), 26–9.

100. BL, Harl. MS 483, fo. 55.

# 3

# 'Lord of the Fens': Oliver Cromwell's Reputation and the First Civil War

S. L. Sadler

It was during the first civil war that Oliver Cromwell became famous. His rising fame rested primarily on his reputation for military success: he had thwarted royalist activists and taken control of Cambridge in the summer of 1642, before the civil war officially began; he defended the Eastern Association when elsewhere parliamentarian fortunes were suffering; and he was rapidly promoted, from captain to colonel. His military success raised his political prestige, and this, combined with his prominence in parliamentary circles, made him an obvious candidate for membership of the committee of both kingdoms that directed parliament's military campaigns from early 1644. His military successes continued thereafter, culminating in the nationally significant battle of Marston Moor in July 1644. By then he had been promoted to lieutenant-general and second in command to the earl of Manchester, general of the Eastern Association's army. Cromwell, rising rapidly in reputation and power, became seen as the unbeatable military hero who had turned the tide in the largest battle of the civil war. He was also a rallying point around which the Independent faction (which had emerged after the victory at Marston Moor) assembled to face down the Presbyterians and their Scottish allies. By the winter of 1644 Cromwell's position in the world had become transformed. From the relative obscurity of the 1620s and 1630s, and his subordinate role during the period of political break-down from 1640 to 1642, he had now emerged as a figure of national importance.

But Cromwell was a complex character, whose reputation among his contemporaries had varied dramatically almost from the beginning of the war, and by the winter of 1644 he had become infamous as well as famous, with enemies among his parliamentarian allies as well as his royalist opponents. On 25 November 1644 Cromwell launched a pre-emptive attack in parliament on the earl of Manchester, accus-ing his general of deliberately avoiding the total military victory that Marston Moor had made possible. This negligence, Cromwell claimed, emanated from Manchester's desire to end the bloodshed through a negotiated settlement with the king, and his support for the introduction of a Presbyterian system in English church government—policies that Cromwell bitterly opposed.[1] There were two strands to his attack. One was the increasing friction between Independents and Presbyterians in general. The other was more specific: the dismal performance of the parliamentarian armies in the autumn campaign of 1644. Parliament's success in crushing the northern royalist army at Marston Moor had apparently signalled the beginning of the enemy's demise, but the lacklustre performance and infighting that followed, especially during the 2nd Newbury cam-paign, let the royalists bounce back. Adding more pressure was a sense that time was running out while the potential rewards of the sum-mer victory slipped through their fingers. England had fought for two years without an adequate infrastructure to sustain the oppos-ing armies. There was a real danger of parliament being forced into a dishonourable peace by a people unwilling, or unable, to bear the price of continued warfare. A few days after Cromwell's blistering attack, Manchester met his challenge head on.[2] He first countered Cromwell's attempts to make him the scapegoat of the autumn cam-paign by presenting his own version of events. Then he also gave an account of Cromwell's character, which was designed to destroy his enemy's credibility. The combined effect was to denounce Cromwell as an unscrupulous, skilful dissembler masquerading as a defender of the godly. He was also portrayed as a threat to social order and to the influence of the Scots and English Presbyterians; and a man guilty of insubordination in his self-serving determination to resolve the con-flict by the sword. Central to Manchester's case was evidence derived from an anonymous 'opponent', which was used to demonstrate that

Cromwell's duplicitous tendencies had been observed from the very beginning of the war in the fenland and fen-edge, where his early military reputation was forged.[3] Thus by the winter of 1644 we have a fully fledged characterisation of Cromwell as the arch-deceiver, as well as Cromwell the parliamentarian military hero. This double-edged reputation continued for the rest of his life and beyond.[4]

The typical image of Cromwell in the early years of the war is of a keen but inexperienced regional commander, with a godly, providential outlook, who quickly learned to hone his natural martial abilities. He was the 'grasper of nettles' in his natural element, rising in status as his successes increased, but still dedicated to service in the field. Older claims of military genius have given way to more sober appraisals of his first modest military endeavours. Whilst still lacking experience of directing entire campaigns by the end of the first civil war, he 'stood out as an inspired and inspiring leader of cavalry'; and despite his successes he was a reluctant soldier, not wedded to the sword.[5] The image is good, but it is incomplete. Cromwell's charisma is acknowledged by military historians, but not fully examined; aspects of his transforming fortunes do not square with what is known, or said; and, as Colin Davis reminds us, sweeping issues under the mat of Cromwell's 'paradoxical' nature is unsatisfactory.[6] This chapter will examine the rhetoric and reality of Cromwell's growing reputation by considering the anonymous 'opponent's' identity and the accuracy of his gloss on episodes in Cromwell's local phase of his military career. In doing so I want to suggest that we need not rely exclusively on Cromwell's own image of these times as relayed by W. C. Abbott, and that a more nuanced sense of his reputation is developed by contextualising aspects of the anonymous 'opponent's' testimony. This shows Cromwell to be a more sophisticated man in the early stages of the war than is generally suggested. But his charismatic sophistication alienated as well as inspired others, handing enemies the ammunition to use against him. What can be drawn from Cromwell seen through both the local lens and the 'opponent's' presentation of Cromwell's record, helps us understand recurring themes in his later career and the continuing debates about his reputation.

# I

The 'opponent' stated that his motivation in offering 'what I have observed and what I have heard and seen' was to unmask Cromwell 'to do this bleeding state service'. (From his point of view discrediting

Manchester's attacker was the same thing.) He finished with a warning:

> But for the absolute Independent he is cruel without mercy, covetous
> without measure; he will have the spirit though it be a false one lying:
> is their best guard, by which he defends himself and offends others, by
> taking away the esteem of a man. Then his will is law to do what he will
> with him. This I can say by experience, the Lord of Heaven deliver every
> honest man out of their hands.[7]

The 'opponent' claimed to have observed Cromwell at first-hand from December 1642. As he knew the environment that Cromwell's career and reputation had been forged in, he said he could show parliament the ambition of the man he now knew Cromwell to be—a man who gloried in his command and promoted religious factionalism.[8]

The 'opponent's' identity is obviously important in assessing whether the depiction of Cromwell that parliament was asked to consider is convincing. Clive Holmes concluded in the 1970s that the 'opponent' was Cromwell's fellow officer, William Dodson, as 'his career alone corresponds to the biographical information which can be deduced from the statement'.[9] If this supposition is correct we have an important local perspective from which to view Cromwell's career during this period. Dodson would certainly make a good witness. He had estates in the Isle of Ely, in March (13 miles northwest of the city of Ely across tracts of fenland, rivers and dykes), and had spent years on draining the Great Level.[10] This is significant because he could thus make well-informed comments on how the shape of the war-zone, the course of the fighting and the dynamic of the action might be affected by the nature of the landscape (now, with agricultural improvement, almost unrecognisable), making him an excellent judge of Cromwell's performance. Additionally, Dodson, like Cromwell, was an active parliamentarian from the summer of 1642 and he was also an officer in parliament's army. Here too Dodson was well placed to observe. What follows draws out connections between Cromwell's view of his development, the 'opponent's' accusations, and the way Dodson's and Cromwell's careers interacted in the locality, concentrating on the period between the spring of 1643 and the autumn of 1644.

## II

Cromwell's first significant military engagement after returning to East Anglia from the battle of Edgehill (23 October 1642) was the siege of Crowland in April 1643. This success was one of a run of victories in defence of the Eastern Association upon which his developing military renown rested. It also consolidated his seizure of the city of Cambridge in the previous summer. Cromwell recalled this phase of his career in 1657, the year he was offered the crown, commenting:

> I was a person that from my first employment was suddenly preferred, and lifted up from lesser trusts to greater, from my first being a captain of a troop of horse. And I did labour as well as I could to discharge my trust, and God blessed me as it pleased him.[11]

For modern students, the siege of Crowland is one of the 'modest military exploits' by which Cromwell became transformed from civilian to soldier.[12] Always the fast learner, it was here that he began to apply the lessons of Edgehill and display his martial aptitude, selecting men who could be transformed into a disciplined force capable of withstanding Prince Rupert's devastating cavalry charges. Furthermore, from the local perspective the siege marked an important territorial advance for parliament.

But the siege is also significant for a less commonly observed reason, as the anonymous 'opponent' claimed his trust in Cromwell began to evaporate around this time. In fact, Crowland formed the first part in the dateable evidence he offered to substantiate his claim that Cromwell was not, as his allies and the press claimed, the local man made good. Instead, the 'opponent' said that Cromwell took the credit for other people's service to parliament at Crowland as well as on later occasions (a charge that had particular resonance for the Scots, indignant at the claims Cromwell made after Marston Moor),[13] and he connected this to the wider claim that Cromwell was a godly fraud, adept at promoting his reputation whilst discrediting rivals. This step in his argument emphasised the nature of local conditions as well as Cromwell's manipulative tendencies, and prepared the way for his revelation that Cromwell was intent on making a factional power base through the creation of a citadel in the natural fortress of the fenland Isle of Ely and its surroundings.[14] In the friction between the usual accounts and the 'opponent's' hostile version a different picture of

Cromwell starts to emerge. To examine it we must turn first to the site of the action.

King's Lynn guarded one of the northern passes through the fens into the Isle of Ely, and Crowland covered the other. In consequence their possession was vital to local activists on both sides, and since January 1643 Crowland had been fortified by royalists. The island on which the town perched was surrounded by fen, accessible from only one side, and the terrain was so difficult to negotiate 'a horse can hardly come to it'.[15] The causeways that had previously prevented people drowning in the morass were now broken. Mists, winter floods and breaking river banks increased the difficulty of movement still further. The safest way to approach the town was by boat. Locals would have known what historians, even with the benefit of hindsight, do not always appreciate: Crowland's strategic potential. For Crowland was a crucial link in the expanse of fen, rivers and meres from Cambridgeshire's borders to The Wash and to the passageway from the Isle of Ely to Holland fen through the Lincolnshire Marshes. There a kind of guerrilla warfare might be attempted by royalists operating between the Humber and the Thames.[16]

Cromwell was in Cambridgeshire, strengthening his hold on the area and recruiting, when the Crowlanders first declared for the royalists, but he did not attack immediately. The delay made sense. The town was at its most inaccessible in winter and he was already occupied at the southern tip of the fen-edge securing Cambridge and its immediate surroundings. Establishing Cambridge as the Eastern Association's headquarters, whilst simultaneously quashing royalists centred on the university, was the more urgent and achievable goal. After moving as systematically as opportunity allowed to secure towns and territory along the natural geographical borders, in late April Cromwell finally turned to Crowland, marching north-east along the western approaches to the fens, from Peterborough towards the section of the River Nene's banks which separated Cambridgeshire from Lincolnshire. Other local forces converged there to meet him.[17]

We know less of Cromwell's first experience of siege-warfare than is desirable for judging his military performance, but press accounts give a general sense of events. The Crowlanders were uncowed by the enemy and the weather increased parliamentarian difficulties, with nothing for miles to break the force of the winds and torrential rain. The parliamentarian troops surrounded three sides of the island with artillery. Captain Dodson sent in his drummer to negotiate, but he was held captive by the defiant royalists. Enraged,

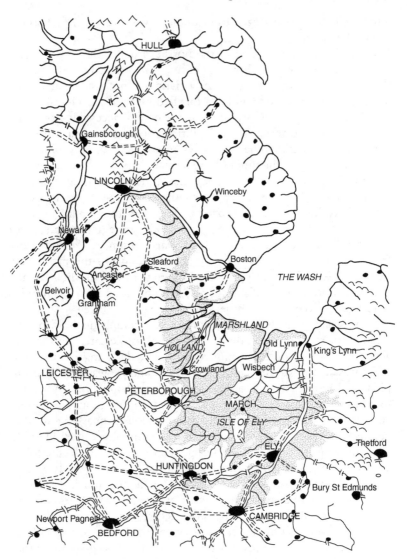

*Map 3.1* **Cromwell and the Fens, 1643–1644** (copyright S. L. Sadler)

the parliamentarians unleashed their artillery (later episodes suggest cannon were mounted on boats). The Crowlanders held firm and by the third day of bombardment many parliamentarians had been forced to retreat from their sodden positions. The situation changed that afternoon, however, when the weather improved. The besiegers assaulted from Crowland's one accessible side. With improved conditions numbers became more significant and the Crowlanders, finally losing confidence, began stealing away. Before daylight on the fourth day the defenders proposed terms of surrender, but they were refused. Eventually the besiegers entered the town and some of the royalist leaders were captured before they could flee. The difficulty of the task was reflected in the casualty reports: only one royalist was killed and one hurt, whereas five parliamentarians died and 18 or 20 were injured, some mortally.[18]

On 28 April 1643 Cromwell's first siege ended in victory. His name was scattered across the press in early May. The parliamentarian newsbook, *Certaine Informations*, claimed that:

> the Spalding men could then do no good upon Crowland, because they wanted ordnance to force it, yet since the heroic and valiant Colonel Cromwell, passing that way from Peterborough, hath regained the town of Crowland, driven the said Captain Welby and his wicked imps from thence, and reduced those parts to their former peace and tranquillity.[19]

So far, this account supports the established picture of Cromwell, but the 'opponent's' view was very different. In fact, the 'opponent' claimed that after he and his men had stood guard before Crowland all winter, 'at the spring [the opponent] took the town in; yet that service, and all other done by me and others, must go in his name or else all was not well'.[20] In short, it was he, not Cromwell, who had captured the town, but his superior had then taken the credit.

The 'opponent's' account must be taken seriously. His evidence leading up to the siege of Crowland can often be verified, suggesting that he was a reliable informant. For example, there is evidence of the rapidly increasing pace of local defence measures relating to the Eastern Association, and of efforts to send soldiers' pay between the tenth and twentieth of December—a period coinciding with the time Cromwell allegedly told the 'opponent' that he had hopes of parliament helping him to secure the area.[21] The 'opponent' also claimed that in the winter 1642–1643 'after some business was done in Huntingdonshire, and the enemy had taken Crowland and fortified it', Cromwell had ordered him to Wisbech to guard against 'the Crowlanders, which I did with mine own troop only'.[22] The dates fit what we can trace of Cromwell's activities and those of the royalists, and such details strengthen the impression that the 'opponent' was indeed William Dodson. Whether Dodson was involved at Huntingdon, or was part of the force which arrived with Cromwell in January, is uncertain, but Dodson's direct connection with Cromwell and Crowland can certainly be substantiated, as Cromwell's own orders confirm it. The military accounts show that Dodson had prepared his side of the pass to face an attack, just as Cromwell had prepared Cambridge. The Wisbech burgesses, for example, lent Dodson 100 pounds towards the expeditionary force against Crowland, and later Dodson became governor of the Wisbech garrison.[23]

The local perspective thus supports the 'opponent'/Dodson's assertion. The familiar image is of a dynamic Cromwell in all places at once, ensuring parliament's success almost on his own. From the alternative perspective, however, the defensive organisation which made the siege of Crowland possible depended on teamwork, albeit under Cromwell's direction. By stationing Captain Dodson at Wisbech to guard against the Crowlanders, Cromwell was free to attend committee meetings, sort the trained-bands, recruit troops, disarm suspects on the Eastern Association's western borders and spark life into the newly formed Association, while confronting threats, real and perceived, from several directions.[24] For example, Cromwell could leave his Cambridge base in mid-March to deal with problems in Norfolk only because Dodson was guarding the northern passes into the Isle and a garrison now protected Cambridge. Queen Henrietta Maria's arrival in Yorkshire raised the stakes over who would control the Great North Road and threatened to establish a link between the marquess of Newcastle's northern royalists and Charles I's Oxford headquarters. No doubt the Crowlanders knew this. In the meantime, the parliamentarian hold on the Great North Road south of Newark slipped; royalists seized Grantham, edging towards the fens the same day Cromwell returned from Norfolk; and on the following day the Crowlanders began causing trouble along the alternative northern route east of the fens.[25]

As the military situation worsened before the siege, the teamwork behind Cromwell's efforts became all the more important. We know that when Cromwell took over effective control of the Eastern Association (as the regional commander, Lord Grey of Warke, left Cambridge with a strong force to join Essex's army in early April) he stood the area on defence, guarding the River Ouse and stationing himself at the crossing point at Huntingdon, which was the nearest staging post on the Great North Road to the Association's headquarters. Cromwell's cavalry could thus advance towards the danger, simultaneously blocking the western approaches to the fens while Dodson at his back faced Crowland's troublemakers and preventing them from seizing more of the Great North Road and making links with those fomenting treachery in the Isle of Ely. The royalist victory at Ancaster Heath on 11 April made the prospect of Newcastle's army marching south impossible to ignore. Raids on Peterborough drove the point home. In response, Cromwell ordered Norfolk infantrymen to reinforce Dodson's dragoons around Wisbech, protecting the Horseshore Pass through Marshland.[26] The terrain dictated these positions, and although Cromwell held overall responsibility, he was heavily dependent on others, including Dodson, in making his preparations possible.

Returning to the siege of Crowland, we can speculate on its potential to create a sense of grievance among those members of the team that had made it possible. The victory could undoubtedly be claimed as a success for Cromwell as the man responsible for defending the region.[27] But the newsbooks also suggested that Cromwell's personal role was decisive in the siege itself.[28] Indeed, the leitmotif of Cromwell's valour and ability to transform apparently intractable situations would soon become familiar. But what we know of the conduct of the siege prompts serious questions. Cannon and infantrymen were most useful for sieges, but most of Cromwell's own men were cavalry. Dragoons, like Dodson's troop, were a flexible, cheap form of cavalry that usually fought on foot in particularly exposed positions. Less flexible cavalry units usually played only a secondary role in sieges.[29] The sodden conditions around Crowland were particularly unforgiving for horses, whose hooves might rot, or legs break while stumbling around in the mud. Cromwell did have some foot soldiers with him, and he perhaps supplied the all-important artillery firepower; but cannons were heavy, difficult to move in dry conditions, and where possible were moved along waterways rather than land-routes. How then, beyond holding overall responsibility for the region's safety and swelling the parliamentarians' numbers, did he become the hero of the action? It is tempting to speculate that Captain Dodson, whose drummer-boy's illegal detention sparked off the violence after a winter of guarding the passes, was justified in his anger at the press reports which credited the victory to Cromwell.

Strategically the outcome of the successful siege was clearer, and in this case Cromwell could take the credit, as he was ultimately responsible for the region's safety. After the fall of Crowland the garrisons guarding the passes between Holland and the Isle of Ely were safe, with the northern bank of the River Nene secured. Instead of bracing themselves against hostile penetration the parliamentarians could go on the offensive, pushing north-west towards the River Trent and the royalist stronghold at Newark. Attack would be the best form of defence for the Isle of Ely. Nationally, Crowland's greatest result was the potential for further gains, but they did not materialise—to Cromwell's intense frustration.[30] Instead, Cromwell's advance north was followed by a three-day riot in the western edge of the fens below Peterborough. The disturbance was only suppressed by the diversion of large numbers of soldiers, and it was suspected that political aims lay behind the rioters' outward protests against drainage.[31] Given they had only just secured nearby Crowland, the local parliamentarians were understandably jumpy. This incident brings us to the effect of hindsight on Cromwell's first victory. We know that in the end the royalists neither carved out a stronghold in the fens, nor seized command of an eastern theatre of the war between the Humber and the Thames, but it is less obvious to us than to contemporaries that the potential risk sharpened parliamentarian anxieties that they would be betrayed, and helped to undermine Cromwell's supposed success. Contemporaries like Dodson knew that despite the fanfare over Cromwell's achievements, the siege of Crowland was a temporary, tenuous victory. The safety of the Isle of Ely remained on a knife-edge.

The immediate result of the riot near Peterborough was the creation of a new parliamentarian garrison at Whittlesey, but the situation remained unstable. Cromwell was no doubt right to disarm his uncle at neighbouring Ramsey Abbey, but perhaps he did not act strongly enough. The story of his unwelcome visit to Ramsey is famous, but its context is not.[32] Sir Oliver's resistance to his parliamentarian nephew, 'opposing him armed all his servants and tenants',[33] although ineffectual, served as a warning that more trouble was brewing. Within days of the Whittlesey riot the press recounted 'some malevolents at Ely had lately made some combustion in that city' including attempting to seize the ordnance there.[34] Once again the riot looked suspicious, even if a political agenda could not be proved this time. If the investigators had known that Henrietta Maria had just advised Charles to make Peterborough his base if he was forced to abandon Oxford, they might have pushed harder. Given the damage the activities the governor of Hull, Sir John Hotham, and his son caused to the campaign between the Nene and the Trent that so frustrated Cromwell, local parliamentarians in the fens were right to be anxious.[35] The later history of Crowland, which was retaken briefly by the royalists in March 1644 and again in October–November, serves to emphasise the continuing dangers in the local situation.[36] Whatever the press might have said, the initial success at Crowland in April 1643 had only temporarily overawed the determined local royalists, it had not defeated them. This fact was painfully obvious in November 1644, as the local forces were once again struggling to retake Crowland at the very time that Manchester and Cromwell were facing each other down at Westminster.

## III

Cromwell's success at Crowland helped to earn him the troubled command of the Isle of Ely (in July 1643), which became the 'opponent's' next area of focus. During the summer the threat to the region was as great as ever. In the early hours of 19 July, the parliamentarians at Huntingdon received intelligence that 400 royalists had appeared before Peterborough, and there were also reports that 'The Colonel [Cromwell] marched out with his ordnance and repulsed them', that the royalist Lord Camden was about to 'set before it', and the town of Stamford had been taken and fortified by a 'far greater force'.[37] In the ensuing manoeuvres, Cromwell ordered Captains Dodson, Walton and Disbrowe to meet the approaching royalists while he, in the most famous part of the episode, combined with Colonels Hobart and Palgrave to surround the royalist garrison at Burghley House near Stamford. Cromwell ignored initial defiance from the besieged, ordered no killing once a parley was requested, and on the surrender of the house took 200 prisoners. Meanwhile, Dodson, arriving first in the attack on the main royalist force, was wounded, knocked from his horse and rescued by Walton. They killed about 50 royalists, routing the rest. The Huntingdonshire committee later commented that Cromwell 'gave great commendation of Colonel Palgrave's men'.[38] The press, however, proclaimed the victory as Cromwell's alone.[39]

The traditional point drawn from this episode is that of Cromwell's disciplined restraint and clemency, but the 'opponent' claimed that it provided further evidence that Cromwell was a social revolutionary:

> At our first being at Stamford after Crowland was taken, there was news brought to Colonel Cromwell that there was some lords of the king's side slain, and he replied that God fought against them, for God would have

no lording over his people, and he verily believed that God would sweep away that lord in power out of this nation.[40]

This supposedly chimed with Manchester's allegation that Cromwell hoped for the overthrow of the aristocracy and the crown, and the allegation is interesting.[41] The strategic significance of the victory at Burghley was that it advanced parliamentarian attempts to create an alternative path northwards towards their allies the Fairfaxes and aided the intended destruction of Newcastle's northern army.[42] For our purposes in testing this early image of Cromwell the dissembler, it is significant for three reasons. First, as we have seen, independent sources confirm Cromwell and Dodson were where the opponent said they were (demonstrating yet another reliable aspect of his claims). Second, the position of the Stamford episode in his testimony may help unlock more than just alleged evidence of Cromwell's socially subversive tendencies. It is sandwiched abruptly between a depiction of Cromwell and his deputy, Henry Ireton, as corrupt, subverting the law and promoting factionalism within the Isle of Ely up to the winter of 1644, and an account of Cromwell's claims for holding the area and their consequences, played out in London in the winter of 1643. Looking at the opponents' frenzied and apparently randomly ordered charges from the local perspective helps makes sense of the order and amplifies his message. His evidence is arranged thematically rather than chronologically. What happened in the Isle could be linked to what Cromwell supposedly said at Burghley, and also created a bridge to what happened in the winter of 1643, the implications of which (as we shall see later) could also be seen as socially subversive. This is the most obvious reading of his evidence, and the local picture suggests the Stamford/Burghley episode forms part of a sequence of events that offers valuable insights in helping us to understand the opponent's characterisation of Cromwell.

Third, the sequence of events highlights Cromwell's understanding of publicity, further contextualising the 'opponent'/Dodson's accusations of political manipulation. Cromwell drafted skilled accounts of his next victory, at Gainsborough on 28 July 1643, and what happened afterwards, for the Suffolk deputies-lieutenants and the Association Committee, commenting disingenuously:

> Thus have you this true relation as short as I could. What you are to do upon it, is next to be considered. If I could speak words to pierce your hearts with the sense of our, and your condition I would.[43]

He described the relieving parliamentarian force's initial clash with the royalists, the destruction of the reserve, General Cavendish's death and the relief of the town, all accomplished before it was noticed that fresh royalists were mustering beyond it. Beating them, his tired forces recovered the hill only to find a terrifying panorama below; 'a regiment of foot; after that another; after that Newcastle's own regiment, consisting in all of about 50 colours, and a great body of horse; which indeed was Newcastle's army'. Leaving the parliamentarian foot to its fate inside Gainsborough, Cromwell led the horse in a retreat that, in his account, became a heroic drama, although he was quick to emphasise that 'the honour of this retreat is due to God'.[44] Within days the Cambridge committee, taking the hint, sent Cromwell's account of the battle to London for publication.[45] Despite Cromwell's genuine achievement in extricating his horse without any casualties, the account was more than bare reportage to serve local committee's intelligence gathering; indeed, through the report the public was again reminded of Cromwell's valour and heroism. In fact, as Cromwell had been forced to retreat back to Huntingdon, and Gainsborough had fallen to Newcastle's men soon afterwards, his 'victory' had come to nothing.

The Gainsborough letter and its publication is well known, but it is not usually connected with the 'opponent'/Dodson's charge that 'all must go' in Cromwell's name. Cromwell must have known from experience that his account, though not necessarily insincere, would make perfect propaganda. His understanding of the importance of print was already apparent. On his return to Cambridge in 1643 he had raided the University press, seizing royal pamphlets and arresting the author and printer; he was repeatedly characterised as valiant Colonel Cromwell in press; and his communiqué after the brief skirmish at Belton House had been passed on for publication.[46] Our knowledge of Cromwell's personality strengthens the supposition that all this was intentional. It is well known that Cromwell was a charismatic military leader. He was the man who studied men more than books, who could inspire others, at least for a time, that his cause was their cause and to share his vision and risk all with him. He was the commander who could train raw troopers to hold their nerve in the face of a royalist cavalry charge, and instil the discipline to charge again or retreat without disorder.[47] To do this he had to be, in modern parlance, a good 'communicator'. It is unlikely the natural 'communicator' recruiting in the market place, inspiring men in the dreadful pause before battle or rallying them in the confusion of conflict, could not transfer his skills into the wider medium of print. It is surely inconceivable that such a good communicator would not understand the possibilities of print. And there can be no doubt that in the composition of his account of Gainsborough we have evidence that Cromwell had the skill and sophistication to bring them into effect. But here we meet a potential paradox.

Cromwell's early use of the press shows him to be a more sophisticated character than is usually depicted. He is usually seen as a forthright, straightforward, impulsive, unwavering one-man parliamentary forlorn-hope, or as a man too inept to deal with measures needing 'sensitivity, tact and gradualism' (an image also drawn from the years immediately preceding the outbreak of war).[48] Yet his skills as a propagandist go to the heart of the controversy about his identity that grew in pace with his fame, and helps make sense of the apparent leap from the man who could be out-manoeuvred and disgraced by a Huntingdon clique in 1630, or the fiery parliamentarian in the Long Parliament of 1640–1642 whose inept intemperance could at times prevent his message being heard, to the charismatic leader whose successes launched him as a newsbook hero and an increasingly significant political figure.[49]

What had changed? The fast learner may have forged a more subtle understanding of how to manage men in the white heat of conflict, perhaps. The war certainly offered him a role as an officer, who expected to command and be obeyed—an expectation that went beyond that of the ordinary politician. This may be part of the key to reconciling the paradox. Add to this his generally acknowledged emotional temperament and his restless search for the best means to achieve his end and we have the other parts of the key.[50] Cromwell's sensitivities were perhaps attuned to an emotional rather than intellectual understanding of situations suited to the urgency of the moment and this is where his sophistication lay. With an expectant audience he could stir people who could not be reached by intellectual argument. In his role as an officer he acquired a style of authority more suited to his personality—and an expectation in others he should be listened to—which, combined with his intuitive understanding of people at an emotional level, launched the previously unguided missile on a more assured (and destructive?) path. This sophistication emanated from his natural abilities as a communicator, combined with a passionate commitment to his cause and a new role in the army, in which he could develop his talents as an effective self-publicist and propagandist.

The flip side of all this is the 'opponent'/Dodson's disenchanted characterisation of Cromwell. Cromwell told a good story, presenting himself in print as the rallying point for the cause. Details like accurate assessments of numbers could be passed over (and we know Cromwell, like so many of his contemporaries, was unreliable there).[51] It seems that his audience could identify with him, become emotionally engaged, and thus inspired to support parliament's armies. But for those fighting alongside him as colleagues (like Dodson), faced with messy details and strategic realities, the picture was much more complicated. It became increasingly hard to reconcile what they knew from first-hand experience with the simple heroism of the Cromwell projected in the press. Disillusion and disenchantment make good breeding-grounds for enmity.

Furthermore, the indecisive action at Gainsborough had left East Anglia vulnerable. Warnings were soon issued of Newcastle's impending invasion and of the need to relieve the forces that had fallen back to Lincoln, if they were to avoid utter destruction.[52] Cromwell wrote, as he prepared to ride out from Huntingdon on 6 August, that:

> It is no longer disputing, but out instantly all you can. Raise all your bands; send them to Huntingdon; get up what volunteers you can; hasten your horses . . . there is nothing to interrupt an enemy, but our horse, that is considerable.[53]

While Cromwell patrolled the western approaches, the earl of Manchester took overall command of the Eastern Association army, and the locality braced itself for the impending attack.[54] But, by the winter the 'opponent' claimed, it was clear to some that Cromwell, not Newcastle, was becoming the greatest threat to the fens.

## IV

William Harlakenden dined with Cromwell at Ely on 4 September 1643. Cromwell told him his scouts brought word of the rapid approach of 8000 of Newcastle's men, and that as a consequence he had sent all his forces towards Lincoln, intending to follow them in the morning.[55] Meanwhile, Manchester gathered forces to besiege Kings Lynn, which had risen against parliament in August, gambling (mistakenly, as it turned out) that Newcastle would easily penetrate the fens to assist them. Cromwell had been appointed governor of the Isle of Ely in late July, and now, in his absence, Henry Ireton took over

command as deputy-governer.[56] While Cromwell followed his cavalry into Lincolnshire, screening Manchester, Harlakenden returned
to Cambridge, writing of difficulties with finances and equipping
soldiers.[57] The situation before Lynn was equally dire, but when
Manchester threatened to storm the town, the royalists realised that
their condition was even more hopeless, and they surrendered. With
the north-eastern gateway into the Isle secured by mid-September,
the parliamentarians could now face Newcastle in the field. But local
parliamentarians remained wary of possible connections between the
rising at Lynn and royalist sympathies in the Isle itself. (They well
knew that the siege of Crowland had not ended royalist unrest and that
the local topography and residual allegiances guaranteed continued
royalist unrest in the area.) However, on 11 October the Eastern Association army, combined with the Yorkshire forces under the Fairfaxes,
inflicted a major defeat on the royalists at Winceby.

In the traditional narrative, the battle of Winceby was the most
significant event of the autumn of 1643. The parliamentarian victory was decisive for the region and saw the culmination of the local
phase in Cromwell's military career. Cromwell's disciplined troops
contributed to the victory and, as a by-product, proved that his
recruiting aims were achievable. The parliamentarian press played up
the victory, relieved that they had a military hero to counter bad
news elsewhere.[58] But in the autumn of 1644 the 'opponent' made
no reference to Winceby, beyond, perhaps, a jibe over Cromwell's
ruthless self-publicity. Instead his suspicions had hardened to opposition while he and his troops stayed behind, guarding the Isle of
Ely. He suggested that the original dangers (external plotting and
internal betrayal) extended to Cromwell's intended aim to establish
a fenland stronghold, and he also attacked Ireton's nefarious influence as deputy. Manipulation of information and reputations, ruthless
activism to the point of lawlessness and corruption, combined with
the charge that Cromwell and Ireton hoped to make a factional
enclave of armed men in the fens.[59] The charges may sound improba-
ble, but the local context demonstrates that Cromwell could plausibly
be depicted in this light, although it does not prove that he was in
reality an arch-manipulator.

The 'opponent's' dates and places were certainly accurate. Dodson
returned from King's Lynn to his quarters at Wisbech in mid-
September to signs of royalist defiance and was probably at the
garrison during the autumn when Ireton was appointed as deputy.
With the royalists now retreating to the midlands, Cromwell returned

to Cambridge in late October and to Ely in mid- or late December.[60] The 'opponent's' charges of financial distress, corruption and lawlessness may have been exaggerated, yet they contained a basis in reality. Cromwell and his captains had parliamentary authority to do what was necessary to defend the region, and his tenacity in ensuring he was listened to when demanding support for his troops is admired by historians; but it should be realised that all this came at a price. The military reorganisation of the summer of 1643 and the steady encroachment of the pressures of war on civilian life made for dangerous divisions in a locality where royalists were waiting for an opportunity to act. The 'opponent' complained that Cromwell had praised Ireton when he was appointed, but that Ireton had immediately started taxing the inhabitants heavily, 'and some of his officers did, as I conceive, take away great sums of money from the subject injuriously'.[61] There is little doubt that the Isle suffered immense strain in shielding the Association and protecting its treasury, and it is known that by December two horse and two foot companies were permanently garrisoned there. Cromwell did not sign the Ely committee's letter to Parliament of 20 December outlining the burden of supporting these garrisons; but he had returned to the city before it was written and it is difficult to imagine that he had no involvement. The garrisons could barely be supported by the 20 parishes along with the cost of raising and equipping field troops and the armed enforcement of war taxation. They were 'constrained' to spend the greatest part of the assessment taxes on these forces and had no hopes of alternative sources of income in the future. Beyond the garrisons' financial expense, the committee claimed that they had recently raised and equipped 440 foot for the earl of Manchester. Like other frontier areas, the Isle needed relief to subsist, and solutions for the endemic financial difficulties of the Association were being sought.[62] Once again, this helps us understand the local context of the 'opponent's' charges against Cromwell.

The 'opponent' claimed that about the time Cromwell and Ireton were seeking vast demands from the committee at Cambridge 'to strengthen that Isle', they spoke of a drainage scheme that they were prosecuting there. Given Dodson's civilian occupation as a fen drainer, his ownership of local land, and his struggles over sequestrations there, he was especially interested and knowledgeable in this matter. Cromwell said he would use soldiers' labour to drain the lands under Sir Cornelius Vermuyden's direction, as it had been before the war. (The siege of Crowland had demonstrated what control of floodwaters could do, and some widening of the river banks on Cromwell's orders had already begun.)[63] It was said that the drainage works would help fortify the Isle, making it invincible, and profitable. Given the pleading of the Isle's committee for relief, the plan had obvious advantages. It may be no coincidence that the royalist press began sneering at Cromwell as 'lord of the fens' (implying he was a social-climbing non-entity) from November 1643. Nor was defensive drainage a fictitious charge, as the road constructed between Ely and Chatteris for his troops became known as Ireton's Way.[64]

The 'opponent's' suspicion—'I well knowing what there aim was'—was confirmed when he enquired how the original under-takers would be compensated. The alleged answer, that 'they did it for their own ends and let them lose their moneys, and this should be for a public good to settle godly men in', sounds plausible. The war presented Cromwell several opportunities to pick at old wounds, in this case drainage compensation with the tables reversed from the 1637 and 1641 confrontations.[65] Besides, we know from other evidence that he needed the money at this time (see Chapter 5). If the opponent was Dodson, this problem may have been as significant as the sectarian discord that usually attracts attention.

Further complications ensued, as old and new sequestrators waged war amongst themselves, intensifying difficulties there. By November 1643 they were so locked in conflict that the central authorities began the regular interventions that would continue for years. Imprisoning or being imprisoned became an occupational hazard on Manchester's as well as Cromwell's orders, and official reprimands frequently followed. Misdirected zeal, conflicting claims to authority and untenable financial burdens—these were enough to give many in the Isle the appearance of being guilty of corruption.[66] The 'opponent'/Dodson's claims are in keeping with the chaos reigning in the Isle and accusations stemming from them. Given the atmosphere in the Isle it would be more surprising if by 1644 the opponent had *not* charged Cromwell and Ireton with corruption and lawlessness. Once again, the 'opponent's' concerns bear testimony to the difficulties in the Isle and lead to the heart of his charges against Cromwell's use and abuse of the fens and bring us to the point where (from his perspective, at least) Cromwell abandoned him.

## V

Cromwell arrived in London 18 January 1644, to argue for financial reforms, to attack Lord Willoughby of Parham's command and to try to transfer Lincolnshire into Manchester's Eastern Association. We can date the continuing contact between Cromwell and Major Dodson through Cromwell's order of 19 January for the Wisbech treasurer to issue £600 'with all possible speed', to allow Dodson to 'satisfy the poor people who have quartered his soldiers and so march away to his charge under Colonel Pickering'.[67] The 'opponent'/Dodson claimed that as Cromwell moved towards Manchester's quarters he heard him say:

> if he had but Marshland and Holland joined to the Isle of Ely he would make it the strongest thing in the world, for there he had three of the finest ports of the world, and that he could keep them against all the strength that could be made against them.[68]

Clearly the potential strength of the fenland territory was not fanciful: locals, royalist plotters and parliamentarian defenders alike understood that potential. But did Cromwell's actions give the impression, as the 'opponent' claimed, that he intended to make an Independent fortress there, and did he really mean to? The answer to the former question is probably yes, while the latter seems doubtful but is ultimately unanswerable.

In the same period, Cromwell appointed Colonel Edward King as governor of Holland and Boston. King's Lynn was now commanded by Cromwell's brother-in-law Walton.[69] With Wisbech, which lay within the Isle of Ely that Cromwell himself governed, the three key ports in the Wash were now held by his allies, and the natural protection of the fens made the area an enclave that could realistically become a haven against the enemy. But who was now the enemy? Walton's Independent views were evident, as was the strength of Independency in Lynn's garrison, but not only was Manchester a Presbyterian, so also was Colonel King, who still had Cromwell's support in December, when he became governor of Lincoln. The apparent balance of power attracts attention, yet Cromwell kept his powder dry by positioning other reliable Independents, such as Lilburne and Berry, in commands where they could inform on King if necessary.[70] This is precisely the pattern of behaviour that could acquire retrospective significance, and, seen through the 'opponent's' lens, it was at this point that his relationship with Cromwell reached its breaking-point.

About four days after Cromwell's conversation about the Isle of Ely, his henchmen visited the 'opponent's' London house, carrying a petition for parliament to secure 'liberty of consciences'.[71] This incident strongly indicates the 'opponent's' identity. His extreme unwillingness to sign showed in his exclamation that 'I would have my hand cut off before I would set my hand to it, and told them if any nation in the world were in the ready way to heaven it was the Scots'. His unusual wording is suggestive. In August 1642 Dodson had threatened to cut the hands off whoever read the proclamation declaring the earl of Essex a traitor at Ely assizes. Evidently the situation seemed equally extreme, and the rift (from Dodson's perspective) was just as decisive. His unwelcome visitors 'told me they thought I had been a godly man, but now they perceive what I was and went away; ever after Colonel Cromwell did slight me' and offered examples as evidence.[72] This rift is months earlier than the point when most historians place Cromwell's alienation from the Presbyterians.[73] For the 'opponent' religious factionalism and his preoccupation with Cromwell's intentions for the fens were now combined.

By the summer of 1644 the 'opponent' was ready to resign his commission and saw in Cromwell's attempts at persuasion a confirmation of his earlier assessment. He had refused to be overruled by Ireton, and he complained that the business in the Isle was not going 'sweetly on' (in fact it was heading for melt-down).[74] Further evidence of the connection between factional ambitions, lawlessness and corruption filled the fretful route home from the battlefield of Marston Moor. This animosity towards Ireton can be explained by Ireton's feud with the additional sequestrators (who were appointed by Parliament the same day Cromwell wrote his account of Gainsborough in the previous summer) that came to a climax while Cromwell, Ireton and Dodson were returning southward from York in July 1644. One of these additional sequestrators, (who later claimed to have been helped at times by Dodson) even quoted John Pym's famous views on tyranny and lawlessness in his printed review of conditions in the Isle. In response, Cromwell backed Ireton to the hilt insisting that 'I will be no governor, nor engage any other under me to undertake such a charge, upon such weak terms!'[75] The crisis point had been reached, and the 'opponent' was now ready to unmask the tyrant.

## VI

In the autumn of 1644, Cromwell wrote of his desperation to go west and deal with the royalist vipers in their nest, and yet shortly afterwards the 'opponent' claimed that Cromwell also aimed to command an Independent citadel in the fens.[76] Hindsight does us a disservice by encouraging the dismissal of this claim because it contained no more than mere knee-jerk localism. Yet, as we have seen, the local perspective shows aspects of the 'opponent's' evidence have some basis in fact. The area Cromwell protected was indeed threatened by dangers from plotters and internal betrayal; Cromwell's siege of Crowland was less significant in reality than in rhetoric; Cromwell was a darling of the parliamentarian press; the military significance of the topography of the fens fitted the alleged site of Cromwell's intended factional stronghold; the Isle of Ely was riven with charges of corruption and power struggles between anxious parliamentarians; Henry Ireton did earn censure from the central authorities for his behaviour there. These can all be established with a degree of certainty.

In the light of this, other aspects of the 'opponent's' interpretation become more convincing. From the local perspective, Cromwell's transformation in experience, power and reputation by 1644 contrasts with the limited level of significant improvement in the locality's problems (despite Cromwell's apparent success in launching his rising reputation). Cromwell solved nothing in the fens, and he never made a secure base there. He periodically overawed the region when it commanded his attention, but from his perspective the local war was a means to a greater end. With his horizon widening, he soon grasped another way of delivering the Israelites out of Egypt: by abandoning the east to gamble on a final solution in the west.

If the identification of the 'opponent' is correct—and it is fairly certain that he was William Dodson—his preoccupation with the fens and his interpretation of Cromwell's behaviour becomes understandable, and his evidence slots an important missing piece into the question of Cromwell's conflicting reputations. For Cromwell, this period is vital, because during it his 'lesser trusts' turned to 'greater' ones, and from his providential viewpoint, his godly mission was becoming ever more obvious. Through the 'opponent's' eyes, however, it represents a period of disillusionment with the charismatic leader he once believed would share his fight to defend the Isle of Ely. Instead, he said that he found Cromwell to be a tyrannical fraud. Dodson operated where parliamentarians had developed a siege-mentality because the landscape invited royalist threats which could not easily be prevented. This pressure created endemic mistrust, which in turn led to vicious disputes and imprisonment, violence and even torture among the parliamentarians. The surviving evidence does not conclusively place Cromwell in the arch-dissembler mould, but it certainly makes the characterisation understandable.

The 'opponent's' view presents a way of testing Cromwell's own claims against the local picture, his later reinvention, and the influential Abbott legacy, in our treatment of Cromwell's identity. What happened in the fens demonstrates patterns and tendencies that would recur throughout Cromwell's life; and he had made enough smoke by 1644, even if there was no fire, to allow some parliamentarians to pick up a royalist jibe and argue seriously that he had ambitions to become a despotic 'lord of the fens'.

## Notes

1. *CSPD 1644–45*, 147.
2. *LJ*, vii. 73,76; C. Holmes, *The Eastern Association in the English Civil War* (1974), 206–9.
3. Huntingdonshire Record Office, 3343/M80, fos. 9, 11 (assessment of Oliver Cromwell's character). This document has no page numbers. For precision I shall refer to the transcript in D. Masson and J. Bruce (eds), *The Quarrel between the Earl of Manchester and Oliver Cromwell* (Camden Society, 1875).
4. For example, J. Morrill (ed.) *Oliver Cromwell and the English Revolution*, (1990), 11–14; Gaunt, *Cromwell*, 7–23; Davis, *Cromwell*, 1–64.
5. Gaunt, *Cromwell*, 44; A. Woolrych, 'Cromwell as a Soldier', 117–18; J. Adamson, 'Oliver Cromwell and the Long Parliament', 55, 73, both in Morrill (ed.), *Oliver Cromwell and the English Revolution*; F. Kitson, *Old Ironsides: The Military Biography of Oliver Cromwell* (2004), 67–8.
6. Davis, *Cromwell*, 4.
7. Masson and Bruce, *Quarrel*, 73, 77.
8. Ibid., 70–7.
9. Holmes, *Eastern Association*, 290, n. 19.
10. Masson and Bruce, *Quarrel*, 71; W.M. Palmer, *Cambridge Subsidy Rolls, 1250–1695* (1912), 68; D. Summers, *The Great Level* (1976), 95.
11. Abbott, iv. 471.
12. Woolrych, 'Cromwell as a Soldier', 97, 117–18.
13. M. Bennett, *Oliver Cromwell* (2006), 85–6.
14. Masson and Bruce, *Quarrel*, 73.
15. Fuller quoted in Kingston, *East Anglia and the Great Civil War* (1902), 101.
16. D. Defoe, *A Tour Through the Whole Island of Great Britain*, ed. P. Rogers (1986), 415; S. L. Sadler, 'Cambridgeshire Society during the First and Second Civil Wars, c.1638–c.1649: Some Aspects of Allegiance' (PhD thesis, Anglia Ruskin University, 1998), 87–95, 181–6, 190–2, 194, 197–9, 201, 212–16, 222–3.

17. Holmes, *Eastern Association*, 70–2.
18. *Diverse Remarkable Passages of God's Providence* (1643), passim.
19. *Certaine Informations, no.* 16 (1–8 May 1643), 123.
20. Masson and Bruce, *Quarrel*, 73.
21. *CJ*, ii. 871, 883–4, 897; *LJ*, v. 306, 369–70, 492–3, 499, 503–4, 505; Abbott, i. 208–9; Holmes, *Eastern Association*, 64; P. Gaunt, *The Cromwellian Gazetteer* (1987), 224.
22. Bruce and Masson, *Quarrel*, p. 73; *Diverse Remarkable Passages* (June 1643), passim; Abbott, i. 22; Kingston, *East Anglia*, 102–7; Gaunt, *Cromwellian Gazetteer*, 106.
23. TNA, SP28/152 (Wisbech parish accounts, question 31); Abbott, i. 224; Holmes, *Eastern Association*, 72.
24. *CJ*, ii. 952; Abbott, i. 211, 213; *Certaine Informations*, no. 3 (30 January–6 February 1643), 19, 21; *The Kingdomes Weekly Intelligencer*, no. 6 (31 January–7 February 1643), 42, 43; *The Kingdomes Weekly Intelligencer*, no. 8 (14–21 February 1643), 62; *Certain Speciall Pasages*, no. 28 (14–21 February 1643), 228; *Certaine Informations*, no. 5 (13–20 February 1643), 40; *Mercurius Aulicus*, no. 9 (26 February–4 March 1643), 107, 118, 119. Kingston, *East Anglia*, 69, 88–90; *A Continuation of Certain Speciall and Remarkable Passages*, no. 34 (23 February–2 March 1643), [final page]; *A&O*, i. 85; Lomas-Carlyle, i. 118–19; Holmes, *Eastern Association*, 66, 69, 72.
25. *CSPD 1641–43*, 454; Kingston, *East Anglia*, 103–4; Bennett, *Cromwell*, 60–1.
26. Abbott, i. 224–5; Holmes, *Eastern Association*, 69–73; P. Bigmore, *The Bedfordshire and Huntingdonshire Landscape* (1979), 197–201; Bennett, *Cromwell*, 60–2; Taylor, *Cambridgeshire Landscape*, 227–8.
27. Woolrych, 'Cromwell as a Soldier', 97.
28. *Special Passages*, no. 38 (25 April–2 May 1643), 313; Lomas-Carlyle, i. 130–1.
29. C. H., Firth, *Cromwell's Army* (1982 edn.), 124–5, 164.
30. Holmes, *Eastern Association*, 73–4; Bennett, *Cromwell*, 62–4.
31. Parliamentary Archives, House of Lords Main Papers, investigation of 17 June 1643, 3–4, 12, 19–20, 22–3, 33–4, 39, 44, 50, 55–6; Sadler, 'Cambridgeshire', 87–94.
32. Sir Philip Warwick, *Memoires of the reigne of King Charles I* (1701), 251; Abbott, i. 227.
33. M.G. Matthews, *Walker Revised* (1948), 207; Parliamentary Archives, House of Lords Main Papers, 17 June 1643, 3–4, 12, 19–20, 22–3, 33–4, 39, 44, 50, 55–6.
34. *Certaine Informations*, no. 18 (15–22 May 1643), 143.
35. M. A. E. Green, *The Letters of Henrietta Maria* (1857), 197–8; *ODNB* (Sir John Hotham (1589–1645) and John Hotham (1610–1645)); Bennett, *Cromwell*, 62–4.

36. *LJ*, vii. 89; *Perfect Diurnal*, no. 9 (December 1644), 3; *A Diary*, no. 31 (5–12 December 1643) 221, 224; TNA, SP28/223, unfol. (November and December payments for service against Crowland, guarding Earith and Ely and soldiers' provision); Lomas-Carlyle, i. 187.

37. *HMC 7th Report*, 555, no. 629; *A True Relation of Collonell Cromwells Proceedings against the Cavaliers, 28 July 1643*, 2; J. Vicars, *Gods Arke Overtopping the World Waves* (1646), 7.

38. *HMC 7th Report*, 55–6, no. 645; Vicars, *God's Arke*, 8; Abbott, i. 239.

39. *The Kingdomes Weekly Intelligencer*, no. 28 (25 July–1 August 1643), sig. Yy2r-v; *A True Relation of Collonell Cromwells Proceedings against the Cavaliers, 28 July 1643*, 2; *Certaine Informations*, no. 28 (24–31 July 1643), 224.

40. Bruce and Masson, *Quarrel*, 75; Bennett, *Cromwell*, 92–3.

41. Abbott, i. 312–13; Gaunt, *Cromwell*, 59.

42. Bennett, *Cromwell*, 64–5.

43. Lomas-Caryle, i. 143.

44. Abbott, i. 246.

45. *The Copy of a Letter Written by Colonel Cromwell to the Committee at Cambridge, Dated 31 July 1643 Concerning the Raising of the Siege of Gainsborough* (1643), passim. This pamphlet omits the last sentence quoted and Cromwell's comments about the necessity of raising more forces against Newcastle: see *HMC 7th Report*, 558, no. 676.

46. *ODNB*, 'Lionel Gatford'.

47. Davis, *Cromwell*, 97–8.

48. Morrill, 'The Making of Oliver Cromwell', 47.

49. Ibid., 32–7, 46–7.

50. Morrill, 'Introduction' in his *Oliver Cromwell and the English Revolution*, 8–14.

51. Bennett, *Cromwell*, 62–3.

52. *HMC 7th Report*, 557, nos. 663, 558, 676.

53. Abbott, i. 251.

54. TNA, SP28/222, fo. 3; Holmes, *Eastern Association*, 94.

55. *HMC 7th Report*, 561, no. 747.

56. Masson and Bruce, *Quarrel*, 73.

57. *HMC 7th Report*, 561, no. 735.

58. Gaunt, *Cromwell*, 52, 228; Bennett, *Cromwell*, 69–70.

59. Masson and Bruce, *Quarrel*, 73–4.

60. BL, Add. MS 15672, fo. 15b; TNA, SP28/223/V (27 October 1643 order for paying Major Ireton's troops and Captains Dodson and Lomax's companies); Gaunt, *Gazetteer*, 224.

61. Masson and Bruce, *Quarrel*, 72–4.

62. Bodl., MS Tanner MS 62/469 (microfilm); TNA, SP28/222, part 1 ('Expenses out of such monies as have been received of the several constables in the same part of the Isle of Ely: toward the pay of

Colonel Cromwell's forces and the provision of red coats for the soldiers, 10 January 1643/4'); Holmes, *Eastern Association*, 98–109.

63. TNA, SP28/222, fo. 3.
64. *Mercurius Aulicus*, no. 45 (week ending 11 November 1643); *Victoria County History of Cambridgeshire* ed. R. B. Pugh, vol. iv. 103.
65. Masson and Bruce, *Quarrel*, 74; Abbott, i. 102–4; Morrill, 'The Making of Oliver Cromwell', 37–8.
66. Sadler, 'Cambridgeshire', 141–53.
67. *CSPD 1625–49*, 657.
68. Masson and Bruce, *Quarrel*, 75.
69. Holmes, 'Colonel King', 455–7; *ODNB*, 'Valentine Walton'.
70. Holmes, 'Colonel King', 66.
71. Mason and Bruce, *Quarrel*, 75.
72. Masson and Bruce, *Quarrel*, 75; BL, Add MS 15672, fos. 33–4.
73. Holmes, 'Colonel King', 462.
74. Masson and Bruce, *Quarrel*, 76.
75. In southern Lincolnshire, Cromwell's ally Colonel King appointed new sequestrators in his campaign to undermine Lord Grey's authority (see Abbott, i. 291; S. L. Sadler, 'The Smoke of War: The Impact of the Civil War on Cambridgeshire', *Cromwelliana* (1996), 20–6; J. Whinnell, *Matters of Great Concernment* (1646) 12, 23. *LJ*, vi. 160–1; *CJ*, iii. 188; *CSPD 1669*, 632, 243; Holmes, 'Colonel King', 457).
76. Abbott, i. 292.

# 4

# 'A Despicable Contemptible Generation of Men'?: Cromwell and the Levellers

Philip Baker

A discussion of Oliver Cromwell's relationship with the Levellers would at first appearance offer a decidedly limited opportunity to say something distinctively new about his career. The nature of that relationship is seemingly well established, and not without good reasons do historians traditionally regard it as one of mutual animosity. In 1647 the Levellers were the first of Cromwell's contemporaries to launch a sustained assault on his personal reputation,[1] and by the 1650s a number of them were embroiled in ill-fated efforts to assassinate him. As a result, Cromwell denounced the Levellers as 'a despicable contemptible generation of men';[2] ensured that they suffered frequent and lengthy periods of imprisonment; and had their leader, John Lilburne, twice stand trial for his life. Indeed, a powerful historiographical tradition that stretches back well over a century casts the two as mortal enemies, as the representatives of two incompatible concepts of government that lay at the heart of the English revolution: the reign of an authoritarian godly clique and direct rule by 'the people'. In 1649, we are told, theocracy ultimately triumphed over democracy when Cromwell's intense fear of popular government led to his routing of almost 1000 mutinous soldiers and the execution

90

of three of their ringleaders at Burford.[3] All this only serves to reinforce the existence of a reciprocal enmity between Cromwell and
the Levellers. Yet what undoubtedly made that loathing all the more
embittered and virulent on both sides was that their relationship had
once been so very different.

For much of the 1640s, Cromwell enjoyed cordial relations with
many of the individuals who by the end of the decade were at the
forefront of the Levellers' campaign. While this is generally acknowledged in the existing literature, these links have been only recently
studied in any detail and, to date, entirely from the perspective of
the Levellers. For example, David Como has demonstrated that a
pamphlet published in 1645 that was in all likelihood the work of
the Leveller William Walwyn had appended to it the final paragraphs
from Cromwell's famous letter written after the parliamentarian victory at Bristol.[4] Similarly, Jason Peacey has argued that until mid-1646
Lilburne was a member of an 'Independent alliance' that included
Cromwell and other leading Independent politicians on whom he
could rely for support and backing.[5] With this in mind, it may therefore be timely to consider the significance of these connections from
the standpoint of Cromwell himself.

This chapter examines the relationship between Cromwell and
the Levellers in the period up to 1649 and starts from the premise
that they were, until that date, natural allies rather than mortal enemies. It uses a variety of sources to explore the origins, nature
and basis of their association, their perceptions of one another and
their main beliefs and ideas. In stripping away the partial content
from retrospective accounts, the chapter reveals how the gradual fragmentation of the parliamentarian cause brought Cromwell
into close contact first with Lilburne and then with other Leveller figures; but it is argued that when Lilburne turned against him
in 1647, Cromwell continued to work and collaborate with men
such as William Walwyn, and that this was possible as he sympathised with and even supported many elements of the Levellers'
reform programme. It goes on to suggest that it was the proposed
method for implementing that programme, rather than its actual content, which Cromwell opposed, and that only when the Levellers
threatened army unity did he temporarily turn against them as a
group, as against the essence of their programme. In these respects
the chapter offers an original reassessment of Cromwell's political
alignments and thinking during the formative years of the English
revolution.

**I**

Cromwell's earliest association with the men who were later pejo-
ratively termed 'Levellers' is well known. On 9 November 1640 he
made his first recorded appearance in the Long Parliament by delivering a petition on the behalf of Lilburne, who was then languishing
in gaol as one of the 'puritan martyrs' of Laudian persecution.[6]
Cromwell's relationship with Lilburne would span some 17 years and
only ended when Lilburne, who was deemed too dangerous to release
after acquittal on a capital charge in 1653, died as his prisoner in
1657. Yet (and in spite of the possible significance of their early connection) the reasons for Cromwell's initial interest in Lilburne have
been surprisingly little discussed. Given that the two men almost certainly did not yet know each other, explanations have been sought
in Cromwell's religious views.[7] While this seems entirely plausible,
his apparent abandonment of Lilburne's case after the latter's release
from captivity suggests that there was a limit to his commitment and
that other factors were also involved.[8] Indeed, as Cromwell seemingly
lacked the patronage of a major parliamentary figure at the beginning of the session,[9] his highly topical interest in Lilburne—and other
godly heroes[10]—may be read as a conscious effort to catch the eye of a
potential patron, to establish a reputation and to make his mark in the
Commons.[11] And if so, his design had some success when as a result
of his speech in support of Lilburne he was added to the powerful
committee that was to investigate the cases of the 'puritan martyrs'.[12]

Regardless of his motives, however, Cromwell's actions undoubtedly secured him the lasting gratitude and affection of Lilburne. Even
in 1647, at a time when their relationship had broken down, Lilburne
affirmed that Cromwell's act 'in delivering me from the very gates
of death, in Anno 1640' was 'engraven upon my heart as with the
point of a diamond'.[13] If Cromwell, for his part, quickly lost interest
in Lilburne, he did not altogether forget him. Some years later, in
October 1643, he used his influence in the parliamentarian army to
secure Lilburne a commission as major in Colonel Edward King's
regiment in the Eastern Association. A number of local men had
expressed their dislike of Colonel King and Cromwell had purposely
commissioned Lilburne in his regiment to watch over and report
on his activities.[14] Within months Lilburne was working to have
the colonel court-martialled and brought before the Commons. The
main thrust of his case was that of military incompetence, but Colonel
King was a rigid Presbyterian and a religious undertone was also in

evidence.[15] Moreover, by August 1644 Cromwell evidently followed Lilburne's lead in attempting to purge the army of those who were both militarily *and* religiously suspect when he called for the Presbyterian Scot, Major-General Lawrence Crawford, to be cashiered.[16]

These disputes were symptomatic of a growing rift between Cromwell and his commanding officer, the (Presbyterian) earl of Manchester, and between the Independents and Presbyterians more generally. While Cromwell viewed the earl as a dilatory military leader, Manchester saw his lieutenant-general as a favourer of dangerous sectaries such as Lilburne, who in May 1644 was commissioned lieutenant-colonel of dragoons in Manchester's own regiment. Lilburne soon fell foul of the earl when he was publicly rebuked for securing the surrender of Tickhill Castle without orders, and it was necessary for Cromwell to persuade him to remain in the army.[17] Thereafter Lilburne proved a loyal and reliable supporter of Cromwell's campaign to discredit Manchester. He reportedly co-managed the securing of hands to a petition that was hostile to the earl, and in November he was among the witnesses who provided evidence of the charges formally brought against Manchester by Cromwell.[18] Nevertheless, it was Cromwell—not Lilburne—whom the earl specifically accused of 'levelling' tendencies at this time, charging his lieutenant-general (no doubt falsely) with having declared 'that he hoped to live to see never a nobleman in England'.[19]

Cromwell's dispute with Manchester was brought to an end by the self-denying ordinance of 1645, and although he was later criticised by Lilburne for not pursuing the earl all the way to the scaffold, at the time Lilburne claimed that Cromwell was deliberately posted away from parliament in order to frustrate his case.[20] Indeed the two continued to co-operate and in April Cromwell received information from Lilburne regarding the activities of the leading Presbyterian, Denzil Holles, whom the Independents later accused of intriguing with royalists.[21] Yet in the same month their relationship altered irrevocably when, and in spite of Cromwell's efforts to convince him otherwise, Lilburne became the only serving army officer to resign rather than accept the requirement to take the Solemn League and Covenant as a prerequisite for service in the New Model Army.[22] For the remainder of the 1640s the two men would meet each other as soldier and civilian.

As the New Model's sequence of crushing military victories in 1645 raised the prospect of peace, both Independents and Presbyterians turned their minds towards the settlement of the nation. For

Cromwell, Lilburne and other Independents and sectaries, the most pressing concern was that any future religious settlement included a provision for liberty of tender consciences. In September Cromwell's letter to the Speaker after the storming of Bristol contained an appeal for the setting aside of religious differences, a goal that had been attained within the army: 'Presbyterians, Independents, all had here the same spirit of faith and prayer; the same pretence and answer; they agree here, know no names of difference: pity it is it should be otherwise anywhere.'[23] A majority of the Commons opposed such sentiments, however, and not for the first time Cromwell's religious views were deliberately omitted from the authorised printing of the letter.[24] Nevertheless, the suppressed passages were published as a separate broadside, and through the same print operation they were appended to an anonymous pamphlet, *Strong Motives*, which has recently been attributed to William Walwyn.[25]

The coming together of Cromwell and Walwyn through their writing should not surprise us. Walwyn was a committed parliamentarian who from an early point in the war attended committees in London that agitated for a vigorous military campaign.[26] Thus *Strong Motives* contains praise for 'our great and victorious army' and for the figure who had been instrumental to its success, 'that worthy and religious commander Lieutenant Generall Cromwell'.[27] Walwyn was the author of a number of works that advocated liberty of conscience,[28] and he noted that the extracts from Cromwell's letter had 'an excellent harmony' with his argument in *Strong Motives* that those calling for a Presbyterian church government should 'endeavour not the compulsion of any in matters of religion, more then they wish others should endeavour to compel them'.[29] The passages from Cromwell's letter were therefore appended to Walwyn's tract as the latter approved of their sentiments. Yet we may also extend this discussion as Cromwell's letters and speeches, and Walwyn's known writings reveal a number of significant common characteristics in their religious thinking.

In one respect, Cromwell and Walwyn shared a number of more general beliefs, with both displaying a core commitment to liberty of conscience and practical Christianity (with its emphasis on charity, community and morality), and complete indifference to all religious forms—principles that were common, if not universal, among other religious nonconformists. But at a more specific level, the two held comparable views on the sovereignty of conscience. As Cromwell told the Scots in 1650, 'we do, and are ready to embrace so much as doth or shall be made to appear to us to be according to the Word of God . . . Faith working by love, is the true character of a Christian'.[30] Similarly, Walwyn believed that 'every man should be fully persuaded in his own mind of the lawfulness of that way wherein he served the Lord'.[31] The attitudes of both men towards the principle of justification through Christ alone are also worthy of comparison. Walwyn maintained that 'The love of God bringing salvation to all men hath appeared, teaching us to deny all ungodliness and worldly lusts.'[32] Cromwell was at times even more forceful on this point: 'What a nature hath my Father: He is Love—free in it, unchangeable, infinite. What a Covenant between Him and Christ, for all the seed, for every one'; 'men that believe in Jesus Christ . . . that believe the remission of sins through the blood of Christ and free justification by the blood of Christ, and live upon the grace of God . . . are members of Jesus Christ'.[33] Here Cromwell's religious thinking appears far more radical than is often acknowledged and much nearer to that of an extreme figure like Walwyn than to many of his later allies and supporters in the 1650s.

## II

We have seen that by 1645 Cromwell, Lilburne and Walwyn were all committed to the realisation of religious liberty, and that Lilburne and Walwyn looked up to Cromwell as a champion of the Independent cause, the 'darling of the sectaries' who had defended the godly and defeated the forces of the king. However, it is in this year that we first detect evidence of a divergence between Cromwell and Lilburne in the political sphere. This did not as yet have an impact on their personal relationship, as the parliamentary Independents continued to defend Lilburne from his Presbyterian enemies whenever possible.[34] Thus in July Cromwell wrote a letter in support of Lilburne's attempt to secure reparations for his punishment by the court of Star Chamber in the 1630s, and the letter Lilburne sent to Cromwell in December was warm and affectionate.[35] Yet here we need to more forcefully distinguish between the members of parliament and the institution of parliament.

In December 1644 Cromwell expressed his fear 'that without a more speedy, vigorous and effectual prosecution of the war . . . we shall make the kingdom weary of us, and hate the name of a parliament'.[36] By October 1645, however, a pamphlet by Lilburne made it evident that the absence of a settlement was having the identical effect. This outlook was encapsulated in the work's title: *'Englands' Birthright Justified Against all Arbitrary Usurpations, whether Regal or Parliamentary, or under what Vizor soever.'* Lilburne's purpose was to highlight the misdeeds of the Long Parliament and to call for its remedy through annual parliaments, legal reform, greater accountability, and the abolition of tithes, monopolies and the excise. As yet such demands and criticism were anathema to Cromwell, who, and in tandem with other army officers, professed as late as mid 1647 that he had no desire to alter the civil government.[37] Moreover, he believed that the justness of the army's cause derived from the authority of the Long Parliament and consequently maintained the utmost respect for the institution and its achievements.[38] By December 1648, of course, Cromwell's views on both these issues had dramatically altered. But until that time we shall see that his veneration of the Long Parliament arguably represented the essential point of divergence between himself and the Levellers.

While Cromwell disagreed with Lilburne's attack on parliament, Presbyterians were naturally horrified by the 'fantastical utopia'[39] depicted in *Englands Birthright Justified* and by 1646 their conflict with Independency was increasingly bitter. The Presbyterian attack on sectarian heresy, *Gangraena*, charted the heretical atrocities of the New Model, which was increasingly perceived as the Independent's army, and revealed how authors such as Lilburne and Walwyn were a threat not only to the nation's religion but also to its magistracy and civil government.[40] In May 1646 a campaign was launched in support of a *Remonstrance* that defended Presbyterian church government and demanded a speedy settlement with the king and a union with the Scots.[41] By July Walwyn and the later Leveller, Richard Overton, had written a rival *Remonstrance* that asserted the supremacy of the Commons over both the king and the Lords.[42] In the following month Cromwell noted that England was 'full of faction and worse'.[43] Furthermore, a Presbyterian majority in the Lords meant that the Independents could no longer protect Lilburne and as a result both he and Overton were imprisoned at the peers' orders. Before the end of the year both men were producing stinging indictments of the entire parliament and Lilburne later alleged that he was 'left in the suds by L.[ieutenant] G.[eneral] Cromwell'.[44] Yet it was not Cromwell's relationship with Lilburne—the traditional preoccupation of studies of his association with the Levellers—that was pivotal during the key year of 1647, but rather his relationship with a group of men around Walwyn.

## III

In 1646 Cromwell moved to a house in Drury Lane, where he became further sensitised to Presbyterian hostility towards the army. 'We have had a very long petition from the city', he wrote to his general, Sir Thomas Fairfax, in December. 'How it strikes at the army ... you will see.'[45] This painted an ominous picture of the balance of power in London, where the Independents and more extreme sectaries—the self-styled 'well-affected'—now appeared an embattled and vulnerable minority. Indeed, in the face of Presbyterian enmity, they increasingly looked towards the army for support and assistance. However, in March 1647 the parliamentary Presbyterians embarked on a new design to settle the nation, one that would see the disbanding of a majority of the New Model and the remainder sent to Ireland. All this ensured a constant flow of sectaries and soldiers to Drury Lane, eager to discuss the looming crisis with the lieutenant-general.[46]

Walwyn was a frequent visitor to Cromwell's house around May 1647 and he describes a meeting between Cromwell, city Independents and himself that resulted in the framing of a petition to the Commons. The so-called 'sharp petition' of 2 June was the fourth and final petition of a series with which Walwyn was involved from March of the same year and, in addition to recounting the recent transgressions of parliament, it contained four specific demands. These were: for a committee of worthy parliament-men to investigate all those in positions of authority and to exclude the unfaithful; to countenance and protect the well-affected, especially in the act of petitioning; to reinstate the former Independent city militia committee (which had been remodelled by the Presbyterians in May); and for parliament to consent to the just and reasonable desires of the army.[47] This final demand related to the fact that in May the New Model had refused parliament's order to disband until it was given adequate security for its arrears and indemnity. Cromwell did not side with the army until June, and Lilburne later alleged that his delay was on account of him being tempted with a bribe by the Commons to betray the New Model.[48] Nevertheless, Walwyn made no such accusation and in fact claimed to have influenced Cromwell's decision to depart the Commons for the army.[49]

Thus while Lilburne and Overton lay incarcerated in prison, Cromwell was actively working with Walwyn and London Independents in an effort to defend the army and the city's well-affected citizenry from the common Presbyterian enemy. And this spirit of co-operation continued over the following months, possibly as part of a larger army design to consult with its civilian supporters.[50] For example, 'very eminent persons of the Army'—perhaps including Cromwell—invited Walwyn to the New Model's headquarters at Reading in July 'to be advised withall touching the good of the people'.[51] Furthermore, other later Levellers were there at the same time. At the beginning of July, John Wildman delivered to the army a paper that called for the restoration of London's Independent militia committee. Wildman may well have represented the group, whose members included Cromwell and Walwyn, who were behind the 'sharp petition', as the paper stated that the issue of the militia was 'a request in our last petition to the House of Commons'.[52] This petition was taken up by the regimental agitators—the officer and soldier representatives of the ranks, who, alongside the general officers, formed the New Model's general council—and Cromwell, too, indicated his support.[53] Indeed, in mid July Cromwell and Colonel John Lambert were appointed to prepare a statement to parliament that called for the reinstatement of the former militia committee—a demand that was acceded to within days.[54]

As the London militia represented a possible counter-force to the New Model, we might expect Cromwell and the army to have supported civilian calls for the militia committee to be wrested from the Presbyterians and put into Independent hands. Yet there is also evidence that the army endorsed a very different set of civilian demands—encompassing social, economic and political reforms—as part of *The Heads of the Proposals*, the terms for settlement that it offered to Charles I in 1647. A draft of the *Heads* was first presented to the army's general council in July, when Cromwell was among those appointed to a committee that was to subject them to further consideration.[55] We have referred to Walwyn's and Wildman's presence at the headquarters in that month, and again in July Wildman and the future Leveller, Maximilian Petty, attended talks at Reading regarding the proposals.[56] In this context it seems significant that in their original published version of August, the *Heads* had appended to them a series of reforms that represented a number of the Levellers' core demands: vindication of the right to petition; the abolition of monopolies and all obstacles to free trade; the (eventual) abolition of the excise; a remedy for the problem of tithes; a reduction in the cost and length of legal proceedings; and an end to imprisonment for debt in cases involving the poor.[57] Moreover, many of these proposals were also contained in the first of the London petitions with which Walwyn was involved in March, the so-called 'large petition'.[58]

Thus while an older historiography saw it as necessary for the Levellers to infiltrate the agitator organisation in order to influence the army grandees, here we see that Cromwell and the general officers openly co-operated with and even countenanced reforms that originated with Walwyn, Wildman and Petty. Yet—and at exactly the same time—Cromwell was attacked by Lilburne for having 'bought and sold, the laws, liberties and justice of the kingdom for your own ends'.[59] Both Lilburne and Overton were increasingly frustrated at their continued imprisonment, and they accused Cromwell of deliberately prolonging their confinement through his removal of the power of the agitators.[60] During the general council's debates in July, however, Cromwell expressed his support for the release of the prisoners and in the same month a request for their liberty was issued to parliament in the name of Fairfax and his council of war.[61] Cromwell may well have done what he could on the behalf of Lilburne and Overton, therefore, and their incarceration was notably never a barrier to his working with the group of men around Walwyn.

## IV

Events in the latter months of 1647 were to substantially alter Cromwell's relationship with the Walwyn group, however. At the end of July an attempted putsch by London's Presbyterian leaders faltered when their remodelled city militia failed to prevent the New Model from entering the capital and restoring order. In the following month, Walwyn was once again at army headquarters when he urged for the Tower of London to be guarded by citizens rather than a regiment of soldiers. Given recent events, the grandees unsurprisingly rejected his proposal, as did the army's Independent allies in London, who subsequently turned against Walwyn. As a result he was thereafter ostracised from Cromwell and the chief officers,[62] though it seems significant that the local issue of control of the Tower, rather than a major ideological dispute, was the cause of the breakdown in the relationship.

The army's entry into London also saw the flight or impeachment of those parliament-men who were complicit in the Presbyterians' design, one effect of which was to end the Presbyterian dominance in the Lords.[63] This raised the likelihood of Lilburne's release, and in early September Cromwell visited him in the Tower. Lilburne had made frequent requests for such a meeting and perhaps Cromwell finally obliged out of a lingering sense of loyalty towards his erstwhile ally. When Cromwell inquired why Lilburne had departed from his friends and turned so vehemently against parliament, Lilburne responded that *he* had fallen out with no one; rather his friends had reneged on their first principles. In spite of this, Cromwell vowed to secure Lilburne's release and even a position for him in the army if only he would remain quiet. This Lilburne simply refused to do unless he received a full vindication for the wrongs he had suffered.[64] Cromwell could have taken little encouragement from such pugnacity, and he no doubt realised that setting free an intransigent Lilburne could have posed a threat to army unity at the very moment that Cromwell and his allies in the Lords were working towards a settlement based on *The Heads of the Proposals*. Thus while Lilburne's allegation that Cromwell thereafter deliberately frustrated his release cannot be substantiated,[65] there is certainly no evidence to suggest that Cromwell positively worked to secure it. Moreover, when the Lords discharged a number of prisoners, including Overton, in mid September, it is notable that Lilburne remained in captivity.[66]

Nevertheless, Lilburne's confinement did not prevent Cromwell and his allies from encountering resistance to their projected settlement from elements within the army and the Commons. And that resistance can be linked to the men who soon emerged as the Levellers and to individuals who openly supported them. Foremost among Cromwell's adversaries was Colonel Thomas Rainborough, who achieved notoriety as the most outspoken advocate of manhood suffrage during the Putney debates. At one level, theirs was a personal dispute born of Cromwell's opposition (for reasons that remain unclear) to Rainborough's appointment to the post of vice-admiral—opposition that provoked Rainborough to make threats against Cromwell's life.[67] Yet it was also determined by Cromwell's willingness to treat with a king whom Rainborough had seemingly turned against in late July when, as part of the delegation that originally presented Charles with the *Heads*, he had experienced at first-hand the king's obdurate nature.[68] A parliament-man himself, Rainborough subsequently allied with the handful of republicans in the Commons and in September this group voted against a proposal that the House form a grand committee to discuss the issue of the king, with Cromwell and Rainborough acting as tellers on the opposing sides.[69]

Within the army hostility towards the projected settlement led to the selection of new agitators—often referred to as agents—who wrote a number of pamphlets calling the army back to its first principles. Whereas the New Model's earlier declarations had demanded the resolution of the army's grievances *before* the subject of the king was entertained, the *Heads* addressed these issues in *reverse* order, leaving the settlement of the army's demands entirely at the will of the man whom it had defeated in battle. The agent's position was most forcefully advanced in a publication of October, *The Case of the Armie Truly Stated*, which insinuated that those at headquarters had reneged on the New Model's engagements in treating with the king, a charge which, despite the absence of any names, was clearly aimed at Cromwell and his son-in-law, Henry Ireton, the chief supporters of the *Heads* within the army. Furthermore, in declaring the sovereignty of the Commons, the agents clearly opposed (*contra* the *Heads*) the preservation of the negative voices of the monarchy and the Lords.[70] According to a hostile account, Cromwell and Ireton roundly turned on the *Case* and its authors when it was discussed in the general council of the army.[71] However, it actually seems that Cromwell was behind the decision to invite its promoters to attend the council, at which the agent Robert Everard 'was marvellously taken up with the plainness of the carriage' and with 'the lieutenant-general's desire for an understanding with us'.[72]

Wildman had certainly made his common cause with the agents by late October, when he attended a meeting with them at which he in all likelihood drafted the *Agreement of the People*.[73] Nevertheless, it is unclear when exactly he turned against the *Heads*. He later claimed that the army drew back from its first principles as early as June and that the *Heads* were presented prematurely by Cromwell and Ireton and thereafter amended entirely as the king willed.[74] But according to Ireton both Wildman and Petty agreed to the retention of the powers of the Lords during discussions over the proposals in July, and as late as September Wildman was recommended for a governorship by the general committee of officers, of which both Cromwell and Ireton were members.[75] In an anonymous pamphlet that appeared on the first day of the Putney debates (28 October), however, Wildman accused Cromwell and Ireton of carrying on the king's design in the name of the army and instructed the soldiery that 'with a word, ye can create new officers'. Yet while Ireton was the focus of his enmity, Wildman held out hope that 'just, honest, sincere and valiant Cromwell' might still repent and once more become a champion of 'the liberties of the people'.[76]

## V

Thus at the outset of the Putney debates, the agents and their civilian advisors, Wildman and Petty, were seeking to *persuade* Cromwell of the justness of their cause rather than defeat him in argument. This is not to ignore that Cromwell and Ireton initially faced the animus of a number of the participants, both in regard to their dealings with the king and in their upholding of the Long Parliament: as Trooper Edward Sexby informed them, 'your credits and reputation hath been much blasted upon these two considerations'.[77] But the focus of the debate quickly moved on to the *Agreement of the People*, and here we need to challenge the prevalent view that Cromwell was diametrically opposed to the document with its call for: the dissolution of the Long Parliament; biennial parliaments and a redistribution of parliamentary seats; and a series of 'reserved powers' which the people were to retain to themselves: freedom of conscience; equality before the law; freedom from impressment; and an amnesty for acts committed during the war.[78] In fact there was much here to which Cromwell could readily consent and he openly acknowledged that 'this paper doth contain many good things in it'.[79] Ireton was even more emphatic: 'there are plausible things in it, and there are things really good in it, and there are those things that I do with my heart desire'.[80] But for both men there was the issue of whether the army was free to embrace the *Agreement* in the light of its existing engagements and a committee was called to discuss this point. This was not a mere diversionary tactic: as Ireton pointed out, the *Case* had implicitly criticised him and Cromwell for allegedly reneging on the army's declarations, and the use of meetings and committees to reach consensus was a well-established procedure within the New Model.[81] Moreover, as the authors of the *Agreement* clearly drew on a number of the army's engagements in composing their paper, with the *Declaration* or *Representation* of 14 June 1647 serving as a direct source,[82] we should not underestimate the level of convergence between the *Agreement* and the army's own political programme.

For Cromwell the problem with the *Agreement* was not so much its content as the method by which it would be implemented. What needed to be considered were 'the ways and means to accomplish

[it]: that is to say whether...those great difficulties [that] lie in our way [are] in a likelihood to be either overcome or removed'. At one level he accepted the principle that the document could gain legitimacy through a literal agreement of the people, but what was to prevent others from drawing up alternate settlements? The result would be utter confusion.[83] More fundamentally, the *Agreement* denied the Long Parliament an active role in the settlement of the nation; indeed it implied that the army would dissolve parliament and impose terms upon the country through naked force. This was still completely contrary to Cromwell's thinking. Throughout the year he continually baulked at the demands of a minority of the soldiery for a purge of parliament by differentiating between those Presbyterian members who opposed the army and the authority of the institution as a whole;[84] and at Putney he emphatically restated his position: 'Either they are a parliament or no parliament. If they be no parliament they are nothing, and we are nothing likewise.' The ramifications were clear: 'therefore the considering of what is fit for the kingdom does belong to the parliament'.[85] Nevertheless, Cromwell's attachment to this standard did not mean that the *Agreement*'s supporters would find himself and the other grandees 'wedded and glued to forms of government'. Rather—and revealing his accord with the underlying principle of the *Agreement*—he reassured them that 'we...concur with you that the foundation and supremacy is in the people, radically in them, and to be set down by them in their representations'.[86]

On the issue of the franchise, it is of course beyond question that Cromwell sided with Ireton in strenuously opposing the doctrine that the vote was the natural right of every individual male. And while this saw him adopt on the second day's debate a more circumspect attitude towards the *Agreement*, it is worth noting that he was quite prepared to admit that the *Heads* may not go far enough in its proposed extension of the franchise, and that, away from Rainborough's talk of the 'poorest he', Petty was quite willing to exclude servants and apprentices from the electorate.[87] Moreover, on other equally controversial subjects Cromwell's words indicate that he was much nearer to the views of Petty and Wildman, who were committed to the removal of the negative voices of the king and the Lords and even their outright abolition. As Cromwell saw it, 'we all apprehend danger from the person of the king, and from the Lords', and he stated his agreement with those who believed 'that there can bee no safety in a consistency with [them]...having the least interest in the public affaires of the kingdom'—an early indication of a developing antipathy towards Charles I and the powers of the upper House. But he thought it was not yet clear that it was God's will to destroy them altogether, and he urged patience on 'those that are of that mind [to] wait upon God for such a way when the thing may be done without sin, and without scandal too'.[88]

Cromwell's and the army's concurrence with much of the content of the *Agreement* is also powerfully reflected in the settlement proposals drawn up by a committee of the general council to which he was appointed and that reviewed the document in tandem with the New Model's previous engagements. Between late October and early November, this committee agreed on a number of propositions that correspond to demands in the *Agreement* and earlier civilian petitions:[89] to put a period to the Long Parliament; to establish biennial parliaments; for the Commons to determine a redistribution of seats and an extension of the franchise; for the power of the Commons to be extended to the enacting and repealing of laws; for all officeholders to be made accountable to the Commons, with peers accountable to the Lords; and for tithes to be replaced. The committee's proposals also retained the concept of reserved powers, with no compulsion in matters of religion, no conscription, and indemnity for acts committed during the war. Yet this projected settlement of the nation was to be undertaken through the agency of parliament, not by a renewal of the social compact, indicating that Cromwell had impressed his assurance in parliament's authority upon the committee.[90]

On 8 November, however, the agitators were ordered to return to their regiments and the army was called to a rendezvous. The most likely reason for this was the increasingly mutinous state of a number of New Model regiments, with some displaying royalist sympathies and others coming under the influence of the agents and their supporters. During the debates Cromwell accused those who sought 'to disoblige the army from [the] commands of the general' of acting in a 'way . . . destructive to the army and to every particular man in the army . . . [We shall hang ourselves], if we doe not conform to the rules of war'. Nevertheless, the concern at the New Model's condition did not disrupt the attempt to agree terms for settlement, as on 9 November Cromwell and Wildman were among those appointed to a committee to examine the *Case* and the *Agreement* in the light of the army's existing declarations.[91] Three days later the king escaped from the New Model's custody at Hampton Court, claiming that his self-preservation forced him to flee from men 'with whom the Levellers' doctrine is rather countenanced than punished'.[92] In this Charles was no doubt creating an excuse for a premeditated action, but his reading of the relationship between Cromwell, the other grandees and the Levellers is perhaps more apt than has often been given credit.[93]

In mid November 1647 the events surrounding the army rendezvous at Corkbush Field near Ware were to cause a major breach in that relationship. Although the New Model had been ordered to three separate rendezvous, the agents and their allies called the soldiery to a general rendezvous at Ware[94]—presumably with the intention of pressurising the grandees into immediately accepting the *Agreement* and then imposing it upon the kingdom. However, in attempting to openly subvert the unity of the army, the agents simply turned Cromwell and the grandees against them. At the Ware rendezvous a number of civilians and soldiers, including Rainborough, were arrested for distributing copies of the *Agreement*, and two mutinous regiments appeared contrary to orders and with copies of the paper adorning their hats. One promptly obeyed an order to remove the papers, but the second refused before Cromwell reportedly snatched the copies of the *Agreement* from them. As a result of their insubordination three soldiers were sentenced to death and one was shot at the head of his regiment.[95] Cromwell's actions at Ware were, nevertheless, directed against the display of mutinous behaviour and the non-compliance with orders rather than against the *Agreement* itself. This is evident from the content of the *Remonstrance* drawn up by a committee headed by Cromwell and Ireton, which each regiment at Ware subsequently approved. While this explicitly condemned those who sought to divide the army, its programme to set a time limit for the Long Parliament, to make provisions for regular sittings of parliaments of fixed duration and for the Commons to be rendered more representative through the freedom and equality of elections was entirely compatible with the content of the *Agreement*.[96]

The open involvement of the *Agreement*'s supporters in the Ware mutiny brought Cromwell's working relationship with that group to an abrupt end. The unity of the army was paramount with Charles's escape prompting renewed fears of war and those who threatened that unity could no longer be countenanced at headquarters. Thus later in November Cromwell reassured the Commons that the mutineers were in custody and that the three rendezvous had successfully united all other troops behind the authority of Fairfax. Moreover, his condemnation of the 'drive at a levelling and parity'[97] within sections of the army lends credence to the allegations of Lilburne and Wildman that it was the army grandees who baptised them as Levellers at Putney.[98] That name may have originated in the *Agreement's* demand for total equality before the law—significantly a proposal that the general council's committee never adopted. During the debates Ireton informed Wildman that if his intent was not only to remove all power from the king and Lords but also to 'take away all kind of distinction of them from other men, then you do them wrong... their having [such] a distinction from other men cannot do us wrong'.[99] And if Cromwell and Ireton were behind the Leveller label, they chose an immensely powerful term which, with its connotations (*contra* the actual demands of the Levellers) of economic and social parity, successfully denigrated those who threatened army unity at a time when its preservation appeared essential to the survival of the parliamentarian cause.

## VI

Charles I's Engagement with the Scots in December 1647 saw Cromwell support a motion in January 1648 that parliament should make no further addresses to the king as the country slid towards a renewal of armed conflict. Yet if Cromwell now accepted the Levellers' view that a personal treaty with the king was a betrayal of the people's trust, they were unwilling to forgive his earlier indiscretions. In January Lilburne accused Cromwell of having earlier struck a bargain to restore the king in return for the earldom of Essex and described how the republican parliament-man, Henry Marten, was so incensed at Cromwell's actions that he had planned to murder him (a story Marten denied). Unfortunately for Lilburne, an informant reported his words to parliament and as a result both he and Wildman were imprisoned.[100] For the first time the Levellers' confinement was orchestrated by the Independents, and one royalist correspondent believed that 'the intent at present is to take Lilburne out of the way... Cromwell his old friend is his adversary, and if Cromwell do not ruin him, I really believe that he will in the end be ruined by him'.[101]

During the second civil war in the summer of 1648, Cromwell once again found himself attacked in print by Lilburne, who denounced him as a 'usurper, tyrant, thief and murderer'.[102] Furthermore, when in August parliament reopened treaty negotiations with

the king, they released Lilburne at the same time, no doubt hoping
that he would destabilise Cromwell's position within the army.[103] This
proved a serious miscalculation, however, as Lilburne had more to fear
from a Presbyterian imposed settlement than from the army grandees,
and he sent Cromwell a letter (via Sexby) in which he pledged him
his support 'to the last drop of my heart blood, (for all your severe
hand towards me)'.[104]

In September of that year the Levellers' *Humble Petition* to the
Commons reaffirmed the social and economic proposals in their earlier manifestoes, demanded an end to the negative voices, though not
the outright abolition, of the king and the Lords, but was notably
silent on the point of the franchise—perhaps in a deliberate attempt
to placate Cromwell. The latter would also have taken solace from
the calls for constant pay and indemnity for the army and for 'justice upon the capital authors and promoters of the former or late
wars'.[105] Over the following months, this Leveller programme was
explicitly endorsed in petitions from nearly twenty New Model
regiments, a campaign that Cromwell and Ireton were rumoured
to countenance.[106] Less circumstantially, when a petition from his
own regiment commended the *Humble Petition* and its promoters,
Cromwell forwarded it to Fairfax with a letter that described the
'very great sense in the officers of the regiments of the sufferings and the ruin of this poor kingdom, and in them all a very
great zeal to have impartial justice done upon offenders; and I must
confess, I do in all, from my heart, concur with them'.[107] Following a meeting between Cromwell and Lilburne and discussions
between the army and London's well-affected, a delegation of officers, Levellers, city Independents and 'honest' parliament-men set
about devising a new draft *Agreement of the People*,[108] and in November
Ireton's army *Remonstrance*, which expressed support for and was in
part influenced by the *Humble Petition*, demanded the execution of
the king and called on parliament to settle the nation through an
*Agreement*.[109]

Given the fallout from the events at Ware, Cromwell's recon-
ciliation with the Levellers is a chapter in his career and in the
history of the revolution that has often puzzled historians.[110] However, our re-examination of their relationship allows us to make
greater sense of the events of late 1648. First, their *rapprochement*
appears all the less surprising if we rightly continue to look upon
them as natural allies. Although they were forced together in 1648 by
parliament's treaty with the king, which threatened to destroy them

and all they had fought for, their re-alliance was clearly eased by
their long-standing personal associations, their earlier working rela-
tionships and the extent of their shared beliefs and ideas.[111] Second,
Cromwell's split with the Levellers in 1647 was not rooted in fundamental ideological differences but in their efforts to divide the
army. Thus with the Levellers respecting military discipline during
late 1648, Cromwell and Ireton were able to join a significant number of New Model regiments in uniting behind their programme.
Third, the recourse to an *Agreement* should not simply be dismissed
as expediency on the part of the grandees. Cromwell continued to
show support for the device if it was presented, rather than imposed
upon parliament, while Ireton's efforts at the Whitehall debates stand
as testimony to his personal commitment to the document.

Nevertheless, Cromwell was aware that the alliance with the Levellers was a cause of anxiety among some supporters of the army, who
as a consequence began to look favourably upon parliament's treaty
with Charles I. One such individual was Colonel Robert Hammond,
and Cromwell's letters to him in November 1648 are revealing. In
stark contrast to his scaremongering to the Commons in the previous
year, Cromwell twice informed Hammond that there was nothing to
fear from the Levellers, although it was 'easy to take offence at [them],
and run into an extremity on the other hand'. Indeed, he predicted
that if there were to be a levelling of the orders of society, it would
not be the work of the Levellers but of those who used them to justify supporting a treaty with 'this man against whom the Lord hath
witnessed'.[112]

Cromwell did not arrive in London from the north of England
until after Colonel Pride's purge of Parliament, and his subsequent
attendance at only a single day of the debates at Whitehall regarding
the final form of the new *Agreement* has been interpreted as evidence
of his lack of interest.[113] Until the end of December he was undoubtedly preoccupied with the issues surrounding the trial of the king,
but his actions also strongly suggest that his preference was for the
introduction of the new constitution *prior* to the trial.[114] Moreover,
the fragmentary records of the debates and the lack of attendance lists
for January make it feasible that Cromwell attended on more than
one occasion. His contributions on 6 January were entirely consistent with his earlier preference for the *Agreement* to be submitted
to the Long Parliament prior to general subscription, and although
his desire to preserve the dignity of parliament in this manner was
opposed by Ireton, it was adopted in the final version of the officers'

*Agreement.*[115] Ireton's defeat on this and other votes determining the form of the *Agreement* are perhaps rightly seen to have cooled his ardour for a written constitution, and the notion that the document was quickly overtaken by events is dramatically symbolised by its presentation to the Commons on 20 January 1649—the first day of the trial of Charles I.[116] While Cromwell was fully committed to that act, Lilburne was resolute in opposing it on the grounds that the erected high court of justice lacked both the legitimate authority and legal basis to proceed against anyone. We have only Lilburne's testimony that he was offered a place as one of the king's judges;[117] but if true it would be entirely within keeping with Cromwell's earlier attempts to keep him on board—or at least quiet—while he pursued the path that in his eyes God had determined to bring peace and settlement to the nation.

# VII

The months following the regicide would bring the rout of the army Levellers at Burford and the first of Lilburne's trials by the commonwealth regime, returning us to the starting point of our enquiry and the mutual enmity between Cromwell and the Levellers. Nevertheless, if Cromwell remains the man who destroyed the Levellers as a group, the picture of him that emerges from this chapter is harder to reconcile with the image of the intransigent 'enemy of revolution'.[118] He was certainly vehement in his condemnation of mutiny within the army, and he dealt mercilessly with a handful of ringleaders at both Ware and Burford. But, as we have seen, his attitude towards military insubordination needs to be distinguished from his general acceptance of elements of the Leveller programme. The degree of consensus between Cromwell and the Levellers has largely been obscured by the historiographical preoccupation with the extension of the franchise,[119] which was never the most important of the Levellers' demands, and after Putney they consistently proposed an electorate exclusive of almstakers, servants, women and children. To be sure, Cromwell opposed the principle that the vote was a natural right, but he was not against the extension of the existing franchise, and on other religious, political, social and constitutional issues that were fundamental to the Levellers, we have seen that there was much with which he sympathised. Moreover, his words and actions continue to support this reading even after the demise of the Levellers as an identifiable group. Into the 1650s Cromwell called on parliaments to 'relieve the oppressed, hear the groans of poor prisoners in England; be pleased to reform the abuses of all professions', and to remedy the 'one general grievance in the nation . . . the law'—all demands the Levellers had advanced.[120] Although during the Putney debates he famously rejected 'temporal things' as 'but . . . dross and dung in comparison of Christ', it is telling that in 1654 he advised his first protectorate parliament that 'in every government there must be somewhat fundamental, somewhat like a *Magna Charta*, that should be standing and be unalterable'.[121] Seven years earlier the identical argument had been used to justify the need for an *Agreement of the People*, for an entrenched constitution that 'shall never be subject to the power of parliaments, or any other'.[122]

Ultimately, Providence never sanctioned the full Leveller programme in the eyes of Cromwell, and when he referred to Levellers in the 1650s, it allowed him, in the words of one contemporary, to 'conjure up at pleasure some terrible apparition . . . [to] affright the people to fly to him for refuge'.[123] By that time both Cromwell and the Levellers would no doubt have vehemently denied that they shared common objectives for the settlement of the nation. But perhaps Cromwell deemed at least some of his erstwhile Leveller allies among those 'many, [and] I fear some good [men]' who in their failing to accept the necessities of God's Providence 'have murmured and repined, because disappointed of their mistaken fancies'.[124]

## Notes

1. J. Morrill, 'Cromwell and His Contemporaries', in Morrill (ed.), *Oliver Cromwell and the English Revolution* (Harlow, 1990), 262–4.
2. J. Lilburne *et al.*, *The Picture of the Councel of State* (1649), 15.
3. S. R. Gardiner, *History of the Commonwealth and Protectorate, 1649–56* (4 vols., repr. 1903), i. 29–30, 53–4; A. Fraser, *Cromwell, Our Chief of Men* (1973), 310, 316–17; B. Manning, *1649: The Crisis of the English Revolution* (1992), 173–7, 214, 215.
4. D. R. Como, 'An Unattributed Pamphlet by William Walwyn: New Light on the Prehistory of the Leveller Movement', *Huntington Library Quarterly*, 69 (2006), 353–82.
5. J. T. Peacey, 'John Lilburne and the Long Parliament', *HJ*, 43 (2000), 625–45.
6. *Procs. LP*, i. 64, 66, 71; *CJ*, ii. 24.
7. For example, see M. Ashley, 'Oliver Cromwell and the Levellers', *History Today*, 17 (1967), 539.

8. In 1645 Lilburne was still seeking the discharge of his Star Chamber fine and the award of reparations when he approached Cromwell for help: see J. Lilburne, *Innocency and Truth Justified* (1645), 63–4.

9. J. S. A. Adamson, 'Oliver Cromwell and the Long Parliament', in Morrill (ed.), *Oliver Cromwell and the English Revolution*, 51–2.

10. G. S., *A Letter from an Ejected Member of the House of Commons, to Sir Jo: Evelyn* (1648), 6.

11. I am grateful to John Adamson for a discussion on this point.

12. *CJ*, ii. 24; W. Notestein (ed.), *The Journal of Sir Simonds D'Ewes from the Beginning of the Long Parliament to the Opening of the Trial of the Earl of Strafford* (New Haven, CT, 1923), 19 n. 35.

13. J. Lilburne, *Ionahs Cry out of the Whales Belly* (1647), 2.

14. Lilburne, *Innocency and Truth*, 41; J. Lilburne, *The Iust Mans Justification* (2nd edn. 1647), 5.

15. Lilburne, *Iust Mans Justification*; Lilburne, *Innocency and Truth*, 41–6; C. Holmes, 'Colonel King and Lincolnshire politics, 1642–6', *HJ*, 16 (1973), 463.

16. Holmes, 'Colonel King', 466–7.

17. Lilburne, *Innocency and Truth*, 21–5, 46.

18. J. Bruce and D. Masson (eds), *The Quarrel between the Earl of Manchester and Oliver Cromwell* (1875), 60; *CSPD, 1644–5*, 148–9.

19. S. R. Gardiner (ed.), 'A Letter from the Earl of Manchester to the House of Lords, Giving an Opinion of the Conduct of Oliver Cromwell' (*Camden Miscellany*, viii (1883)), 2.

20. Lilburne, *Iust Mans Justification*, 20; [J. Lilburne], *Englands Birthright Justified* (1645), 17 and 32.

21. House of Lords Record Office, Main Papers, 30/6/45, fos. 260, 262v-3.

22. Lilburne, *Innocency and Truth*, 46.

23. Abbott, i. 374–8, quotation at p. 377.

24. Abbott, i. 378 n. 172. For an earlier example of the suppression of Cromwell's religious views by the Commons, see Abbott, i. 360 n. 130.

25. Como, 'Unattributed Pamphlet'.

26. Walwyn's activities are usefully summarised in K. Lindley, *Popular Politics and Religion in Civil War London* (Aldershot, 1997), 396.

27. [W. Walwyn], *Strong Motives* (1645), 4.

28. For example, see [W. Walwyn], *The Compassionate Samaritane* (1644); [W. Walwyn], *A Helpe to the Right Understanding of a Discourse Concerning Independency* (1645).

29. [Walwyn], *Strong Motives*, 7 and sig. A.

30. *A Declaration of the Army of England upon Their March into Scotland* (1650), 9; J. C. Davis, 'Cromwell's Religion', in Morrill (ed.), *Oliver Cromwell and the English Revolution*, 191–2, 194, 195, 198, 207.

31. [W. Walwyn] *Good Counsell to All* (1644), 84.

32. Ibid., 81–2.
33. Abbott, ii. 602; iv. 271–2.
34. Peacey, 'John Lilburne', 629–32.
35. Lilburne, *Innocency and Truth*, 63–4; Lilburne, *Ionahs Cry*, 12–13.
36. Abbott, i. 314.
37. Ibid., 460.
38. Abbott, i. 292; Adamson, 'Cromwell and the Long Parliament', 73–5.
39. *The True Informer*, no. 27 (19–25 October 1645), 211.
40. T. Edwards, *Gangraena* (3 parts, 1646), especially part III.
41. *To the Honourable the House of Commons . . . the Humble Remonstrance and Petition of the Lord Major, Aldermen and Commons of the City of London* (1646).
42. [R. Overton and W. Walwyn], *A Remonstrance of Many Thousand Citizens* (1646).
43. Abbott, i. 410.
44. Peacey, 'John Lilburne', 634–40; J. Lilburne, *The Free-mans Freedome Vindicated* (1646); R. Overton, *An Arrow Against all Tyrants* (1646); Lilburne, *Iust Mans Justification*, 26 for the quotation.
45. Fraser, *Cromwell*, 179; Abbott, i. 420.
46. I. Gentles, *The New Model Army in England, Ireland and Scotland, 1645–53* (Oxford, repr. 1994), 169.
47. W. Walwyn, *Walwyns Jvst Defence* (1649), 4–6; [W. Walwyn], *Gold Tried in the Fire* (1647), sig. A1-A2, and pp. 11–12 for the 'sharp petition'. A. Woolrych, *Soldiers and Statesmen: The General Council of the Army and its Debates, 1647–8* (Oxford, 1987) and B. Taft, 'Journey to Putney: the Quiet Leveller', in G. J. Schochet *et al.* (eds), *Religion, Resistance and Civil War* (Washington, DC, 1990), 63–81, have adopted different perspectives and reached substantially different conclusions in examining the events of 1647 with which we are concerned in this and the following two sections.
48. Lilburne, *Ionahs Cry*, 4.
49. Walwyn, *Jvst Defence*, 6.
50. Cf. Woolrych, *Soldiers and Statesmen*, 154–5. In the light of the evidence presented here for Cromwell's interaction with civilians, I cannot agree with Woolrych that the generals must have opposed close army-civilian co-operation.
51. Walwyn, *Jvst Defence*, 6.
52. Worcester College, Oxford, Clarke MS 41, fos. 167-v, quotation at fo. 167. I owe the latter point to Elliot Vernon.
53. Worcester College, Oxford, Clarke MS 41, fos. 165v–166v, 185; *Clarke Papers*, i. 171, 174, 179 and n.
54. *Clarke Papers*, i. 183–4; *A Declaration of the Engagements . . . from His Excellency Sir Tho: Fairfax, and the Generall Councel of the army* (1647), 96; *CJ*, v. 254; *LJ*, ix. 349.

55. *Clarke Papers*, i. 216–17.
56. For Wildman's and Petty's involvement with the *Heads*, see *Clarke Papers*, i. 351–2, 356–7.
57. *A Declaration from His Excellencie Sr Thomas Fairfax, and His Council of War* (1647), 12–13.
58. [Walwyn], *Gold Tried*, 4–5, where the numbered points 3–4 and 6–10 all have largely corresponding clauses in the demands appended to the *Heads*.
59. Lilburne, *Ionahs Cry*, 9.
60. Lilburne, *Ionahs Cry*, 8–10; R. Overton, *An Appeale from the Degenerate Representative Body the Commons of England* (1647), 7–10, 30–1.
61. *Clarke Papers*, i. 186 and 188; *Declaration from Fairfax and the Generall Councel*, 97.
62. Walwyn, *Jvst Defence*, 1, 6–7.
63. J. S. A. Adamson, 'The English Nobility and the Projected Settlement of 1647', *HJ*, 30 (1987), 569–70.
64. H. G. Tibbutt (ed.), 'The Tower of London Letter-book of Sir Lewis Dyve, 1646–7' (*The Publications of the Bedfordshire Historical Record Society*, 38 (1958)), 85–7.
65. J. Lilburne, *Tvvo Letters VVrit by Lievt. Col. John Lilburne* (1647), 4.
66. *LJ*, ix. 436; *A Perfect Summary*, no. 9 (13–20 September 1647), 70.
67. Bodl., MS Clarendon 30, fo. 67v; Tibbutt (ed.), 'Dyve's Letter-book', 89.
68. C. H. Firth (ed.), *The Memoirs of Edmund Ludlow* (2 vols., Oxford, 1894), i. 159–60.
69. *CJ*, v. 312.
70. E. Bear *et al.*, *The Case of the Armie Truly Stated* (1647).
71. [J. Wildman], *A Cal to All the Souldiers of the Armie* (1647), 4–5, 7.
72. *Clarke Papers*, i. 234, 342, 343, quotations at pp. 343 and 342.
73. *Clarke Papers*, i. 240.
74. 'John Lawmind' (= J. Wildman), *Putney Proiects* (1647).
75. *Clarke Papers*, i. 356–7; Worcester College, Oxford, Clarke MS 66, fo. 6.
76. [Wildman], *A Cal*, 7, quotations at pp. 7 and 6 (both second pagination).
77. *Clarke Papers*, i. 228.
78. [J. Wildman?], *An Agreement of the People* (1647); cf. M. A. Kishlansky, 'Consensus Politics and the Structure of Debate at Putney', *Journal of British Studies*, 20 (1981), 50–69, who argues that the 'intense ideological differences revealed during the debates' led to the failure of the genuine effort to reach a consensual position (52).
79. *Clarke Papers*, i. 291, and see ibid., i. 237 and 369 for his further praise of the *Agreement* and the *Case*.
80. *Clarke Papers*, i. 242.

81. *Clarke Papers*, i. 239–40, 241–4, 248–51; Kishlansky, 'Consensus Politics', 52.
82. This point is argued at length in my forthcoming article with Elliot Vernon, 'What Was the First *Agreement of the People?*'
83. *Clarke Papers*, i. 237–8, 369, quotation at p. 237.
84. *Clarke Papers*, i. 72–3, 192–3, 202–3; Adamson, 'Cromwell and the Long Parliament', 75.
85. *Clarke Papers*, i. 369 and 370.
86. Ibid., 277 and 278.
87. Ibid., 309, 328, 332, 336, 342.
88. Ibid., 379 and 382.
89. Cf. J. Morrill and P. Baker, 'The Case of the Armie Truly Re-stated', in M. Mendle (ed.), *The Putney Debates of 1647: The Army, the Levellers and the English State* (Cambridge, 2001), 122, which I now think failed to adequately distinguish between the content and the means of implementing the *Agreement*.
90. *Clarke Papers*, i. 363–7, 407–11; *Perfect Occurrences*, no. 44 (29 October–5 November 1647), 312.
91. *Clarke Papers*, i. 410–15, quotations at ibid., i. 371; *A Copy of a Letter from the Com. Gen. Regiment, to the Convention of Agents* (1647).
92. *A Declaration by the Kings Majestie Concerning His Majesties Going Away from Hampton-Court* (1647), 2.
93. Cf. Woolrych, *Soldiers and Statesmen*, 273, who maintains that Charles's accusation would appear 'staggering' to 'the reader of the Putney debates'.
94. E. Sexby *et al.*, *A Copy of a Letter Sent by the Agents of Severall Regiments* (1647), 3.
95. *LJ*, ix. 527–8; R. Scrope and T. Monkhouse (eds), *State Papers Collected by Edward, Earl of Clarendon* (3 vols., Oxford, 1767–86), ii, appendix, p. xlii.
96. *Clarke Papers*, i. 413; *A Remonstrance from His Excellency Sir Thomas Fairfax, and His Councell of Warre* (1647).
97. D. Underdown (ed.), 'The Parliamentary Diary of John Boys, 1647–8', *Bulletin of the Institute of Historical Research*, 39 (1966), 151–3, quotation at latter.
98. J. Lilburne, *The Legall Fundamentall Liberties of the People of England* (1649), 36; [J. Wildman], *The Leveller* (1659), 15.
99. Worcester College, Oxford, Clarke MS 65, fo. 83v is preferable here to Firth's transcription, which includes a number of errors.
100. [W. Frost], *A Declaration of Some Proceedings of Lt Col. Iohn Lilburn, and His Associates* (1648), 12–15; *CJ*, v. 437–9; Underdown (ed.), 'Diary of Boys', 156–8.
101. Peacey, 'John Lilburne', 644; Bodl., MS Clarendon 30, fo. 279.
102. J. Lilburne, *The Prisoners Mournful Cry* (1648), 8.

103. *CJ*, v. 658; *LJ*, x. 405 and 407.

104. Lilburne, *Legall Fundamentall Liberties*, 28.

105. *To the Right Honorable, the Commons of England in Parliament Assembled. The Humble Petition of Divers Wel Affected Persons* (1648), 3–7, quotation at latter.

106. Gentles, *New Model Army*, 267–8; *Mercurius Pragmaticus*, no. 28 (3–10 October 1648), sig. Pp10.

107. *Severall Petitions presented to his Excellency the Lord Fairfax* (1648), 2–3; Abbott, i. 690.

108. Lilburne, *Legall Fundamentall Liberties*, 28–35.

109. [H. Ireton], *A Remonstrance of his Excellency Thomas Lord Fairfax* (1648), 62, 64, 67, 69.

110. For example, see G. E. Aylmer (ed.), *The Levellers in the English Revolution* (1975), 38.

111. Even Barbara Taft, who successfully challenged the view that the army simply distracted the Levellers with talk of an *Agreement* while it carried out its political revolution, still refers to the 'differences' and 'distance between' them: see her 'The Council of Officers' *Agreement of the People*, 1648/9', *HJ*, 28 (1985), 170.

112. Abbott, i. 676–7, 698–9, quotations at pp. 676–7, 699.

113. Taft, 'Officers' *Agreement*', 183.

114. J. Morrill and P. Baker, 'Oliver Cromwell, the Regicide and the Sons of Zeruiah', in J. Peacey (ed.), *The Regicides and the Execution of Charles I* (Basingstoke, 2001), 30–2.

115. *Clarke Papers*, ii. 170–1; *A Petition from His Excellency . . . Concerning the Draught of an Agreement of the People* (1649), 5–6, 28.

116. Taft, 'Officers' *Agreement*', 173, 176–8, 182–5; *CJ*, vi. 122.

117. Lilburne, *Legall Fundamentall Liberties*, 42–3.

118. For an example of this view, see H. N. Brailsford, *The Levellers and the English Revolution*, ed. Christopher Hill (2nd edn. Nottingham, 1983), xii, 12, 417.

119. For example, Christopher Hill described 'the problem of the electorate' as the 'one fundamental problem' that underlay 'all the disputes between Oliver Cromwell [and] the Levellers': *God's Englishman: Oliver Cromwell and the English Revolution* (repr. Harmondsworth, 1979), 198.

120. Abbott, ii. 325; iv. 274.

121. *Clarke Papers*, i. 370; Abbott, iii. 459.

122. [Wildman?], *Agreement*, 11–12, and see p. 9.

123. Richard Baxter, *Reliquiae Baxterianae*, ed. Matthew Sylvester (2 parts, 1698), i. 70. For Cromwell's references to Levellers in the 1650s, see Abbott, iii, 435–6, 585; iv. 267.

124. Lomas-Carlyle, ii. 426, makes better sense of this passage than Abbott, iii. 591.

# 5

# Cromwell and Ireland before 1649

Patrick Little

Oliver Cromwell's ten-month stay in Ireland is perhaps the most controversial period of his entire career. The arrival of the English expeditionary force at Dublin in August 1649 made a decisive difference to a war that had dragged on for almost eight years. The siege of Drogheda, to the north of the Irish capital, ended in the cool, calculated massacre of almost the entire royalist garrison there; the siege of Wexford in the south-east brought yet more indiscriminate killing as Cromwell's troops ran amok. The port of New Ross quickly surrendered; Waterford held out and was bypassed; and Cromwell had arrived in the south-western province of Munster by the onset of winter. In 1650 local campaigns saw the taking of the Confederate Catholic capital of Kilkenny by storm, and culminated in the bloody siege of Clonmel, where Cromwell's troops were repulsed with significant casualties. The Irish war continued for three more years, but it is generally agreed that by the time of Cromwell's departure in May 1650 the Catholic Irish had been broken. The job of stamping out the last pockets of resistance, and of clearing the land for English settlers— recently described as 'ethnic cleansing on a scale unknown in western European history'—was left to others.[1] Cromwell was in Ireland for just 40 weeks. It was a brief interlude in his 18-year public career, but one that has tarnished his reputation in the eyes of later generations, not least in Ireland, where nineteenth-century nationalists turned Cromwell into the exemplar of English prejudice and inflexible bigotry, and helped to create a 'black myth' that endures to this day.[2]

The dictates of chronology and biography mean that most historians pick up the story only in the spring of 1649, when Cromwell was appointed as lord lieutenant of Ireland. His earlier involvement in Irish affairs is only treated as a precursor for later events, and Cromwell's own words while in Ireland have formed the basis for most accounts of his attitudes in the longer term. For Sir Charles Firth, Cromwell 'knew nothing of Irish history' before 1649, and even after his arrival on the island he 'shared the general ignorance of his contemporaries about the causes of the rebellion', claiming that the Catholic Irish had been treated leniently, and that the rebellion in 1641 was entirely unprovoked.[3] The theme of ignorance has been taken up by other historians, notably David Stevenson, who said that Cromwell's attitude showed

> no sign of any distinctive outlook, any special insights into the Irish problem. He simply shared the attitudes of most Englishmen. Ireland had to be reconquered, as historically subordinate to England, as a potential strategic threat, and as the home of barbarous papists whose crimes must be punished, whose religion must be suppressed.[4]

The religious dimension of Cromwell's attitude towards Ireland has proved the most influential. Robert Paul saw Cromwell's reaction to the 1641 rebellion and the massacres that followed as formative, creating a hostility that 'did not diminish with the course of years, and it became hardened into the one great religious prejudice of Cromwell's life—a hatred of things Catholic, and, in particular, an overwhelming detestation of the Catholic Irish'.[5] Recent biographers have also tended to emphasise Cromwell's religious bigotry when dealing with Ireland, and to trace this back to his reactions to the outbreak of rebellion at the beginning of the decade.[6] While there is no doubt that Cromwell's attitude towards Ireland was religious at heart, the reality is more complicated than has usually been allowed, involving not only God but Mammon, and the awkward relationship between them. In this chapter I shall examine Cromwell's relationship with Ireland before he ever set foot on Irish soil, in the hope of putting his invasion in 1649 into its proper context.

# I

The starting point is the Irish rebellion of October 1641, as there is no evidence for Cromwell's opinions on Ireland—or on many

other matters—before this date. The sudden uprising by the Ulster
Catholics, and in particular stories of the wholesale massacre of
Protestant settlers, clearly made a deep impression on Cromwell. The
traces of this remained with him, providing a ready excuse for the bru-
tality of the attack on Drogheda in September 1649, which he saw as
'the righteous judgement of God upon these barbarous wretches, who
have imbrued their hands in so much innocent blood'.[7] In January
1650 he went further, telling the Irish clergy that

> they [the English] had lived peaceably and honestly amongst you. You had
> generally equal benefit with them, and equal justice before the law . . . You
> broke this union! You, unprovoked, put the English to the most unheard-
> of and most barbarous massacre (without respect of sex and age) that ever
> the sun beheld.[8]

These comments tie in with other evidence from the months following the outbreak of rebellion, which reveals Cromwell supporting
measures against Catholics, both in England and Ireland.[9] The reaction in England to news of the rebellion was one of alarm, and
concrete measures to send troops to suppress the insurgency soon
followed, despite the immense logistical difficulties involved and the
delicate position of parliament, which was unwilling to raise men and
money without the authority of the king and the co-operation of the
lord lieutenant of Ireland, the earl of Leicester.[10] The war effort was
put on a firmer footing in the spring of 1642 with the appointment
of commissioners for Irish affairs (including Cromwell) to manage the
transport of men and supplies to Ireland, and the passing of the adventurers' act, under which investors were encouraged to put up money
in return for lands in Ireland, to be confiscated once the rebellion had
been suppressed.

Cromwell's involvement in the Irish adventure—both as an MP
supporting the legislation and as an investor—is well known.[11]
According to Karl Bottigheimer, Cromwell invested £300 in the
original adventurers' act of March 1642, and £300 more under the
ordinance for the 'sea adventure' in the following June. By the time
that the Irish lands were eventually allocated in 1653–1654, Cromwell
had invested a further £250, as the total acreage he was allowed
was 1257 acres in the barony of Eglish, King's County, in the Irish
midlands.[12] The date of this final instalment is uncertain, but there is
no doubt that in 1642 Cromwell paid at least £600 to the adventurers' scheme. This was the same as the amount put up by the leading

parliamentarian, John Pym, and twice as much as Cromwell's wealthy cousin, Oliver St John, and the scale of this investment has always been seen as a sign of his passionate commitment to the suppression of the Catholic rebellion.[13] This was a considerable sum for someone of Cromwell's social and economic status—even more so when a further £500 promised by him for 'the defence of parliament' in June 1642 is taken into account. Colin Davis was understandably puzzled by this: 'the sums offered by Cromwell appear to have been considerable and it would be interesting to know where they came from if he was contributing in his own right or if he was acting for others'.[14] Recent research by Andrew Barclay and Simon Healy has solved this conundrum. In the autumn of 1640 Cromwell had agreed to sell his leases of the dean and chapter lands of Ely to the archdeacon of the diocese, and as there is no evidence that he reinvested this money in land in England, it can be assumed that he commanded considerable cash resources in the spring of 1642.[15] The implications of this are important. In 1640 Cromwell had taken the highly unusual step of cashing in his main estates, thus jeopardising his own future and that of his young family. Still more startling, he had then bet a large slice of the money on rank outsiders: the prospect of the Irish rebellion being put down quickly, and, even less certain, parliament winning any confrontation against the king. As Bottigheimer has pointed out, the Irish adventure was not a good investment. If the Irish triumphed, the investors would lose everything; if there was a negotiated peace, the mass confiscations upon which the scheme was based were unlikely to occur; and even if total victory was achieved, the longer the rebellion dragged on the more land would be 'wasted', and rendered worthless. In short, 'everything hinged upon the rapidity of reconquest'.[16] Cromwell's investment in the Irish adventure was thus a huge gamble. It was not, as has been suggested, 'more than his annual income is supposed to have been'—it was the majority of his capital, and as a result his financial position was now very fragile.[17] Yet the stakes were not just financial. Cromwell was also making a religious statement, almost putting his financial survival into the hands of God. This curious mixture of money and religion is a theme that would recur throughout his dealings with Ireland in the 1640s.

A further aspect of Cromwell's early involvement in Irish affairs that should be noted at this stage is his apparent agreement with those who identified the southern province of Munster as the key to the Irish situation. From April 1642 the adventurers' main plan was to send a brigade of 5000 men to Munster, and through the summer there developed a 'special relationship' between the adventurers and the province. This turned out to be a damp squib. Troops were raised and Lord Wharton was chosen as the commander; but the approach of civil war in the late summer made England a more urgent priority than Ireland. First money was withdrawn from the adventure and then the troops themselves were co-opted for English service. Although as many as 2000 men were indeed despatched to Munster under Lord Kerry, the majority of the Munster brigade was diverted to form the nucleus of parliament's army at Edgehill in October.[18] Cromwell's activities in parliament suggest that he was an advocate of the Munster scheme. In June 1642, for example, he attended the adventurers' committee on behalf of the House of Commons, asking for £10,000 to be sent to Munster from the first money collected by them, and in July he was named to a committee to treat with Irish Protestants who had presented proposals for the reinforcement of the province.[19] Also in July, Cromwell was chosen to attend the House of Lords to arrange a conference 'concerning the removing of some forces out of Ulster and Leinster for the reducing of Limerick' and received assurances from the upper chamber that they would take care of 'the drawing of forces into Munster'.[20] Cromwell's involvement in the supplementary scheme known as the 'sea adventure' in the early summer of 1642 also points to Munster as being something of a priority for him. The sea adventure involved the raising of further money, again in return for Irish land, in order to mount an expedition to harry the Irish coast, taking castles and ports and defeating rebel forces. The amount raised—£43,000—was modest compared with that of the main adventure, and the number of investors small, with only 171 subscribing.[21] It is interesting that Cromwell was among this number, and he was also prominent in managing the passage of the necessary legislation through parliament in May and June.[22] Like the main adventure, the sea adventure was doomed to failure. The force raised set sail under the command of Alexander Lord Forbes in July, bound for the port of Kinsale in County Cork. The Protestant commander in Munster, Lord Inchiquin, was offended by the high-handedness of Lord Forbes, and relieved when the expedition moved off round the coast to plague Galway and Clare instead.[23] The failure of both the sea adventure and the Munster brigade was not the fault of Cromwell or the other investors, and should not detract from its significance as the first scheme to use Munster as a spring-board for the reconquest of Ireland. This was a plan that would reappear, at regular intervals, later in the 1640s, and on each occasion Cromwell was involved.

## II

With the onset of civil war Cromwell, like most of his fellow MPs, found himself preoccupied with events in England, but as the war drew to an end in the autumn of 1645, Ireland once again became the focus for his attention. In some ways, Cromwell's primary motive for involvement in Irish affairs during the mid-1640s was the same as that in 1641–1642, combining a deep commitment to the defeat of the Catholic rebels with a concern to protect his financial investments. But the financial side of this had become more complex—and more pressing—during the civil war: not only did Cromwell have a substantial investment in the Irish adventure, it was also likely that he would need Ireland to provide him with an income in the short term. It was assumed that the end of the English war would naturally lead to the disbandment of the armies, and the redundancy of their officers, and the salaries enjoyed by Cromwell and other officers would thus come to a sudden end. This was not a trivial matter. By the end of 1645, Cromwell's financial position had become precarious. As early as September 1643 he had told Oliver St John of his inability to provide sums to keep his men quiet, as 'I have little money of my own to help my soldiers. My estate is little. I tell you, the business of Ireland and England hath had of me, in money, between eleven and twelve hundred pounds; therefore my private can do little to help the public'.[24] Cromwell's investment of £1100 in the spring and summer of 1642 has already been noted; but how much more did he have to disburse in the uncertain days of 1642 and 1643? Although he was entitled to a military salary that progressively increased as he was promoted from captain to colonel to lieutenant-general, he probably received only a proportion of this money. We know that pay for Cromwell's troops (and probably his own salary) was received regularly from August 1642 until January 1643,[25] but then the records become more sporadic—perhaps reflecting the irregularity of the payments made. If his warrants as lieutenant-general are complete, the sums assigned for his personal use were £60 in February 1644, £60 in March 1644, £40 in April, £182 in August and £151 in December–January 1644–1645: a total of £493 over roughly a year, when, as lieutenant-general, he could expect £4 a day, amounting to £1460, during the same period.[26] This fits in with his later claim that he was owed £1500 as lieutenant-general under the earl of Manchester (until April 1645), as well as two years' arrears of salary as governor of Ely.[27] A letter from Cromwell's mother, arranging for £50 to be sent to him in July 1643, supports the idea that he was short of money in this period;[28] and in this context, the later allegations of Archbishop Williams, who told Charles I in December 1644 that '[Cromwell's] fortunes are broken, that it is impossible for him to subsist', might contain more than a grain of truth.[29] Unlike many other gentleman officers, Cromwell did not have the luxury of mortgaging his family estates—that money had already been cashed in 1640. The regular pay associated with the New Model Army from the spring of 1645 would have been a lifeline, but it is unlikely that it allowed Cromwell to do more than pay the interest on his mounting debts. Furthermore, Cromwell's position in the New Model was only on sufferance, as he was spared the loss of his command only as long as parliament chose to exempt him from the terms of the self-denying ordinance. As John Adamson comments, 'even after Naseby, the continuance of his position in the army hung by a thread; all was contingent on the parliamentary strength and factional fortunes of his allies at Westminster'.[30] It might be added that Cromwell's financial fortunes were as precarious as his political survival during this period. It was essential that he prolonged his military career; and as the English war ended, that meant finding a senior position in the army in Ireland.

The situation in Ireland had deteriorated since the beginning of the English civil war. With money raised by the adventurers and other schemes siphoned off to fund the conflict in England, the Irish Protestants found themselves at a huge disadvantage. Although campaigns against the Catholic rebels continued, in the spring of 1643 negotiations for a truce were on foot, and these resulted in the cessation of arms signed in September of that year. The truce was backed by the king, who hoped to bring Irish troops over to England, and was championed by the marquis of Ormond, who was made lord lieutenant by the king in the following November. Parliament and its supporters rejected the cessation altogether, but the war in England meant that the Protestants who refused to observe the cessation received little further support in their increasingly desperate struggle against the Catholic Irish. Apart from the Ulster Scots, who held their own in the north, the only major pro-parliamentarian enclave was a small area around the towns of Cork and Youghal in Munster. The Munster Protestants were nearly annihilated in a major Confederate offensive in the spring of 1645, and after the victory at Naseby had eased the position in England there were demands in London that something must be done before southern Ireland was entirely in the hands of the Confederates and the royalists. Foremost among those who called for action were the adventurers, and it was from their ranks that the idea sprang of appointing a new chief governor (whether a lord lieutenant or a lord deputy), to challenge Ormond's authority, and to provide a focus for raising a strong expeditionary force to reconquer Ireland.[31]

Cromwell's name was closely associated with these moves. On 4 December 1645 Sir Hardress Waller, a man with substantial estates in Munster and a colonel in the New Model, reflected in a letter to his fellow Munsterman, Sir Philip Percivalle, that:

> Tis certain our greatest hopes for Ireland is from this army, about which I have had many free and serious discussions with Lieutenant-General Cromwell, whose spirit leads much that way, and especially for the support of Munster and to begin the war there, which, were he sent over, I should look upon as the work done, and therefore I offer it to you as a matter very serious whether we should not all petition to have him our deputy.[32]

There was an element of wishful-thinking in Waller's words, as it is unlikely that Cromwell was senior enough—both socially and politically—to be a serious contender to become lord deputy at this time; but his letter reveals Cromwell's continuing interest in Ireland, and that he was already formulating a plan of campaign, focused once again on Munster. At the end of December, Sir Philip Percivalle reported to Waller that the strongest candidate for the top job was Viscount Lisle, son of the previous lord lieutenant, the earl of Leicester, but that there had been moves that

> your friend there [Cromwell, then in the west with Waller] might be designed for that service as the only expedient and (as I understand by some that wish well to the service and to him) it was stayed by them for some reasons, wherewith I doubt not but they have ere this acquainted him, they having frequent opportunities of sending.[33]

Percivalle's account fits fairly closely with that of the royalist, Sir Edward Nicholas, who told the marquis of Ormond in January 1646 that the candidates for the lieutenancy included Viscount Lisle and Lord Inchiquin, and that 'Cromwell (who is lieutenant-general of the army in the west under Sir Thomas Fairfax) hath been offered by the two Houses to be sent over general of the army, but he hath refused it'.[34]

Although it is clear that Cromwell was not a candidate for the lieutenancy, parliament's decision to reward him at the same time as Lisle's appointment as lord lieutenant was announced is telling. Lisle was formally nominated on 21 January 1646, and two days later Cromwell was granted £500 in cash ('as a respect from this House'), he was promised that his post as lieutenant-general in England would continue for a further six months, and, more significantly, that he would receive lands of inheritance from the confiscated estates of the earl of Worcester.[35] This land grant had been promised since December 1645, but this was the first sign that parliament intended to be true to its word.[36] It is also interesting that on the same day that Viscount Lisle was formally accepted by both Houses as 'chief governor' on 26 January, the Commons passed the first and second readings of the ordinance for Cromwell's lands.[37] This compensation came not a day too soon. A letter from Oliver St John of 18 February is full of urgency. He sent Cromwell the newly passed ordinance allowing him the lands, and also a rent-roll and other information which meant he could get his hands on at least some of the profits. Although the paperwork was incomplete, St John told Cromwell that he 'endeavoured to pass this for the present, rather than to have stayed longer to make up the whole' and added that bailiffs could now be appointed 'to husband the lands to your best advantage, which would be done speedily'. He had not waited for the other promised estates to be confirmed, as he 'desired for present to pass this, than to hazard the delay'.[38] St John had long been acquainted with the financial difficulties of his friend, and his haste in securing income in February 1646 suggests that financial disaster had only just been averted.[39]

## III

The rewards given to Cromwell in the spring of 1646 undoubtedly improved his financial position, but they did not reduce the frustration felt by him, and those around him, that the Irish war was not being pursued with sufficient vigour. Sir Hardress Waller, for instance, was deeply disappointed with the choice of Viscount Lisle as lord lieutenant, saying in February that 'I do not hear the work is like to be carried on by such as carry a two-edged sword in their hearts as well as their hands'.[40] As in his earlier letters, Waller probably thought Cromwell a better bet, and there are certainly indications that Cromwell remained keen to further the Irish war. In April 1646, for example, the former royalist, Colonel John Buller, was eager to be commissioned as lieutenant-colonel in a new regiment bound for Ireland, and told his brother that 'I am promised Sir Thomas Fairfax, Lieutenant-General Cromwell [and] Sir Hardress Waller their letters in my behalf unto the parliament'.[41] At the end of July 1646, once news of the catastrophic defeat of the Ulster Scots at Benburb in the north of Ireland and of a dangerous new offensive in Munster had reached Westminster, it was proposed that a number of supernumerary English regiments be sent to Ireland to strengthen the Protestant position. The move was championed by Lisle and his supporters, and Cromwell acted as teller for the motion that the matter should be referred to a grand committee to discuss it further.[42] Instead, it was proposed that six regiments of the regular New Model Army should be sent to Ireland. It has been suggested that this plan was backed by the Independents, but in reality it originated with the rival Presbyterian party, whose 'design was to weaken or rather dissolve the army', and the diarist, Thomas Juxon, saw it as '[Sir Philip] Stapilton's motion, who never loved them [the army]'.[43] Edmund Ludlow commented that the motion was championed by those 'who earnestly endeavoured to break the army . . . pretending the necessity of relieving Ireland'.[44] The motion was only narrowly defeated, with the leading Presbyterians, Denzil Holles and Sir Philip Stapilton, telling for the yeas, and their Independent rivals, Sir Arthur Hesilrige and Sir John Evelyn of Wiltshire, telling for the noes.[45]

The alternative plan, promoted by the Independents, was to send other troops, mostly drawn from units outside the New Model, such as Edward Massie's brigade, and Cromwell was the principal spokesman for this scheme. In the debate, 'the lieutenant-general pressed largely and passionately' and even made the startling offer 'to relinquish £10,000 voted to him . . . that money might be for levying men'. Like his ostentatious investment in the adventurers' scheme, this was Cromwell putting his money where his mouth was—whatever the personal cost might be. Cromwell's gesture was all the more dramatic as his formal commission as lieutenant-general (and the pay that went with it) had expired in the same month.[46] His prominence in the same debate, and his lack of an official command in England, made Cromwell the obvious commander for this new expedition to Ireland, and he certainly seems to have taken responsibility for the choice of officers. For example, Cromwell was at pains to deny that the plan was a partisan one, designed to favour only Independents, and protested that only one Presbyterian officer, a Scotsman, had been cashiered as 'labouring to disaffect the army from the parliament'.[47] The committee of Irish affairs responded to this debate on 1 August, when it ordered that Cromwell, with three other Independent MPs and also the bellicose Ulster Adventurer, Sir John Clotworthy, were to investigate what companies remaining in the English counties, rather than units of the New Model, could be recruited for Ireland.[48]

Recruitment of these new regiments was very slow, but Cromwell's commitment to the Irish war continued during the second half of 1646 and the early weeks of 1647. On 11 August he was named to the committee to borrow money for the Irish service, in response to the alarming news that Ormond had finally signed his long-negotiated treaty with the Confederate Irish.[49] On 1 October, when Clotworthy was ordered to facilitate the crossing of new troops to Ulster, Cromwell was one of the MPs sent to the committee of accounts, to urge them to settle Clotworthy's (admittedly highly suspect) financial dealings, presumably to allow him to handle further government funds.[50] It is uncertain how far Cromwell was involved in the various calls for parliament to take a more robust line on the Irish war during this period, although the presence of Sir Hardress Waller and Sir John Clotworthy in the line-up of Irish Protestants who, in December 1646, called for Lisle to take troops to Ireland forthwith, provides an indirect link with the lieutenant-general, who was already associated with such a plan.[51] At the core of this Irish Protestant scheme was a new offensive in Munster, and this intervention succeeded in putting the province back at the top of the Irish agenda. Preparations were made to equip an expeditionary force to sail to the province under Viscount Lisle during the early weeks of 1647, and Cromwell's involvement in Irish affairs also appears to have increased during the same period. During the winter of 1646–1647 Cromwell had joined the new Derby House committee, which took over the lead role in the conduct of Irish affairs, and in January he was added to the committee for public accounts, when its remit was expanded to include claims for service in Ireland.[52] In the same month, his eldest son, Richard, was commissioned as captain of Lisle's lifeguard—a prestigious appointment that was no doubt intended as a compliment to his father.[53]

Seasoned commentators greeted news of Lisle's departure for Munster in February 1647 with cynicism. Thomas Juxon claimed that the Independents who backed the design send upon that account such men for the conduct of the Irish business as they do pre-intend and know shall come to nothing, but consume men and money; and all this for support of the faction, and it may be to the intent Cromwell may hereafter go and have his own conditions.[54]

Juxon almost certainly exaggerated the political calculation that lay behind Lisle's Munster expedition, but he was right to see Cromwell's ambitions as bound up with it. An Irish command was still the most attractive option for Cromwell, and this time it was for political as well as financial reasons. From mid-February 1647 it was clear that the Independent interest at Westminster was losing ground to its Presbyterian enemies, and that the chief target of the latter was the New Model Army. From 18 February there were various proposals to disband the army or send it to Ireland. On 8 March, the Presbyterian majority forced through measures to remove all senior officers except for Fairfax from the army in England—a move clearly aimed at Cromwell[55]—and this came only two days after a vote to send 12,000 New Model soldiers across the Irish Sea.[56] The latter was in some ways a re-run of the July 1646 proposal that Cromwell had opposed so vehemently, but it may not have been entirely partisan on this occasion, as when parliament voted not to renew Lisle's commission as lord lieutenant, and promised a shake-up of the whole Irish command, Cromwell was named as one of the candidates. On 2 April 1647 Percivalle told Lord Inchiquin of a Commons' vote that lords justices would be appointed to run the civil government in Ireland, and that 'Sir William Waller and Massie are in nomination by one party, and Major [General] Skippon and Cromwell by the other, for the martial commands'.[57] But with a compromise agreement made on the same day, appointing Skippon and Massie as leaders of the New Model regiments to Ireland, Cromwell's ambition to go to Ireland was finally quashed.[58]

Cromwell's importance as a member of the Independent faction at Westminster, and his role in the army's showdown with parliament, make his activities in the spring of 1647 of particular interest. Yet, as Peter Gaunt puts it:

> Cromwell played a low-key role during March and April 1647, with little evidence of parliamentary activity . . . Cromwell's name largely disappears from the *Commons' Journal* and his failure to act as a teller in divisions or to be nominated to committees may be an indication that he was physically absent from the chamber.[59]

Contemporaries also found his behaviour puzzling. The Leveller leader, John Lilburne, considered that Cromwell had undermined the army's petition in mid-March, 'and will not suffer them to petition till they have laid down their arms whensoever they shall command them', and linked Cromwell's reluctance to declare himself to his earlier grant of lands, for 'the House of Commons bribed you with a vote of £2500 to betray and destroy us'.[60] Lilburne was not alone in suspecting that Cromwell was acting hypocritically during March. Colonel Wogan said that when it came to disbanding the New Model or sending them to Ireland 'Cromwell seemed to be as forward for this as any in the House'; while John Wildman, writing a little later, said of Cromwell and Ireton that 'both in private opposed those gallant endeavours of the army for their country's freedom'.[61] The most convincing explanation is that Cromwell was simply delaying his decision until the matter of the commanding officers for the new Irish expedition had been chosen. As John Adamson emphasises, Cromwell was at pains

> to prevent an open breach between parliament and the New Model . . . for the disbandment of the New Model was the necessary prelude to the formation of a new expeditionary force to quell the Irish rebellion, an enterprise which Cromwell ardently supported. It was only after April, when plans for the new force were announced by Holles . . . that he, and the army, came to resist disbandment and enlistment for Ireland on the terms then proposed'.[62]

Before that time, the attitude of both senior officers and ordinary soldiers to the Irish service was equivocal—unlike their reaction to the disbandment of regiments without the payment of arrears, which was generally detested. On 15 April, for example, when commissioners from the Derby House committee met to discuss the situation with Fairfax, 200 officers drew up their own demands. Instead of simply refusing to go to Ireland, they insisted that if their old generals should go with them 'it would conduce much to their encouragement and personal engagement', and cried 'Fairfax and Cromwell, and we all go!'[63]

## IV

From the beginning of April 1647, Cromwell and his allies were once again distracted from the Irish war by pressing matters at home.

There are, however, signs that Cromwell was still committed to the reconquest of Ireland. On 14 September 1647 he wrote to the governor of Dublin, Michael Jones, congratulating him on his spectacular victory at Dungan's Hill, and professing 'the mutual interest and engagement we have in the same cause'.[64] It was surely not a coincidence that the only time that Cromwell attended the Derby House committee during this autumn was on the very next day,[65] nor that Munster was the focus of the debate, with 7000 suits being sent to the army there, and the nominations for new commissioners to co-ordinate the government of the province being discussed.[66] Despite such moves, the Irish situation worsened. Jones wrote to Cromwell at the end of October asking for further help 'by hasting hither the supplies of money and provisions, together with the forces designed for this service', which he hoped would bolster the Protestant position in Leinster, at least.[67] By this stage, the mutinous state of the New Model had again delayed any hopes of again mounting a serious expedition to Ireland, and it was only in the spring of 1648 that any further action was contemplated. Michael Jones in Dublin was especially vociferous in his complaints, as parliament's interest slackened, and in February 1648 he twice called for new leadership to revivify the war effort, telling Speaker Lenthall that 'I have formerly represented to your honours the necessity of a commander-in-chief, which again I very earnestly desire may be taken into consideration, as mainly tending to the well-being of this great work, requiring some person of countenance and abilities above mine'.[68] In February 1648 there were only two men with 'countenance and abilities' greater than the victor of Dungan's Hill: Fairfax and Cromwell.

Although this crisis in confidence affected the whole of Protestant Ireland, once again the primary focus was Munster, where Inchiquin's position had worsened, partly as a result of friction between him and the dominant Independent party at Westminster, which was reluctant to keep his troops supplied or reinforced. It is difficult to be sure how far Inchiquin or the Independents were to blame for the rapid break-down in relations between them, but in March 1648 Inchiquin allowed his officers to draw up a remonstrance, complaining of their treatment, and warning that without immediate supplies they would have to begin negotiations with the Confederates for a local truce. In the same month, Inchiquin was in talks with the Scots, whose own conflicts with the English parliament were leading inexorably towards the second civil war.[69] Inchiquin's defection to the king in early April was apparently forced by a mutiny within his own officer corps. According to one royalist,

> the spirit moved the Independents to think of securing some of the towns when the army should be abroad and my lord of Inchiquin with them, and to send away a ship to hasten supplies to Youghal, which they intended to seize upon, and the supplies being once landed they hope soon to persuade the major part of the army to desert Inchiquin, and to join with them.

The plan was discovered, however, and 'the chief contrivers' imprisoned. How far the mutinous officers were acting on their own initiative, and how far they had been encouraged by the Independents to lead a rising, is not certain, although it is interesting that the four ringleaders included Lord Broghill's uncle, Sir William Fenton, and Sir John Temple's kinsman, Colonel Edmund Temple, as well as Lt-Col Phaier and Maj. Purdon.[70] Inchiquin did not immediately defect to the king; instead he sent 'a pre-emptory letter to the parliament for supplies', knowing full well what the answer would be.[71]

Cromwell was closely involved in the Westminster side of the latest Munster crisis. During the early months of 1648, his attendance at the Derby House committee suddenly picked up: he was there twice in January, once in February, but six times in March and five times in the first half of April.[72] His renewed enthusiasm can be seen in his 21 March 1648 letter to the committee:

> The two Houses of parliament having lately bestowed one thousand six hundred eighty pounds per annum upon me and my heirs, out of the earl of Worcester's estate; the necessity of affairs requiring assistance, I do hereby offer one thousand pounds annually to be paid out of the rents of the said land...for the space of five years, if the war in Ireland shall so long continue, or that I live so long; to be employed for the service of Ireland, as the parliament shall please to appoint...and whereas there is an arrear of pay due unto me whilst I was lieutenant-general unto the earl of Manchester, of about fifteen hundred pounds audited and stated; as also a great arrear due for about two years being governor of Ely; I do hereby discharge the state from all or any claim to be made by me thereunto.[73]

This was yet another instance of Cromwell putting up large sums of money as a sign of his selfless commitment to the cause and his trust in Providence. There may have been an element of leading by

example in Cromwell's promise, as when the Derby House committee discussed it on the same day, they immediately ordered Arthur
Annesley and Sir John Temple to speak with the London citizens
to gain favourable rates for a loan for the Irish war.[74] The offer was
reported to parliament by Sir John Evelyn of Wiltshire on 24 March,
and Cromwell received the thanks of the Commons for his generosity on the next day.[75] Although the royalist newsbook, *Mercurius
Pragmaticus*, had a very different take on the episode, it is interesting
that the editor recognised the religious motives behind Cromwell's
financial pledge:

> What think ye of the noble bounty of King Cromwell, who is
> become sparkish and deals away his hundreds and thousands like an
> Emperor[?] ... This is the man of God, the chariot of Israel and the
> horsemen thereof, that looks for a translation like Enoch or Elias, and
> therefore for the more easy passage hath rid himself of all worldly encum-
> brances by will and testament and (as becomes so great a prince) made the
> two kingdoms of England and Ireland his executors; to whom he gives all
> his arrears and leaves a legacy of £1,000 per annum for the maintenance
> of the war in Ireland, being no man of this world any longer.[76]

Cromwell's offer coincided with new efforts by the Derby House
committee, aware of the effects of neglect, to mount a new campaign in Ireland. News of the failure of the officers' mutiny (which
was current in London by 30 March 1648) only increased the sense
of urgency.[77] On 28 March three new commissioners were ordered
to go to Munster to take over the government of the province,
money was raised for paying the arrears of the troops there, and
provision made 'in case that any mutinies should be made against
them [the commissioners] by the soldiers there'.[78] On 30 March it
was ordered that £5000 would be provided for the commissioners to take with them to Munster.[79] Final arrangements were made
for the Munster commissioners, and the order granting the £5000
was signed by Cromwell among others, in the committee on 3
April.[80] On the same day, the committee drafted a further ordinance to finance the Irish war, with £50,000 to be raised from the
houses of Irish rebels.[81] There are even hints that Cromwell expected
to be the commander of the new force. On 3 April he wrote to
Richard Norton about the marriage settlement of his eldest son,
Richard, with Dorothy Maijor, and added in the postscript that he
should 'not lose a day herein, that I may know Mr Maijor's mind,
for I think I may be at leisure for a week to attend this business,

to give and take satisfaction; from which perhaps I may be shut up afterwards by employment'.[82] In the last days of March it was reported that Cromwell was closeted with the former lord lieutenant, Viscount Lisle. According to one royalist source, Cromwell had a narrow escape from some 'roaring boys' at Charing Cross, 'but mistaking the coach, he being in my Lord Lisle's, recovered his home'.[83] Although unsubstantiated, this story fits with the preparations in early April, especially as the focus for the new expedition, like Lisle's in February 1647, was Munster. Clement Walker also made a connection between Cromwell and Lisle, when he included Cromwell with Lisle, Temple, Broghill and others who had made it there business to undermine Inchiquin 'that they might send schismatics of their own party to lord it there'.[84] But if Cromwell anticipated a commission as general of an expeditionary force in April 1648, he was to be disappointed. The defection of Inchiquin to the royalist side by the middle of April brought the Derby House committee's preparations—and Cromwell's attendance at its meetings—to a sudden halt.[85] The provisions and money destined for Munster were redirected to Michael Jones in Dublin, and although there was talk of sending 2000 men to encourage a new uprising against Inchiquin, the project was not pursued further. With the onset of the second civil war, and the Scottish invasion of England that accompanied it, any English intervention in Ireland was left on hold.

## IV

The second civil war and its aftermath, the trial and execution of the king, and the creation of a new republic, combined to delay the English response to Ireland for another 12 months. It was only in March 1649, with the fall of the last royalist outpost, Pontefract Castle,[86] that the Rump Parliament was prepared to mount a new expedition. Cromwell was nominated as its commander by the council of state and parliament in mid-March. On 23 March the matter was before the general council of the army at Whitehall, at the prompting of a group of officers which included Cromwell's old crony, Sir Hardress Waller. Cromwell's speech to them referred back to the situation in 1647, saying that he would accept the command 'if their lordships did think that the naming of a commander-in-chief might be some satisfaction to persons, to officers and soldiers to go', but only if there was 'a just and fitting provision for them before they went'. There would be no more talk of disbanding the New Model without payment of arrears, or sending them to Ireland under unpopular officers. Cromwell also emphasised the importance of the province of Munster, which, he implied, was the seat of rebellion:

> in all which provinces we have an interest, but in Munster [we have] none at all; and though that interest we have in these three provinces it is not so inconsiderable, yet if these Confederate forces shall come upon them, it is more than probable, without a miracle from heaven, that our interest will easily be eradicated out of those parts.

Interestingly, the first response to Cromwell's speech came from Waller, who said 'that he thought the work would not go forward till it be known whether the commander-in-chief named will go or not'. This endorsement of Cromwell was a repeat of the view that Waller had held since December 1645, that only Cromwell could tackle the Irish problem effectively.[87] Although Cromwell asked for time to consider his position and seek God's approval, there was no real doubt that he would accept the command. The horrified reaction of some sections of the New Model Army at news of the proposed expedition to Ireland in 1649 was also redolent of the situation in 1647, although this time the officers sided with Parliament, and the mutiny was put down by force. Everything was right for a strong, well-funded expedition to Ireland, and Cromwell was determined not to be disappointed this time.

Cromwell's preparations for the new Irish campaign were made with his earlier experiences of Irish affairs in mind. Above all, he recognised the importance of recruiting Irish Protestants. He had maintained his correspondence with Michael Jones at Dublin during the second half of 1648, and it continued into 1649.[88] On his appointment as lord lieutenant, Cromwell brought in Irish advisers, contacting directly the commanders in Ulster and Connaught as well as Leinster.[89] The council of state was also in consultation with various of Lisle's old councillors, including Sir William Parsons and Sir Gerard Lowther.[90] Importantly, agents were also sent into Munster, to sound out the loyalties of the Protestant garrisons there, in what looks suspiciously like a re-run of the abortive mutiny against Inchiquin in March 1648. Significantly these agents included one of the 'chief contrivers' of the earlier attempt, Colonel Robert Phaier, through whom Cromwell made contact with officers in the garrisons of Cork and

Youghal.[91] Lord Broghill, who would be a key figure in any mutiny against Inchiquin, was brought out of retirement in August. Stories of Broghill being intercepted by Cromwell in London *en route* to join the king can be discounted, and it is telling that on 4 August 1649 Broghill was granted £500 by council of state—a week before news of Michael Jones's victory against Ormond at Rathmines reached London.[92] Sir Hardress Waller's influence has already been seen in the army council in March; in April he consulted with Cromwell about the recruitment of a 'person' (possibly Colonel Townsend) to act as an agent in Munster, and in late May there are indications that he was treated by the council of state as one of the key officers in the army, second only to Fairfax and Cromwell.[93]

Cromwell's reference to the payment of arrears and his concern at the state of Munster when talking to the army council in March 1649, as well as his concern to draw in Irish Protestants to advise him on the war, provide an important link back to the earlier occasions when he was a candidate for an Irish command. It is also interesting to note that the Lisle lieutenancy appears to have formed something of a model for Cromwell's own office. In June 1649 the earl of Leicester, the father of Viscount Lisle and himself a former lord lieutenant of Ireland, noted in his diary that Cromwell's commission 'is drawn after the copy of that which my son had, but he had it not for three years'.[94] In July, Cromwell was granted £3000 as 'transportation' money: the same as had been granted to Lisle in 1646–1647.[95] It is also significant that Lisle was very much involved in preparations for the new Irish campaign, and that, in June 1649, he was awarded £2434 from the money owed to him for his 'entertainment' as lord lieutenant two years' before.[96] Finally, although historians have usually not questioned that Dublin had always been the target of Cromwell's invasion force,[97] there are reasons for believing that, like Lisle over two years before, Cromwell intended to send a few regiments to reinforce the capital, while concentrating his main forces in Munster. Although this possibility was raised by Gardiner over a century ago, it is usually discounted, most recently by James Scott Wheeler, who points out that the artillery was sent to Dublin and the main royalist or Confederate field armies were known to be in Leinster and Ulster.[98] Despite these arguments, it is curious that Cromwell's army mustered at Milford Haven in South Wales—an odd embarkation point for Dublin; and while Cromwell took a small force northwards, the majority of his ships—77 as opposed to 35—were originally sent to the Munster port of Kinsale under Cromwell's son-in-law, Major-General Henry

Ireton. According to the general-at-sea, Richard Deane, the imbalance of forces was even greater, as the 84 ships he brought into Dublin at the end of August had only been brought there after a failed attempt 'to recover Munster and the bay of Kinsale'. As Robert Blake, patiently waiting off Kinsale, told the other general-at-sea, Edward Popham, 'I doubt not but you have heard that a considerable part of the army on the way hither were by contrary winds forced into Dublin'.[99]

Deane's comments in a further letter to Popham of 22 September 1649 suggest that the original plan had indeed been changed at the last minute. Popham had apparently complained that Cromwell 'is not like with his army to march to Munster this two months' and asked Deane to approach both Cromwell and Ireton 'and say you are sorry they are no more sensible of that place'. In reply, Deane protested that the landing point had been changed, but the overall strategy remained the same:

> my lord and the gentlemen with him are as sensible of the consequence of Kinsale and the ships as we can possibly be, and first we endeavoured with the greatest part of the army to have landed when Ireton and I were as high and [sic] Youghal, but the wind took us short and we were forced for Dublin, where they had so deep a resentment of the business of Munster that they had appointed four regiments of foot to be reshipped and Ireton with two thousand horse and dragoons to have gone through all the enemy's quarters by land thither, and sent for me and desired me to provide shipping accordingly.

This alternative plan was delayed because of a renewed threat from Ulster, which necessitated the taking of the hostile garrisons at Drogheda and Trim, and the reinforcement of existing units in the north. 'But', Deane continued, 'now it hath pleased God to give them Tredagh [Drogheda], Trim and Dundalk . . . they have nothing in their eyes so much as Munster'.[100] Deane was soon proved to be correct. Despite the ill winds, there are signs that Cromwell's strategy in Ireland was not entirely blown off course. Munster remained the goal. Once Drogheda had been taken, and the northern approaches to Dublin secured, the main army marched quickly south, through Leinster and to the border of Munster, where he was met on 6 December by Lord Broghill, who had finally managed to arrange a successful mutiny of the garrisons against Lord Inchiquin. Although the abortive siege of Waterford had delayed Cromwell's progress to the south west, he had arrived in Munster with a haste that suggests that securing the province had been his priority all along. And once there, he was in no hurry to leave. In fact, as John Morrill has observed, 'he spent thirty-four of his forty weeks [in Ireland] clearing Munster of royalist garrisons',[101] and did not return to Dublin afterwards, instead taking ship for England from Youghal on 26 May 1650.[102]

Cromwell's focus on Munster requires explanation. He was not merely following strategic convention, as before 1646 'it was axiomatic that the main effort would be in Ulster in conjunction with the Scots'.[103] Nor did he have any personal interest in the province. The only, very weak, family ties linking Cromwell with Ireland, were with Ulster, not Munster.[104] Instead, the roots of the plan seem to lead back to the spring of 1642, when the adventurers tried to send a brigade to Munster and also backed the 'sea adventure' against the Munster coast, starting at Kinsale. This also seems to have been a strategy that Cromwell himself favoured from the winter of 1645–1646, perhaps influenced by those with vested interests—especially the Munster landowners, Sir Hardress Waller and (latterly) Lord Broghill. Cromwell may also have been encouraged by the plan laid down by Viscount Lisle, although Lisle himself may well have been relying on men like Broghill when drawing up his own strategy.[105] The scheme reappeared in the spring of 1648 and again when Cromwell was drawing up his own plan of invasion in 1649, and on both occasions he may have been influenced by Irish Protestants. The Munster plan reinforces the point that in 1649 Cromwell was not working in isolation, or in ignorance, and he was willing to take advice from those who knew more about Ireland than he did. As we have seen, there were other important factors influencing Cromwell at various points in the 1640s, including his own personal position as a major investor in the Irish adventure, and his concern to retain a military command when the English civil war came to an end—both for financial and political reasons. Perhaps the important, and most enduring, influence on him was religion. There is no doubt that hatred of Catholicism, and fear that the 'popish plot' might spread to England, had been behind his attitude to Ireland since the outbreak of rebellion in 1641. But this should not be artificially separated from his other concerns. Cromwell's insistence on making extravagant financial commitments to the Irish war effort—in 1642, 1646 and 1648—points to his whole-hearted approach to the reconquest of Ireland. The demands of the 'living God' affected Cromwell's financial and political, as well as his religious, position.[106] Even monetary gain, power, ambition and worldly success could be acceptable if each element was guided by Providence. Oliver St John's comments to Cromwell when the Worcester lands were granted to him in February 1646 put this in a nutshell: 'all things are ours because we are His; and who knows but that for His sake ere long you must again forsake them, and that blessing is reserved to that time?'.[107]

After August 1649, Cromwell continued to believe that the Irish campaign, and his own part in it, had been pre-ordained. Cromwell's repeated references to Providence, whether at Drogheda, Wexford or when castigating the Irish Catholic clergy, should be seen in this context. Cromwell believed that God had brought him to Ireland, after humbling him by eight years of false-starts and missed opportunities, and he had no doubt that the successes, when they came, were divinely inspired. As he told his friend, Richard Maijor, on 2 April 1650:

> The Lord is pleased still to vouchsafe us His presence, and to prosper His work in our hands; which to us is the more eminent because truly we are a company of poor, weak and worthless creatures. Truly our work is neither from our brains nor from our courage and strength, but we follow the Lord who goeth before, and gather what He scattereth, that so all may appear to be from Him.[108]

## Notes

1. *ODNB*, 'Oliver Cromwell'.
2. T. Barnard, 'Irish Images of Cromwell', in R. C. Richardson (ed.), *Images of Oliver Cromwell* (Manchester, 1993), 180–206.
3. C. H. Firth, *Oliver Cromwell and the Rule of the Puritans in England* (1966 edn.), 58–9.
4. D. Stevenson, 'Cromwell, Scotland and Ireland', in J. Morrill (ed.), *Oliver Cromwell and the English Revolution* (1990), 150; see also Coward, *Cromwell*, 19.
5. R. S. Paul, *The Lord Protector: Religion and Politics in the Life of Oliver Cromwell* (1955), 52, 207–8.
6. See, for example, Coward, *Cromwell*, 72–6; Gaunt, *Cromwell*, 115–24; Davis, *Cromwell*, 6, 30–1, 107–110.
7. Abbott, ii. 127.
8. Ibid., 197–8.
9. *CJ*, ii. 349; *PJ*, ii. 268.
10. See R. Armstrong, 'The Long Parliament Goes to War: The Irish Campaigns, 1641–3', *Hist. Res.* 80 (2007).For the background see R. Armstrong, *Protestant War: The 'British' of Ireland and the Wars of the Three Kingdoms* (Manchester, 2005), ch. 2; P. Little, 'The English

Parliament and the Irish Constitution, 1641–9', in M. Ó Sióchrú (ed.), *Kingdoms in Crisis: Ireland in the 1640s* (Dublin, 2001), 108–9.

11. For his role in parliament, see *CJ*, ii. 468, 569; *PJ*, i. 395.
12. K. S. Bottigheimer, *English Money and Irish Land: The 'Adventurers' in the Cromwellian Settlement of Ireland* (Oxford, 1971), 70, 179.
13. Bottigheimer, *English Money and Irish Land*, 70.
14. Davis, *Cromwell*, 18, 203.
15. The value of the leases was about £400 p.a., and at 5–7 years' purchase this would have provided Cromwell with a lump sum of perhaps £2000–3000.He may have still been liable for Sir Thomas Steward's debts, and this would have diminished this sum considerably; on the other hand, he may have retained money from the sale of his Huntingdon lands in the early 1630s. See A. Barclay, *Oliver Cromwell: The Unknown Politician* (forthcoming) and chapter one, above.
16. Bottigheimer, *English Money and Irish Land*, 45–6, 49, 56–7.
17. Firth, *Cromwell*, 58–9; restated in *ODNB*, 'Oliver Cromwell'.
18. Bottigheimer, *English Money and Irish Land*, 79–80; Armstrong, 'The Long Parliament Goes to War', 90–1.
19. *CJ*, ii. 610, 672; *CSPI 1633–47*, 368.
20. *LJ*, v. 218; *PJ*, iii. 222.
21. Bottigheimer, *English Money and Irish Land*, 52.
22. *CJ*, ii. 588, 590, 600, 606–7, 609–10, 627, 629; *LJ*, v. 85, 92; *PJ*, ii. 372, 375, 384; *PJ*, iii. 14.
23. Bottigheimer, *English Money and Irish Land*, 81–2.
24. Abbott, i. 258–9.
25. TNA, SP 28/1a/159, 271; SP 28/2a/159, 232; SP 28/2b/391; SP 28/3a/223, 378; SP 28/4/161; SP 28/5/43.
26. TNA, SP 28/12/275–6, 279–80; SP 28/14/20, 164; SP 28/17/372; SP 28/18/217; SP 28/21/115; SP 28/26/119; another account lists Cromwell as being owed £840 for 48 weeks' pay as lieutenant-general (January–December 1644) and £705 as colonel and captain during the same period (see Abbott, i. 272).
27. Abbott, i. 588.
28. Huntington RO, Cromwell-Bush MSS, 3 July 1643 letter (currently on display in the Cromwell Museum, Huntingdon).
29. J. Hackett, *Scrinia Reserata: A Memorial Offered to the Great Deservings of John Williams D. D.* (1693), part 2, 212; see also J. Nalson, *An Impartial Collection of the Great Affairs of State* (1682–3), ii. 510. I owe these references to Andrew Barclay.
30. J. Adamson, 'Oliver Cromwell and the Long Parliament', in Morrill (ed.), *Oliver Cromwell and the English Revolution*, 65.
31. For this period see R. Armstrong, *Protestant War*, passim; and Bottigheimer, *English Money and Irish Land*, ch. 4.
32. *HMC Egmont*, i. 265.

33. Ibid., 268.
34. T. Carte, *History of the Life of James of James, 1st Duke of Ormonde* (2nd edn. 6 vols., Oxford, 1951), vi. 351–2 (Bodl., MS Carte 16, fo. 489v).
35. *CJ*, iv. 413, 416.
36. *CJ*, iv. 360b: The earlier resolution was on a list of 'desires' sent to the king.
37. *CJ*, iv. 418; *LJ*, viii. 127.
38. *TSP*, i. 75.Cromwell had also been promised lands confiscated from the marquess of Winchester.
39. His urgency may well have also been occasioned by the marriage of Elizabeth Cromwell to John Claypole. The wedding had taken place on 13 January 1646, but the marriage settlement, which allowed the bride a portion of £1500, was not signed until 9 March, after the Worcester lands had been voted to her father (Abbott, i. 398).
40. *HMC Egmont*, i. 280.
41. R. N. Worth, *The Buller Papers* (privately printed, 1895), 97.
42. *CJ*, iv. 631.
43. Abbott, i. 409–10; but cf. K. Lindley and D. Scott (eds), *The Journal of Thomas Juxon, 1644–1647* (Camden Soc., 5th ser. 13, 1999), 131.
44. *Ludlow Memoirs*, i. 141.
45. *CJ*, iv. 631, 632.
46. G. E. Aylmer, 'Was Oliver Cromwell a Member of the Army in 1646–7 or Not?', *History*, 56 (1971), 185–6. As Aylmer shows, Cromwell continued to be paid intermittently, and was treated by the army as one of its own, even if his official position was in doubt.
47. M. F. Steig (ed.), *The Diary of John Harington, MP, 1646–53* (Somerset Record Society, 74, 1977), 30.
48. *CSPI 1633–47*, 485.
49. *CJ*, iv. 641.
50. Ibid. 679.
51. For this see P. Little, 'The Irish "Independents" and Viscount Lisle's Lieutenancy of Ireland', *HJ*, 44 (2001), 955.
52. *CJ*, v. 63.
53. *CCAM*, 59; this identification is suggested by Richard's further appointment, by September 1647, as captain of Fairfax's lifeguard (C. H. Firth and G. Davies, *The Regimental History of Cromwell's Army* (2 vols., Oxford, 1940), i. 47–8).
54. Lindley and Scott (eds), *Juxon Diary*, 147.
55. Abbott, i. 429; Paul, *Lord Protector*, 109.
56. Firth, *Cromwell*, 153–4; *CJ*, v. 107.
57. *HMC Egmont*, i. 384.
58. Abbott, i. 438; *CJ*, v. 133.
59. Gaunt, *Cromwell*, 72; see also S. R. Gardiner, *History of the Great Civil War, 1642–1649* (4 vols., 1893), iii. 241; Paul, *Lord Protector*, 114.

60. Abbott, i. 435.
61. Ibid., 436–7.
62. Adamson, 'Oliver Cromwell and the Long Parliament', 74.
63. Abbott, i. 439.
64. Ibid., 505.
65. TNA, SP 21/26, p. 104.
66. *CSPI 1647–60*, 764.
67. Trinity College Dublin, MS 844, fo. 5 (27 October [1647]).
68. Bodl., MS Nalson 6, fo. 182r (26 February 1648) (printed in *HMC Portland* i. 445); see also Bodl., MS Carte 67, fo. 149.
69. J. A. Murphy, 'The Politics of the Munster Protestants, 1641–1649', *Journal of the Cork Historical and Archaeological Society*, 76 (1971), 16.
70. Bodl., MS Carte 22, fo. 67v; see also ibid, fo. 53r.
71. Bodl., MS Carte 22, fo. 53r.
72. TNA, SP 21/26, 124–153.
73. Abbott, i. 588.
74. *CSPI 1647–60*, 775.
75. Abbott, i. 588; *CJ*, v. 514; *A Perfect Diurnall*, no. 243 (20–27 March 1648), 1960.
76. *Mercurius Pragmaticus*, no. 1 (28 March–4 April 1648), sig. A3.
77. Mr Denham, writing to Ormond from London on 30 March 1648, noted that 'my Lord Inchiquin has committed four principal Independents officers' (Bodl., MS Carte 22, fo. 53r).
78. TNA, SP 21/26, p. 144; *CSPI 1647–60*, 775.
79. *CSPI 1647–60*, 775.
80. Abbott, i. 593.
81. *CSPI 1647–60*, 776.
82. Abbott, i. 592.
83. BL, Richard Browne corresp. 2, vol. x (6 April 1648, Nicholas to Browne).
84. Walker, *The History of Independency* (26 May 1648), 58.
85. *CSPI 1647–60*, 777–8; TNA, SP 21/26, 153–4.
86. Abbott, ii. 35.
87. *Clarke Papers*, ii. 201–7.
88. Trinity College Dublin, MS 844, fos. 29r–32v, 77–8v.
89. Abbott, ii. 59, 83 (for contacts with Sir Charles Coote).
90. *CSPD 1649–50*, 53, 132.
91. *CSPD 1649–50*, 77, 112, 121, 131; Abbott, ii. 88.
92. Little, *Broghill*, 2–3, 52–3, 59–60; *CSPD 1649–50*, 273, 584.
93. Abbott, ii. 53; *CSPD 1649-50*, 77, 166.
94. *HMC de Lisle*, vi. 589.
95. Abbott, ii. 86–7; *CSPI 1633–47*, 586.
96. TNA, SP 28/61, fo. 2; see also *CSPD 1649–50*, 164, 575.

97. Firth, *Cromwell*, 253; Paul, *Lord Protector*, 209; Gaunt, *Cromwell*, 115; Davis, *Cromwell*, 30–1; Roger Howell Jr, *Cromwell* (1977), 138.

98. S. R. Gardiner, *History of the Commonwealth and Protectorate* (4 vols., 1903), i. 94–5, 97, 105; James Scott Wheeler, *Cromwell in Ireland* (Dublin, 1999), 71–3.

99. *HMC Leyborne-Popham*, 21, 24–6; 34–6.

100. Ibid., 40–1.

101. *ODNB*, 'Oliver Cromwell'.

102. Abbott, ii. 256.

103. P. Lenihan, *Confederate Catholics at War, 1641–49* (Cork, 2001), 90.

104. Lord Cromwell of Ardglass, whom Oliver acknowledged, and assisted, as a distant relative in October 1646, was seated in Ulster (see Abbott, i. 417).

105. Little, 'Irish "Independents" ', 956–7.

106. See J. C. Davis, 'Living with the Living God: Radical Religion and the English Revolution', in C. Durston and J. Maltby (eds), *Religion in Revolutionary England* (Manchester, 2006).

107. *TSP*, i. 75.

108. Abbott, ii. 235.

# 6

# Oliver Cromwell and the Solemn League and Covenant of the Three Kingdoms

Kirsteen M. MacKenzie

During the negotiations for the surrender of Edinburgh Castle in September 1650, an earnest debate took place between Oliver Cromwell and Sir Walter Dundas, governor of the castle, regarding the Scottish ministers sheltering within its walls. Two major issues were debated: the ministers' freedom to preach the gospel and the obligations of both the English and the Scots under the Solemn League and Covenant. In a letter to Cromwell, Dundas declared: 'The contents of these papers do concern the public differences betwixt you and these of the three kingdoms, who have faithfully adhered to the Solemn League and Covenant.'[1] 'These of the three kingdoms' not merely referred to the ministers in Edinburgh Castle, who remained loyal to a covenant whereby the subscribers pledged to promote and defend the reformed religion in England, Scotland and Ireland, but also referred to an actual 'covenanted interest' in all three kingdoms.[2] Not only did the ministers lament the treatment of their own religion at the hands of Oliver Cromwell and his English army in Scotland, they also feared for 'the ministers of Christ in England and Ireland'.[3] Scottish covenanters saw themselves as part of a wider covenanted interest, with adherents in all three kingdoms; they thought that the welfare of the covenanted people of the other two kingdoms was just as important as their own.

The concept of a covenant for religion was an integral part of Scottish religious life and culture, with origins extending well before the National Covenant of 1638. 'Bands' or 'bonds' between the people and God for the defence of the Protestant religion had been an important feature of the Scottish reformation in the later sixteenth century. The National Covenant of 1638 declared itself to be consistent with and in adherence to the oath taken by the king in 1580 and the people of Scotland in 1581 to uphold the true Protestant faith that, with the religious legislation passed by the Scottish parliament during the reformation, gave the Scots the legal and cultural justification for their Covenant. The National Covenant of 1638 was built on this previous oath or 'band' between James VI and his people in order to protect the Scottish reformed faith that Charles I and his Laudian policies challenged.[4] The National Covenant was a public band between God, the crown and the people of Scotland in defence of the 'pure' Scottish reformed faith as enshrined in Scottish law against 'popish' influences, and it laid down that the crown and its subjects were to protect the reformed faith for eternity.[5] The British implications of the Scottish Covenant were profound. The National Covenant of 1638 found support amongst British settlers in Ulster as well as those who wished for a further Protestant reformation in England, particularly English parliamentarians. The Irish rebellion of 1641 triggered an invasion of Ulster by covenanting forces seeking to protect settlers from attacks by the Irish. With this army came a Scottish Presbyterian church structure with ministers ready to preach the Scots' reformed gospel to the planter population. Therefore, the Scottish covenanters, or 'new Scots', came to have a committed presence in Ireland.[6] At home, the Scottish covenanters continued to strive for godly reformation throughout the 1640s.[7] Furthermore, the covenanters sought to protect this, the 'second Scots reformation', by building contacts with the king's opponents in the English parliament—a move that, in September 1643, culminated in the Solemn League and Covenant. For English Presbyterians this was not only a treaty of military convenience but, as Edward Vallance has shown, a renewal 'of God's original Covenant with man and his chosen nation, England'.[8] For Scots, moreover, the Solemn League and Covenant was not only an alliance between the godly of Scotland and their maker, but also an alliance for the benefit of the godly in both England and Scotland. From their perspective, the Solemn League and Covenant was a statement of an ambitious pan-Protestant reformation across the three kingdoms which had its roots in the Scottish reformation of the sixteenth century. John Knox, for example, came to believe that it was the duty of England and Scotland to protect and nurture the reformed faith in both nations, in addition to encouraging reformation in Ireland.[9] The Solemn League and Covenant built on such ideas by declaring that 'in this common cause of religion and peace of the kingdom' the signatories would assist and defend all those that 'entered into the League and Covenant'.[10] The alliance was therefore to be one of mutual co-operation and assistance between the English parliament and Scottish covenanters. To facilitate this, Scottish covenanters sat on the committee of both kingdoms (to help co-ordinate the joint military effort) and Scottish Presbyterian ministers sat in the Westminster Assembly (advising members upon the new English church).[11] By the mid 1640s, with their armies spread across the three kingdoms, a regime in Scotland and involvement in the wars in England and Ireland, the Scottish covenanted interest was a genuinely 'three kingdoms' interest.[12]

As the exchange with Sir Walter Dundas suggests, Oliver Cromwell was not a natural supporter of the covenanting interest. He did not take the Solemn League and Covenant of the three kingdoms until February 1644, nearly five months after it had first been published. Cromwell might have been too busy fighting to take the oath, but it is more likely that he was reluctant to do so, as his enthusiasm for liberty of conscience went hand-in-hand with a belief that rigid Presbyterianism should not be imposed on individuals. As David Stevenson states, Cromwell 'resented and feared the price the Scots demanded in return' for military assistance, believing that the Scottish covenanters, and above all their strict adherence to the Covenant, posed a serious threat to England. Cromwell soon emerged as a leading figure amongst those English parliamentarians who grew to resent Scottish intervention in English affairs during the wars of the 1640s. This hostility was further complicated by Cromwell's growing conviction that he, at the head of his godly troops, was an instrument of God's Providence. Thus, although his involvement in the defeat of the royalist engagers in 1648 raised the possibility that he could co-operate with the godly of Scotland in friendship (as we shall see), for this to work the Scots had to accept that his role was providential in exactly the same way as he did. Cromwell continued to promote this image of himself as he came to Scotland to defeat the forces of Charles II in 1650. He saw himself not as an invader but as a liberator, who would show the Scots that their strict adherence to the Covenant was misguided, and that they should abandon their Presbyterian system and embrace liberty of conscience instead.[13] This can be seen most clearly in his famous letter to the kirk ministers in August 1650, in which he challenged their position: 'Is it therefore infallibly agreeable to the Word of God, all that you say? I beseech you, in the bowels of Christ, think it possible you may be mistaken.'[14]

Cromwell's attitude to the Scots and their Covenant has been explored elsewhere.[15] This chapter seeks instead to look at the relationship between them from the other side, by examining Cromwell through the eyes of the Scottish covenanters from 1643 to 1653. It will tackle Cromwell's military and political reputation in the mid 1640s and will explain why Scottish covenanters first regarded him as an ally and then as an enemy of the 'covenanted interest'. The changing and sometimes conflicting faces of Cromwell, from the first civil war to the royalist Engagement of 1648 and the conquest of Scotland from 1650 to 1651, will be explored. Across this period, Cromwell was variously seen as an instrument of Providence, an instrument of God's wrath, a covenant-breaker and, eventually, as harbinger of the coming millennium. The chapter will also explain the Ulster Presbyterian reaction to Cromwell's siege at Drogheda in 1649, by putting it into its immediate context. Lastly, it will address the covenanting perspective on Cromwell as ruler of the three kingdoms from 1653, and his image as a usurper and an obstacle to the workings of God's Providence.

## I

In February 1644 Oliver Cromwell was appointed to the newly formed committee of both kingdoms, which took over the management of the joint war effort. Yet between February and July 1644, he never actually sat on the committee, as he was busy taking part in the military operations of parliament's Eastern Association, which by this stage was looking to join forces with the Scottish covenanting army that had crossed the border in January.[16] Even before this, there were tensions between Cromwell and the Scots. For example, Cromwell had already worked with Sir John Meldrum, an experienced Scottish soldier, during the skirmish at Gainsborough in July 1643.[17] In this action, Meldrum brought around 300 cavalry from Nottingham to join Cromwell, considerably strengthening his force; but in the three letters in which Cromwell gives his account of the battle he only mentions Meldrum in passing. He states that he met up with Meldrum's Nottingham forces before the skirmish, but there is silence on the specific activities of Meldrum that day, as Cromwell was anxious to play up his own actions and to praise those of his kinsman, Edward Whalley.[18] Therefore we have no direct evidence about the relationship between Meldrum and Cromwell on the day of battle; but Cromwell's silence gives the impression that he had deliberately slighted his Scottish colleague.[19]

Cromwell also worked with Scottish officers in the employment of the English parliament immediately after the main covenanter force crossed the border, and once again tensions are apparent. In early March 1644 he collaborated with the devout Scottish Presbyterian, Major-General Lawrence Crawford, on an operation to take Hilsden House in Buckinghamshire. As they neared Bedford a Baptist officer, Lieutenant-Colonel William Packer, disobeyed orders and was arrested by Crawford. Cromwell was absent at the time, but Packer soon complained to him, and Cromwell sent Colonel Rich to admonish Crawford for his actions, on the grounds that he knew that Packer was a 'godly man'.[20] From Crawford's perspective, far from upholding a spirit of military co-operation between Scottish and English officers, Cromwell had arrogantly overruled the decision of a senior Scottish colleague. In addition, by tolerating the undermining of Crawford's position by a subordinate officer, and supporting those whom Crawford would have seen as misguided or even totally irreligious, Cromwell had come into conflict with the covenanting principles of godly reformation. This row is usually seen within the context of the public dispute between Cromwell and the earl of Manchester some months later at the end of 1644. Yet, although it is clear that the Packer episode caused bad feeling between Crawford and Cromwell in March 1644, it seems to have been a personal, not a public, dispute between two people. This can be seen in the reactions of the Scottish commissioners in London, who seemed unaware of the ruffled feathers between the two men. As far as they were concerned, Cromwell and Crawford had worked together to gain Hilsden House in a spirit of military co-operation befitting the Solemn League and Covenant.[21]

There were also questions as to Cromwell's attitude during Sir John Meldrum's failed siege of Newark at the end of March 1644. Some accused 'Cromwell, the great Independent' of withholding reinforcements to Meldrum, hinting that he was not fully co-operating with his Scottish ally in military affairs. However, in this case Cromwell was defended not by a fellow Englishman or Independent, but by Robert Baillie, a Scottish Presbyterian minister and member of the Westminster Assembly. Viewing events from London, Baillie believed

Meldrum was to blame. This was evident in the letters Meldrum sent to London reporting his actions, which made it obvious to Baillie that Meldrum had been too eager to besiege the town and did so before he was properly prepared.[22] In another account of the siege, by Lieutenant-Colonel Berry, the blame was said to lie with Lord Willoughby of Parham's soldiers, who had turned against parliament and joined the royalists, and also with Prince Rupert, who had betrayed the articles of peace. Cromwell was not criticised in any way for failing to support his Scottish colleague.[23]

Scottish covenanting opinion on Cromwell's role in the victory of Marston Moor in July 1644 should be seen in the light of these earlier incidents, and not in the context of disputes that were to follow after the battle. As Barry Coward has commented, 'Cromwell believed that he and his cavalry had won the battle and that his allies, Fairfax, Leven and the Scots, had played a relatively insignificant (at best) supporting part in the victory.'[24] According to Cromwell, it was God's victory, and he implied that the instrument that God had used to achieve victory was Cromwell himself.[25] Yet a letter from the covenanting forces at York, written in the aftermath of the battle, gives an alternative account of Cromwell's role that day. The author also ascribes the victory to God, but adds that the success of left wing cavalry was due to the actions of Cromwell working alongside the Scottish commander, David Leslie. Cromwell's success was portrayed as a joint effort with a Scottish covenanter, and therefore as a success of the two kingdoms working together under the Solemn League and Covenant. Another covenanter hoped that the victory 'ought never to be forgot in the three kingdoms as one of the greatest acts of God's great power'. For such commentators, Cromwell was still a valuable ally whose actions were deemed providential, since his part in the shared victory assured the covenanters that the Solemn League and Covenant was blessed by God.[26] Nor were the Scottish forces at York alone in their interpretation of Cromwell's actions that day. Robert Douglas, a minister with the covenanting forces in England, noted that both English parliamentarians and Scottish covenanters had jointly achieved victory. Cromwell charged very well but was hurt and had to retire from the battlefield leaving David Leslie to deal successfully with the royalist forces. In this account success was again attributed to both men in a spirit of military of co-operation.[27]

News of the victory at Marston Moor was proclaimed from Scottish pulpits, but Cromwell's role in the victory was not singled out. Instead, it was portrayed as a major covenanting victory, a sign of God's blessing upon their Solemn League and Covenant. In Sir Thomas Hope of Craighall's local church in Fife, the minister declared that the authors of the victory were the Scottish covenanters with the English commanders, the earl of Manchester and Sir Thomas Fairfax, following their lead.[28] This view can also be seen in the kirk records of the period. For example, the Presbytery of Kirkcaldy in Fife was ordered to declare a day of thanksgiving 'received at our army in England'; in the highland Presbytery of Strathbogie, a thanksgiving was to be observed for the 'great mercy of God towards our army'. There was no specific mention of Cromwell's actions in their orders for thanksgiving.[29] It is in this context that Robert Baillie's comments about Cromwell's role in the battle should be read. Baillie complained that 'the Independents sent up on quick-like, to assure, that all the glory of that night was theirs; that they, and their General-Major Cromwell, had done it all alone';[30] but, like the other Scottish covenanters, Baillie knew full well that the victory had been achieved through the actions of his countrymen as well as the English parliamentarians. Indeed, by August 1644 he had received further reports from Sir Adam Hepburn and Sheldon Crawford, eyewitnesses of the battle, confirming that Cromwell could not have been successful without the full support of Leslie's horse.[31] This perception of a joint victory, which was a powerful reaffirmation of the Covenant, was not just the preserve of the Scots. As Allan Macinnes states, after the battle Manchester and Fairfax, with Leven, wrote to the committee of both kingdoms stating their continued adherence to the Solemn League and Covenant.[32] Therefore, Baillie's comments about Cromwell were not unusual or exceptional, but very much a judgement that many contemporaries, particularly his fellow covenanters, would have shared.

The military campaigns of the earls of Essex and Manchester after Marston Moor were a great disappointment, and their failure revealed serious divisions within the command of parliament's army. Foremost among the critics was Oliver Cromwell, who attacked Manchester's conduct, saying that he had not been vigorous enough in pursuit of the war. Major-General Crawford's narrative, written as a defence of Manchester's campaign, is often dismissed on the grounds that the author held a personal grudge against Cromwell, not least because of the Packer affair. However, if Crawford's Scottish Presbyterian background and the relationship between the Scottish covenanters and the English parliament at the time are taken into account, a new perspective on Cromwell can be suggested: one which goes beyond personal grudges. In planting many religious Independents in the army, Cromwell was seen as 'highly mutinous'—a judgement no doubt influenced by Crawford's previous experience with Packer. In addition Crawford alleged that Cromwell was reluctant to take part in joint military operations with his Scottish colleagues. Crawford was in effect implying that Cromwell was undermining the military co-operation as envisaged in the Solemn League and Covenant.[33] The need for unity between the commanders in the army, both English and Scottish, was clearly of increasing concern to the Scottish commissioners in London by October 1644. They observed that the English parliament and the army were 'divided into several factions' and this was a danger 'to us and the cause of God'. Instructions were drawn up whereby Sir Archibald Johnston of Wariston, an author of the National Covenant of 1638 and member of the committee of both kingdoms, was to:

> unite the armies and settle a good understanding betwixt the lord general [the earl of Essex], my Lord Manchester and Sir William Waller amongst themselves and with us in pursuance of the ends expressed in the Covenant and Treaty for settling religion and peace, and preventing all new factions and designs tending to the divisions of the kingdoms.[34]

Cromwell's dispute with Manchester was thus one of many fractures in the command which Scottish covenanters believed could destroy their hopes for settling religion throughout the three kingdoms. It was, however, a serious one. Robert Baillie, for example, now began to see Cromwell as a major threat to the establishment of a permanent Presbyterian settlement. His view was justified by Cromwell's action in obtaining an order from the House of Commons, on behalf of the committee of both kingdoms, proposing that liberty of conscience must become part of the religious settlement of England. According to Baillie, this 'high' order was totally unexpected, and he hinted that Cromwell had subverted expected procedures on such religious issues, which were a matter for both kingdoms, and the Scottish commissioners had been kept in the dark.[35] From the covenanter perspective by the end of 1644 Cromwell had emerged as a dangerous troublemaker, bent on destroying the principles of unity and reformation which they had strived for under the Solemn League and Covenant.

By December 1644 the committee of estates in Edinburgh had digested events in London and stated 'wherein we find expressions alleged to have fallen from Lieutenant-General Cromwell so destructive to the very ends of our mutual League and Covenant as we cannot but in a high measure resent the same'. They were disgusted by his contempt for the privileges of the English parliament, which both Scots and the English had a duty to maintain under the Covenant. Cromwell was condemned as a man who hated the Scots, favoured English Independents above all others and was correspondingly critical of the Assembly of Divines, calling its members persecutors of the godly. The committee of estates also believed that Cromwell was intent on destroying the alliance between the English parliament and the Scottish covenanters. Therefore, they asked the commissioners in London to bring proceedings against Cromwell as an 'incendiary'.[36] In doing so, the committee of estates was not asking for anything extraordinary from the English parliament, but simply upholding the terms of the Solemn League and Covenant, which declared that if anyone sought to impede reformation, or create any factions within the kingdoms, he/she should be brought to trial and punished. In the event, the Scottish commissioners in London were advised against this extreme course by their English allies, and proceedings against Cromwell were dropped.[37]

In the same period, new proposals were put forward to unite the command of parliament's armies, and the English Presbyterian allies of the Scottish commissioners insisted that Scots should be consulted, so as not to overturn the established practices of parliament's military management through the committee of both kingdoms.[38] Independent moves to create a unified English army could only be seen as a challenge to this alliance. However, it is evident that the self-denying ordinance and the New Model Army were initially not the most pressing worries for the Scottish commissioners, who concentrated instead on trying to gain Charles I's backing for the peace propositions of Uxbridge, including a commitment to the establishment of the Presbyterian religion in the three kingdoms. However, by March 1645 the detailed proposals surrounding the creation of the New Model Army began to give the Scots serious concern, as they realised that such moves would threaten the unity of the 'covenanted interest' between England and Scotland. There were two reasons for this. Firstly, there was the inevitable disruption and dislocation that would come with the reorganisation of parliament's forces to create the new army. Many Scottish soldiers were being cashiered, and some mutinied. It was proposed by parliament that only three Scots officers would remain in the new army, and Cromwell's old adversary, Major-General Crawford, was to be demoted to the rank of colonel. Secondly, in the same month it became apparent that the English officers in the new army were men 'not zealous of the reformation and uniformity of religion between the kingdoms'.[39] These developments brought a belated reaction. In May 1645 Scottish commissioners objected to Cromwell's appointment as lieutenant-general, seeing it as 'prejudicial to the service of both kingdoms', and proposed that Colonel Vermuyden be appointed to the position, receiving orders from Alexander Leslie, earl of Leven. This proposal for a joint military effort between the two countries was, however, rejected out of hand by the English parliament. It was now clear to the Scottish commissioners in London that Cromwell's exemption from the self-denying ordinance was a measure aimed at them.[40] Furthermore, there was no denying the fact that the New Model Army's victory at Naseby in June 1645 was a purely English achievement, obtained without the assistance of the covenanter army. The contrast with the great covenanted victory at Marston Moor could not have been starker. It is telling that the Scottish covenanters did not remark on Oliver Cromwell's contribution to the success at Naseby; nor did they join in the day of thanksgiving.[41]

The victory at Naseby fitted very badly with covenanter interpretations of God's Providence over the past year. Their preferred version of events can be seen in a pamphlet published in Edinburgh in July 1645 describing the triumphs of the covenanting forces in England. The string of providential successes had begun with a skirmish at Bowdon Hill in March 1644, continued with Marston Moor in July, and in October culminated with the successful siege of Newcastle. Newcastle was hailed as 'a famous and renowned victory', allowing the Scottish covenanting forces to carry on with the work of godly reformation.[42] Another pamphlet written in the same year by another Scot, David Buchannan, continues to detail and embellish on the good that Providence had bestowed on the Scottish forces in England. He argued that the Scottish army had been strategic in preventing Scottish royalists and their Irish allies from invading England and that their work had lifted the burden off parliament's southern armies. In addition, he also asserted that God was angry with both nations and, as evidence of this, cited the destruction of the work of reformation. Scotland had helped the English parliament remove prelacy from the Church of England, but parliament was now destroying reformation by allowing the proliferation of sectaries. He argued that the Solemn League and Covenant was being undermined by the many warring factions in both kingdoms. The appointment of Scots in 'inferior employments' in the New Model also gave rise to the fear amongst them that the Solemn League and Covenant was breaking apart. The New Model was a force wherein the English predominated, and therefore co-operation between godly Scots and English as equals could not take place—a situation that conflicted with the Covenant. David Buchanan certainly acknowledged that the victory at Naseby was providential, but stated 'I do not find piety more really in them', and that the New Model's religious zeal was a guise under which 'knavery and faction' were encouraged. Interestingly, he does not mention Oliver Cromwell—or anyone else—by name, perhaps fearful of causing further divisions between the kingdoms. Nevertheless, despite (or perhaps because of) the success of the New Model army at Naseby, Oliver Cromwell was now seen as the leading enemy of the 'covenanted interest'.[43]

## II

Three years would pass before Oliver Cromwell and the covenanters would again come together to work on political and military issues. By then, like at Marston Moor, Cromwell was seen as an ally whose actions could be considered to be 'providential'. How did Cromwell move from enemy to ally between 1645 and 1648? Military success, a sure measure of God's approval, was one factor. Cromwell had defeated the Scottish royalists under the duke of Hamilton at Preston in August 1648, and the defeat of Hamilton was a 'providential' sign for those who had opposed the Engagement in Scotland.[44] As William Row, minister of Ceres in Fife, noted:

> The woeful defeat of the engagers in England made a great change on the face of affairs, and no small revolution in Scotland; for all that were not satisfied in point of conscience with the Engagement, and had suffered upon that account, made use of the opportunity offered for shaking off the yoke laid upon them by the engagers.[45]

Those who opposed Hamilton's Engagement in Scotland were men closely allied to the kirk. The commission of the kirk had denounced the Engagement believing that the Presbyterian faith had not been secured in the treaty. A small group of noblemen in the Scottish parliament, led by Archibald Campbell, marquis of Argyll, had actively tried to stop Scottish royalists from invading England, believing that it would bring chaos to both kingdoms. One staunch Presbyterian, Major Strachan, had even joined Cromwell's forces before Hamilton left Scotland, believing that co-operation with 'backsliding' covenanted Englishmen was more favoured by God than an invasion of England by malignant royalists. Therefore, when Hamilton was decisively defeated by Cromwell at the battle of Preston, the result was seen as the work of Providence, showing the folly of the Scottish royalists in their invasion of England—which was itself a serious breach of the Solemn League and Covenant.[46] Once again Cromwell was part of a covenanting dynamic, as a providential figure; not because of any gifted military ability but because God had used him as an instrument to show that the Engagement was an action against God and His Covenant.

Cromwell's relationship with the anti-engagers in Scotland should be seen within the context of the continuing obligations of both kingdoms under the Solemn League and Covenant. Cromwell was in Scotland between mid-September and early October 1648 to assist the anti-engagers to defeat the remainder of their opponents in Scotland. For Cromwell it was an opportunity not to renew a Covenant but to secure England from further invasions from the north. The anti-engagers had hoped their opponents would lay down their arms and that Cromwell would not have to enter Scotland after all. As a result, they wrote to Cromwell assuring him that the engager forces would be disbanded and insisting that they had a desire to 'preserve the union between the two kingdoms'. In addition, they offered to co-operate with him in England to regain the border towns of Berwick and Carlisle from the royalists to 'observe inviolably the Covenant and the treaties between the kingdoms to be mutually aiding to each other against the common enemy'.[47] They also offered to send their own forces to put down 'malignants' in England, and proposed that the anti-engagers and the English parliament could bring their common enemies to trial.[48] All this was in accordance with the Solemn League and Covenant, but there were limits to the anti-engagers' co-operation with Cromwell. In particular, there was a fear amongst the Scottish populace that Cromwell's military assistance could turn into an English invasion. If so, the Scottish would 'rise as one man against him'.[49] Cromwell was thus seen as an unwanted as well as an uninvited guest when he crossed the border in the wake of Hamilton's defeat. He was treading a thin line, tolerated only for his military power, which could help the anti-engagers. By ignoring Scottish declarations that they could defeat their enemies on their own, Cromwell was increasingly seen as a foe, whose military might threatened to conquer Scotland and destroy the 'covenanted' union between the two kingdoms.

There was an atmosphere of mistrust between the anti-engagers and Cromwell in 1648, despite the public show of unity. One account of Cromwell's stay in Edinburgh, printed in London at the time, states that he was thanked by the commission of the kirk for putting down the engager forces and that he had supper with the leading anti-engagers. According to the author there was 'mutual love between each other' which it was hoped would bring a successful peace to both nations.[50] The reality was rather different. Cromwell had made it clear to the anti-engagers 'how far the late Engagement had tended to the detriment of England', and he therefore demanded the exclusion of the engagers from power. This was not a balanced negotiation for the sake of both nations, but one expressly anglocentric—purely for the benefit of England. Cromwell had a meeting with some leading ministers of the kirk, including Robert Blair, minister of St Andrews, who began to ask leading questions in order to draw out Cromwell's real views on the Solemn League and Covenant. The ministers hoped that the success of Cromwell in Scotland would lead to a renewal of the union between the two nations and an opportunity to promote reformation in England. The ministers were honest with Cromwell, and stated that his army was now the only stumbling block to achieving a covenanted reformation in England. In response, Cromwell declared that he would preserve the king and his posterity, but interestingly denied that he was in favour of religious toleration and would not answer a question on Presbyterian church government. Cromwell's fondness for liberty of conscience was well known to Robert Blair, who had met Cromwell after Marston Moor. The ministers of the kirk knew that Cromwell was not being entirely truthful, and they did not trust him.[51]

The ministers' suspicions were justified when Charles I was executed in January 1649. To the covenanters this was a despicable act which was a breach of the Covenant, as it broke the pledge to preserve the king and his posterity; it also turned Cromwell from an untrustworthy ally of the 'covenanted interest' to an outright enemy once again. The kirk regime was determined to stand by their Covenant and upon hearing of the death of Charles I it 'ignored' the existence of the English republic and declared his son King Charles II of Britain, Ireland and France. In doing so they still continued to uphold the union between the two countries as envisaged in the Solemn League and Covenant. Conversely, the English republic was a regime that saw itself as under siege by supporters of the Stuarts, both at home and abroad, and which, for survival, had to conquer Scotland and Ireland strictly on English terms, thereby removing any possibility of an equal union between the two kingdoms as envisaged in the Covenant.[52]

## III

The actions of Cromwell at the Irish town of Drogheda in September 1649 can be regarded as one of the first major tests of the English republic's military might against the monarch's loyal subjects in the three kingdoms—and one in which, according to one contemporary, Cromwell's 'resolute' opponents 'in the righteous judgement of God met with a scourge from unjust hands'.[53] This apparently confusing statement came from the pen of Patrick Adair, Presbyterian minister of Cairncastle, County Antrim. Chillingly, his words echoed Cromwell's own statement about Drogheda being 'a righteous judgement of God'.[54] Yet, for Adair, this judgement was achieved by the 'unjust' hands of Oliver Cromwell. How could the success of Cromwell at Drogheda be attributed to God, yet Cromwell himself considered 'unjust'? Furthermore, how could Cromwell's opponents be called admiringly resolute, but yet their death be a sign of divine judgement?

Adair's comments, paradoxical as they may first appear, accurately reflect the Ulster Presbyterian position at that time. In September 1649 the Antrim Presbytery wrote to Robert Douglas in Edinburgh describing their 'lamentable' condition. An ally of the Presbytery, Viscount Montgomery of the Ards, had just betrayed them and joined with the 'malignant' royalist party. The republican sectaries were on the march and there was widespread 'backsliding' from the Covenant in Ulster. The Presbyterians saw themselves as the only 'honest party' working hard to continue reformation against a sea of enemies.[55] Their 'necessary representation' issued in the wake of the king's execution declared that they would not recognise the English republic, and asserted that they were 'so deeply engaged by their Solemn League and Covenant' that they were bound only to recognise rule by the monarch and both Houses of parliament. From Adair's viewpoint, the soldiers at Drogheda fighting for the king were to be commended, but God had poured his wrath upon them. Although sharing the same basic sentiment as Oliver Cromwell, for Adair this was not a judgement upon 'barbarous wretches', who had killed many Protestants in 1641, but a condemnation of the ungodliness of the governor of

the town, Sir Arthur Aston, and his soldiers. Aston was an English
Catholic and a staunch royalist, and, in disgust, the Antrim Presbytery
classed him as a papist and uncovenanted malignant. The godly were
warned not to comply with these people under any circumstances for
fear of incurring God's wrath. Aston was not the only one condemned
in this manner by Adair, who thought that the defeat of the marquis
of Ormond at Rathmines near Dublin in August 1649 was due to the
'ungodly' behaviour of the royalist soldiers who were 'minding their
drinking, cards and dice more than their work'.[56]

Cromwell was thus both a respected instrument of God used to
punish Aston for his wicked ways, and a man castigated for being
'unjust'. Cromwell's reputation was already well established in Ulster,
not just for his role in the execution of the king, but also for his
importance in promoting sectaries in England, which had destroyed
the work of reformation. For Adair and his friends, Cromwell and
his sectaries were also instruments of Satan sent to Ireland to test
the faith of the Presbyterians. Adair's comments about Cromwell as
'unjust' therefore do not come from any disapproval of Cromwell's
military conduct at Drogheda. Although Cromwell may have been
severe, Adair certainly had no sympathy when it came to the punishment of 'ungodly malignants'—rather his disapproval came from a
sense of betrayal over the breaking of the Covenant. Cromwell had
overturned the rightful and therefore 'just' settlement of the three
kingdoms. This settlement had boundaries, a divinely appointed religion, a form of worship characterised by strict discipline with a wish
to preserve the established privileges of the king and the English parliament over Ireland. By way of contrast Cromwell was bringing with
him 'universal toleration' in religion and had imposed English government by military force, solely deriving its powers from a purged
House of Commons. These were 'innovations' with no clear boundaries. Cromwell had overridden the natural order and by implication
was no longer constrained by what was naturally just.[57]

## IV

Oliver Cromwell was formally declared to be in breach of the
Covenant as he approached Scotland, at the head of an English army,
in July 1650. In addition to his earlier crimes, he was breaking apart
the mutual covenant of co-operation by declaring a war of aggression against Scotland.[58] Wariston, writing in the early months of
the invasion, condemned Oliver Cromwell as boastful, arrogant and

aggressive. Cromwell threatened to bring ruin on the Scottish army, he was supremely confident of victory, and, to the disbelief of Wariston, he was even 'sending up bragging news for a diurnal in London'. Clearly irritated, Wariston declared: 'I hope we can bring God with us, who can soon take order with that proud piece of clay.'[59] Cromwell also struck fear into the inhabitants of Edinburgh who began to move their possessions north of the Firth of Forth for safekeeping. The kirk responded to the invasion by assuring its parishioners that the nation was being unfairly targeted, that it was Cromwell who was in the wrong because he was breaking the Covenant.[60] The kirk was quick to state that it was an 'unwarrantable war, and hath not its rise from the spirit of truth and consolation, and is not grounded upon the Word of God'. In short, for Scottish Presbyterians, Cromwell was a man who had started an unnecessary and illegal war in conflict with the mutual union between the two countries established by the Solemn League and Covenant. Like their brethren in Ireland, the Scots thought that Cromwell had been sent to test their faith. They pledged to stand by their faith regardless of the 'trials' and tribulations which he and his sectaries as instruments of God's wrath would pour on them. Cromwell 'unjustly' persecuted those who adhered to the Covenants, trying to prise people away from a faith that had been divinely established for the people of Scotland. Furthermore, Cromwell had taken the Covenant himself, and was therefore still bound to defend and protect the Scottish Presbyterian faith. In the eyes of the covenanters, Cromwell and his army were overconfident and arrogant men who believed that they could achieve 'immunity from death and hell, from the overflowing scourge, by success and prevailing in all their unrighteous undertakings'.[61]

The kirk, assured of its godliness through its adherence to the Covenant, hoped that Cromwell would be punished by God for his over inflated ego. Their reaction to Cromwell's success at the decisive battle of Dunbar in September 1650 was therefore one of complete despair. It was now clear that God had sent Cromwell not merely as an unwelcome irritant to the godly of Scotland, but as a severe instrument of punishment for all their sins, and after Dunbar God had allowed the English to run amok throughout the land. The Scottish nation was being gradually enclosed by the English army and landlocked, hemmed in for divine punishment. This explains the reactions of ordinary Scottish people. Upon hearing of Cromwell's arrival in Edinburgh immediately after Dunbar, many of the inhabitants fled for fear of complying with the enemy. Compliance was a sin in the

eyes of the kirk, which would provoke wrath from the Lord.[62] In
October 1650 Patrick Oliphant was hauled before the Synod of Perth
and Stirling on the grounds that he had offered Cromwell 'conditions' when he was taken prisoner after the battle. He was eventually
cleared of these allegations.[63] John Nicoll, a Scottish diarist record-
ing Cromwell's campaign in Scotland, recognised that the conquest
was not just a military offensive but a war of intelligence. There were
also rumours circulating that Cromwell had been offering money in
exchange for intelligence about the Scottish army which 'did corrupt
many'.[64]

Defeat at Dunbar also had the effect of widening the existing divisions within the Scottish kirk. The resolutioners, who comprised the
majority of the kirk, believed that the defeat was a sign from God and
as a result they should allow the royalist engagers back into the army
to fight for the king. On the other hand the rival faction, known as
the protesters, believed the defeat had revealed God's wrath that the
army was not 'godly' enough. Cromwell was astute enough to realise
that he could take advantage of these divisions. His efforts concentrated on the west of Scotland where the more extreme protesters
decided against a purge of the main army and raised a separate army,
filling it with those whom they considered to be godly. Cromwell
hoped that because of their distance from the main body of the kirk,
they would join him.[65] In January 1651 Oliver Cromwell invited
John Livingstone, protester minister of Ancrum, for discussions at
Cromwell's quarters in Edinburgh. Livingstone politely declined the
offer, believing that God was still present in Scotland and that his
conscience dictated that he should stay with his congregation rather
than get involved in politics.[66] For Livingstone, the Covenant was
still in force and he was bound to look after God's people. Cromwell
came to Glasgow in April 1651 to have discussions with the more
'godly' ministers. On hearing of Cromwell's arrival, John Spreul, the
town clerk, resolved to avoid the debates between Cromwell and the
kirk over religion, and keep his own company instead.[67] Nevertheless, Cromwell attended church services in Glasgow. One eyewitness,
Gabriel Semple, a young entrant to the ministry, saw Cromwell at
church and described him as very grave and reverent, listening politely
whilst James Durham prayed for the king. According to Semple,
Durham prayed for Charles 'to make him so good, that he might
stop the mouth of his enemies'.[68] A week later, Cromwell entered
into a religious conference with ministers in Glasgow. One of the
main points of the dispute was the validity of the English conquest

of Scotland, and in particular the state of the union between the two nations. Patrick Gillespie and James Guthrie, prominent members of the protesting party in the west, argued that invading Scotland was contrary to the Solemn League and Covenant. Cromwell's officers replied that parliament had dissolved the Covenant between the two nations, but the ministers were adamant that the Covenant was inviolable as long as there was one Englishman and one Scotsman alive.[69] For all ministers the debates were something they did not instigate, did not want to take part in and did not want to continue: but they could not be avoided.[70]

Upon his return from Glasgow, Cromwell had discussions with Wariston regarding the return of the Scottish registers. During these discussions, the two men also debated the legality of the invasion of Scotland. Cromwell believed that the invasion was justified on the grounds that it was similar to the Scottish entry into England in 1640. Wariston vehemently denied this and stated that the Scottish army had crossed the border only on the grounds of self-defence. In 1640 England had already been aggressive towards Scotland by refusing to negotiate, imprisoning their representatives and raising an army, which at that time was already on the march to attack them. This was in direct contrast to the Cromwellian invasion of 1650, which was an act of pure aggression for 'we had not done all these previous things against them'.[71] Ironically, the following summer saw a Scottish army again cross the border into England, only to be crushed at Worcester on 3 September 1651. In the months that followed, the defeated Charles II fled into exile in Europe, the Scottish government dissolved itself, and the English parliament formally incorporated the Scottish kingdom into their new republican state.

## V

The political incorporation of Scotland was outwardly successful, with the majority of burghs and shires assenting (however reluctantly) to the union; to uphold the pretence of legality, Scots were even allowed to sit in the English parliament. In 1653 Oliver Cromwell issued invitations to two different Presbyterians, Sir James Hope and Alexander Brodie, to take up seats in the Barebone's Parliament. In May 1653 Brodie was courted by the English government in Edinburgh, making him feel extremely uncomfortable, as he was determined to avoid employment under the regime. For Brodie, changes in civil government were the result of 'sin and much guiltiness' in Scotland and he feared that such changes would inevitably lead to corruption in religion. When he received his summons to go to London, Brodie went into a period of religious reflection, believing the invitation to be a 'snare' to test his faith. He eventually decided that he could not accept the invitation because the English were destroying religion and he questioned the legitimacy of the English government in Scotland.[72] In contrast, Sir James Hope quickly accepted his invitation to sit in the Barebone's Parliament. As Arthur Williamson has argued, Hope realised that Charles II could not fulfil the pledges in the Covenant and therefore concluded that constructing a union between England and Scotland under Cromwell was better for the godly in both countries because they would eventually unite.

Oddly, Sir James Hope's comments on Oliver Cromwell came in the form of a dream at the end of 1652. In this dream Cromwell was lying in a bed ill and very weak, and Hope told him that expectations regarding union had not been fulfilled. Following on from this, Cromwell's head appeared to Hope on a plate, or table, dripping in blood and after this he saw Cromwell and his officers in a room dressed in black. Hope and his brothers followed them downstairs to church, holding a candle to light the way, and, upon getting to the 'close head', Cromwell vanished. At that moment, Hope saw many people joyfully on their way to church holding candles. Arthur Williamson believes the dream was optimistic, showing that despite the darkness the Scottish people would be saved, but perhaps more plausibly it reveals Hope's doubts over Anglo-Scottish union. Cromwell was a weak man, not one of conviction; he would not create the union between the two nations that Hope had envisaged. The image of Cromwell dripping in blood perhaps reflected a deep-seated fear that if the godly in both nations were not united there would be no lasting peace. Cromwell's disappearance before they reached the church perhaps mirrors the Presbyterian view that Cromwell had no interest in Presbyterianism and the Covenants, regardless of Hope and the godly people of Scotland lighting the way. Dreams are difficult to read, and this interpretation can hardly be substantiated with any firm evidence, but we do know that Hope had pinned his dreams on a union between the godly of both nations. Later on he fell out with Cromwell over the dissolution of the Barebone's Parliament, his dreams had been torn to shreds and his doubts had become reality.[73]

The declaration of Oliver Cromwell as lord protector in December 1653 was a non-event in Scotland. The sombre atmosphere of the occasion may have reflected the fact that Scotland was still a nation under captivity and suffering. This can also be seen in a sermon given by a protester minister in the same year, taking as his text Isaiah 57 v.13. God was angry, punishing people for their sins; the destruction of the Lord's ordinances had brought down Charles I as it had the kings of Judea in the Old Testament; but like the Israelites, God would promise his people deliverance from captivity; the Cromwellian invasion was a punishment for tolerating royalist malignants in the armies of Charles II.[74] Another minister, Robert Law (who was entered by the protesters to his charge), commented:

> Oliver Cromwell the general of the English forces makes himself protector over Britain and Ireland Anno 1652, summons parliaments to sit and dissolve them at pleasure, and in a word ruled with absolute power and authority than ever any king before him did.[75]

This passage, written later, and obviously inaccurate in its dating of events, nevertheless encapsulates how the kirk as a whole regarded Cromwell's authority over the three kingdoms. As William Row, resolutioner minister of Ceres, acknowledged, Cromwell had power and authority through the military might he had exerted over the Rump Parliament.[76] If we contrast Cromwell's position with the Presbyterian ideal of a 'covenanted monarch', it is obvious that Cromwell had no cultural, traditional or legal claims or constraints on his power in Scotland. For the resolutioner faction in the kirk, Cromwell was not the 'natural' sovereign over the three kingdoms. The resolutioner position on Cromwell was also revealed in the form of Charles II's coronation at Scone in January 1651. Robert Douglas lectured Charles II on his responsibilities as a 'covenanted monarch', and his sermon outlined the power the king could exercise and its limitations. Charles II was crowned at Scone because he was the son and rightful heir to Charles I, from the ancient royal line, and his subjects had desired him to be crowned. This was contrasted with the 'unnatural' actions of the English in declaring a republic. Crowning Charles II meant that he and his subjects had renewed the Solemn League and Covenant with God. Charles was answerable to God and was bound to retain the Scottish Protestant religion as enshrined in Scottish law.[77] In contrast, Cromwell had no hereditary line from which he could claim power in Scotland and the Scottish people had not desired his authority over them.[78] He was not bound by Scottish law, nor traditional religious practice. Military force, not covenanted authority, was the root of the protector's power in Scotland.

## VI

In general, Cromwell's relationship with the Solemn League and Covenant and the Scottish Presbyterians goes far beyond a debate over toleration and Presbyterian bigotry. Looking at it from a covenanter perspective, Cromwell, initially an ally, became a troublemaker who destroyed the principles of unity and reformation that were integral to the success of the Solemn League and Covenant. By doing so Cromwell was destroying the aspirations of many godly Scots— indeed, he seemed to lack any cultural sensitivity and understanding of the Covenants or the Scottish reformation whatsoever. Furthermore, Cromwell was seen as a divine instrument to punish God's people. This is a world away from the image of God's Englishman, a man blessed by God fulfilling England's providential destiny. Within this context it is easy to see why Cromwell's authority was never truly recognised by the majority of Scottish Presbyterians. He was a man who had overturned the natural order in the three kingdoms and as such was considered a law unto himself, with his power resting only on the sword.

It is true that Cromwell and the Covenanters both saw God's Providence at work in their own actions. However, they interpreted Providence in very different ways. Cromwell's view of Providence was based upon his personal belief that he was an instrument of God— as proven by his military success in the 1640s and early 1650s and later by his political ascendancy, culminating in his investiture as protector in 1653. For the Scottish covenanters, however, providential success was based on their own achievements, firstly in creating the National Covenant of 1638 to defend the reformed religion against Charles I, and secondly in securing the divine and eternal Solemn League and Covenant between the English parliament and themselves in 1643. The political and military victories of the covenanting forces in Scotland, England and Ireland during the 1640s confirmed that the covenanters were instruments of God and doing God's work. Therefore, Cromwell's behaviour and his interpretation of Providence were completely alien to the covenanters, and many of the events that are often regarded as favourable and important in the life of Oliver Cromwell, such as the battle of Naseby in 1645, had little or no significance for the Scots. Other events, such as the defeat of the royalists in 1648, were significant for both, but for different reasons. For Cromwell, the battle of Preston was the confirmation of his status as an instrument of God, whilst for the covenanters it marked the renewal of co-operation between England and Scotland as envisaged in the Solemn League and Covenant. The Cromwellian victories at Drogheda and Dunbar were also interpreted in very different ways by the two parties. Despite their similar belief systems, Scottish Presbyterians could never recognise Cromwell as he saw himself, as a man doing God's work and an instrument of Providence. Indeed, for the most part they regarded Cromwell as the destroyer of God's work, who had wilfully tried to break the divine and eternal Solemn League and Covenant between the godly of the three kingdoms.

When Cromwell died on 3 September 1658, he was not mourned in Scotland, but it did not escape the notice of Presbyterians that his death came on the same date that God had visited his wrath upon the Scottish nation at Dunbar in 1650 and Worcester in 1651. William Row noted that it was divine Providence that had caused Cromwell to die on his own 'lucky day', that God had decided to call judgement upon him for his actions.[79] Wariston certainly saw Oliver Cromwell's death and the succession of Richard Cromwell as protector as a turning point—a sign that God was bringing about a major change of affairs in the three kingdoms. For him, it heralded the longed-for resurgence of the covenanted interest. He compared it to 1638, the year of the National Covenant, and 1645, the year of the victory at Philiphaugh and the total defeat of the royalists in Scotland. In September 1658 the signs were also good: the Scottish royalist interest was at its lowest ebb, and, with the death of Cromwell, the other main obstacle to the covenanted reformation had at last been removed.[80]

## Notes

1. *TSP*, i. 159–63.
2. Gardiner, *Constitutional Documents*, 267.
3. *TSP*, i. 159.
4. S. A. Burrell, 'The Covenant Idea as a Revolutionary Symbol: Scotland 1596–1637', *Church History*, 27 (1958), 338–49; A. H. Williamson, *Scottish National Consciousness in the Age of James VI: The Apocalypse, the Union and the Shaping of Scotland's Public Culture* (Edinburgh, 1979), 47, 64–85, 140–46, J. Morrill 'The National Covenant in its British Context', in Morrill (ed.), *The National Covenant in its British Context, 1638–51* (Edinburgh, 1990), 11; M. Steele, 'The Politick Christian':

The Theological Background to the National Covenant', in Morrill (ed.), *The National Covenant*, 38-41, 53-9.

5. A. I. Macinnes, *Charles I and the Making of the Covenanting Movement* (Edinburgh, 1991), 173-6.

6. D. Stevenson, *Scottish Covenanters and Irish Confederates: Scottish-Irish Relations in the Mid-Seventeenth Century* (Belfast, 1981), 43-119; E. M. Furgol, 'The Military and Ministers as Agents of Presbyterian Imperialism in England and Ireland 1640-48', in J. Dwyer, R. A. Mason and A. Murdoch (eds), *New Perspectives on the Politics and Culture of Early Modern Scotland* (Edinburgh, 1982), 95-115; M. Perceval-Maxwell, 'Ireland and Scotland, 1638-1648', in Morrill (ed.), *The National Covenant*, 193-209; R. Gillespie, 'An Army Sent from God: Scots at War in Ireland, 1642-1649', in N. MacDougall (ed.), *Scotland and War, AD 79-1918* (Edinburgh, 1991), 113-32; R. Armstrong, 'Ireland's Puritan Revolution? The Emergence of Ulster Presbyterianism Reconsidered', *EHR*, 121 (2006), 1048-74.

7. J. R. Young, 'The Covenanters and the Scottish Parliament, 1639-51: The Rule of the Godly and the Second Scots Reformation', in E. Boran and C. Gribben (eds), *Enforcing Reformation in Ireland and Scotland, 1550-1700* (Aldershot, 2006), 131-158.

8. E. Vallance, *Revolutionary England and the National Covenant: State Oaths, Protestantism and the Political Nation, 1553-1682* (Woodbridge, 2005), 100; E. Vallance ' "An Holy and Sacramentall Paction": Federal Theology and the Solemn League and Covenant in England', *EHR*, 116 (2001), 50-75.

9. C. Kellar, *Scotland, England and the Reformation, 1534-1561* (Oxford, 2003), 21-2, 29, 36-41, 78-107, 117-18, 149-50, 154-5, 176, 185-7, 204; A. H. Williamson, *Scottish National Consciousness*, 3, 11-14, 20, 33, 35, 68.

10. Gardiner, *Constitutional Documents*, 270.

11. D. Laing (ed.), *The Letters and Journals of Robert Baillie, A.M. Principal of the University of Glasgow M.DC.XXXVII–M.DC.LXII* (Edinburgh, 1841), ii. 198-9, 265, 307, 318; D. Stevenson, 'The Early Covenanters and the Federal Union of Britain', in R. Mason (ed.), *Scotland and England, 1286-1815* (Edinburgh, 1987), 163-4; D. Stevenson, *The Scottish Revolution, 1637-44: The Triumph of the Covenanters* (Newton Abbott, 1973), 285-8.

12. D. Stevenson, *Scottish Revolution*, 276-98; D. Stevenson, *Revolution and Counter Revolution, 1644-51* (1977), 3-4; A. I. Macinnes, *The British Revolution, 1629-1660* (2005), 148-66.

13. M. Bennett, *Oliver Cromwell* (Abingdon, 2006), 75; Davis, *Cromwell*, 198; D. Stevenson, 'Cromwell, Scotland and Ireland', in J. Morrill (ed.), *Oliver Cromwell and the English Revolution* (Harlow, 1990), 149-55, 158-61, 163-66.

14. Abbott, ii. 303.
15. See, in particular, D. Stevenson, 'Cromwell, Scotland and Ireland', passim.
16. *CSPD 1644*, 17–295, *CJ*, iii. 503–4; A. Marshall, *Oliver Cromwell Soldier: The Military Life of a Revolutionary at War* (2004), 103–9.
17. *ODNB*, 'Sir John Meldrum'.
18. Abbott, i. 240–6; *ODNB*, 'Edward Whalley'.
19. This is difficult to confirm because another account of the skirmish, this time by Lucy Hutchinson, describes the significant activities of the Nottingham forces and she praises Colonel Francis Thornhagh, a good friend of John Hutchinson, for his actions. She does not, however, discuss the actions of Meldrum that day nor single him out for special praise. Therefore, Cromwell's accounts of the skirmish may be personal, but this does not necessarily indicate any animosity towards Sir John Meldrum or his nationality (see N. H. Keeble (ed.), *Memoirs of the Life of Colonel Hutchinson with a Fragment of Autobiography* (1995), 114–15, 348).
20. D. Masson and J. Bruce (eds), *The Quarrel between the Earl of Manchester and Oliver Cromwell: An Episode of the English Civil War* (1875), 59.
21. H. W. Meikle (ed.), *Correspondence of the Scots Commissioners in London 1644–1646* (Edinburgh, 1917), 9.
22. Laing, *Letters and Journals*, ii. 153.
23. *A Briefe Relation of the Siege of Newark, as it Was Delivered to the Councel of State at Derby-House by Lieutenant Col. Bury* (1644), 4.
24. Coward, *Cromwell*, 33.
25. Marshall, *Oliver Cromwell Soldier*, 118–20.
26. *The Glorious and Miraculous Battell at York* (Edinburgh, 1644), 1.
27. J. Maidment (ed.), *Historical Fragments Relative to Scottish Affairs from 1635 to 1664* (Edinburgh, 1833), ii. 62–3.
28. T. Hope, *A Diary of Public Correspondence of Sir Thomas Hope of Craighall, 1633–1645* (Edinburgh, 1843), 207.
29. W. Stevenson (ed.), *The Presbytrie Booke of Kirkcaldie* (Kirkcaldy, 1900), 272; J. Stuart (ed.) *The Presbytery Book of Strathbogie* (Aberdeen, 1843), 59.
30. Laing, *Letters and Journals*, ii. 203.
31. Laing, *Letters and Journals*, ii. 203; Masson and Bruce, *Quarrel*, xiv.
32. Macinnes, *British Revolution*, 164.
33. Masson and Bruce, *Quarrel*, 59–70.
34. Meikle, *Correspondence*, 44–5.
35. Laing, *Letters and Journals*, ii. 225–32.
36. Meikle, *Correspondence*, 51–2.
37. Gardiner, *Constitutional Documents*, 269.
38. Macinnes, *British Revolution*, 167.
39. Meikle, *Correspondence*, 53–64.

40. Ibid., 75.
41. Stevenson, *Presbytery of Kirkcaldy*, 286–7; Stuart, *Presbytery of Strathbogie*, 63.
42. W. Lithgow, *A True Experimentall and Exact Relation upon that Famous and Renowned Siege of Newcastle* (Edinburgh, 1645), 1–16.
43. D. Buchannan, *A Short and True Relation of Some Main Passages of Some Things, Wherein the Scots are Particularly Concerned* (1645), 2–104.
44. A. F. Mitchell and J. Christie (eds), *The Records of the Commissions of the General Assembly 1648–9* (Edinburgh, 1896), 66.
45. T. McCrie (ed.), *The Life of Mr Robert Blair Minister of St Andrews* (Edinburgh, 1848), 204.
46. McCrie, *Life of Robert Blair*, 296; Stevenson, *Revolution and Counter Revolution*, 81–95; *A Great Victorie Obtained in the Kingdome of Scotland* (1648), 1.
47. *The Transactions of Severall Matters Between Lieut: Gen. Cromwell and the Scots* (1648), 13–15.
48. *Transactions of Severall Matters*, 16.
49. *A Letter Sent from Lieutenant General Cromwell to the Marquis of Argyll* (1648), 1–6.
50. *A True Account of the Great Expressions of Love from Noblemen, Ministers and Commons of the Kingdom of Scotland unto Lieutenant General Cromwell, and the Soldiers and Officers under his Command* (1648), 3–8.
51. McCrie, *Life of Robert Blair*, 210.
52. Macinnes, *British Revolution*, 193–205.
53. P. Adair, *A True Narrative of the Rise and Progress of the Presbyterian Church in Ireland* (Belfast, 1866), 174.
54. Abbott, ii. 127.
55. NLS, Wodrow Folio xxv (i), no. 59; 'The Presbytery of Bangor in Ireland to Mr Robert Douglas, 1649', fo. 114; R. Armstrong, 'Viscount Ards and the Presbytery: Politics and Religion among the Scots of Ulster in the 1640s', in J. R. Young and W. P. Kelly (eds), *Scotland and the Ulster Plantation: Explorations in the Scottish Settlement of Ulster* (Dublin, forthcoming). I am indebted to Dr Robert Armstrong for allowing me to consult a copy of his chapter before publication.
56. Adair, *True Narrative*, 174; *Articles of Peace Made and Concluded with the Irish Rebels, and Papists, by James Earle of Ormond*, 44–5.
57. *Articles of Peace*, 41–3.
58. B. Whitelocke, *Memorials of English Affairs* (Oxford, 1853), iii. 213.
59. D. Hay Fleming (ed.) *Diary of Archibald Johnston of Wariston ii* (Edinburgh, 1919), 6–10.
60. D. Laing (ed.), *A Diary of Public Transactions and Other Occurrences, Chiefly in Scotland from January 1650 to June 1667* (Edinburgh, 1836), 19.

61. A. F. Mitchell and J. Christie (eds), *The Records of the Commissioners of the General Assemblies of the Church of Scotland . . . 1650, 1652* (Edinburgh, 1909).
62. Laing, *Diary of Public Transactions*, 30–1.
63. NAS, CH2/449/1 (Synod of Perth and Stirling 1639–1661), fos. 130, 151.
64. Laing, *Diary of Public Transactions*, 27–8.
65. D. Stevenson, *The Covenanters and the Western Association, 1648–1650* (Ayr, 1985), 149–186.
66. J. Nickoll (ed.), *Original Letters and Papers of State Addressed to Oliver Cromwell* (1743), 46.
67. Maidment, *Historical Fragments*, i. 9–10.
68. NLS, MS 5746 (autobiography of Gabriel Semple minister of Jedburgh), 184–5.
69. NLS, MS 5746, p. 185
70. Laing, *Letters and Journals*, iii. 166.
71. *Diary of Archibald Johnston of Wariston* ii. 47–8; Bennett, *Oliver Cromwell*, 190.
72. D. Laing (ed.), *The Diary of Alexander Brodie of Brodie* (Aberdeen, 1863), 41–67.
73. A. H. Williamson, 'Union with England Traditional, Union with England Radical: Sir James Hope and the Mid-Seventeenth Century British State', *EHR*, 110 (1995), 303–22; J. Balfour Paul, 'The Diary of Sir James Hope 1646–1654' (*Miscellany* iii, Scottish History Society Edinburgh, 1919), 153–4.
74. New College Edinburgh, Ers 14 (Sermons preached by Mr James Erskine and Mr John Carstairs Anno 1653), 13–29.
75. C. Kirkpatrick Sharpe (ed.), *Memorialls: Or the Memorable Things that Fell Out within this Island of Brittian from 1638 to 1684* (Edinburgh, 1818), 6; H. Scott (ed.), *Fasti Ecclesiae Scoticanae*, iii. 355.
76. McCrie, *Life of Robert Blair*, 305.
77. Robert Douglas, *The Form and Order of the Coronation of Charles the Second, King of Scotland, England, France and Ireland* (Aberdeen, 1651), 1–39.
78. Cf. L. Bowen, 'Oliver Cromwell (*alias* Williams) and Wales' (below, Chapter 7).
79. McCrie, *Life of Robert Blair*, 335; Laing, *Diary of Public Transactions*, 217.
80. J. D. Ogilvie (ed.), *Diary of Archibald Johnston of Wariston* iii. (Edinburgh, 1940), 102.

# 7

# Oliver Cromwell
# (*alias* Williams) and Wales

Lloyd Bowen

---

Oliver Cromwell was 'God's Englishman', and his stature as an English national hero has remained largely untarnished since the nineteenth century. Yet he also had important links with Wales which have been almost completely ignored in both popular and academic literature.[1] This chapter teases out some implications of these neglected intersections of Cromwell's life with Wales and ideas of Welshness. It does not, however, argue for any intense 'special relationship' between Cromwell and the principality. He rarely mentioned Wales in his letters and speeches, and only (briefly) visited the principality twice: in the spring of 1648 when he journeyed through south Wales to suppress the royalist risings in Pembrokeshire, and again in July/August 1649 while *en route* to Ireland. Nevertheless, his particular interest in religious reform in the principality constitutes an important running thread through Cromwell's political career from his emergence in the House of Commons in the early 1640s to his rule as lord protector. It will be suggested here that the degree to which his Welsh ancestry remained significant throughout his life has been rather overlooked, and that this background may help us understand the interest Cromwell took in the moral and spiritual reformation of Wales in general, and his sponsorship of puritans in south east Wales in particular. It is also often forgotten that Cromwell became a major landholder in Monmouthshire and Glamorgan after 1648, and this chapter will discuss how his possession of these lands throws up some intriguing continuities with his sponsorship of further reformation in Wales in 1642. It will also be argued that Cromwell had ties with a small band of Welsh radicals from the early 1640s, and that these, and Walter Cradock in particular, became key pillars of Cromwellian policy in Wales. Furthermore, his leading Welsh counsellor, Colonel Philip Jones, was the primary conduit through which Cromwell perceived and understood Wales, especially during the protectorate, and this had significant ramifications for policy in the region.

# I

Cromwell was descended from south Walian stock, a fact which is sometimes cursorily acknowledged in accounts of his life before the narrative moves quickly on to his emergence from East Anglian obscurity. Commentators who discuss his Welsh roots often indulge in pseudo-biological determinism in an attempt to explain aspects of his enigmatic character. C. V. Wedgwood believed that Cromwell's Welsh background offset his East Anglian stolidity, endowing him with 'a fanaticism, a vision, a hidden fire, blazing out suddenly to consume all opponents', adding, 'these and perhaps other less admirable qualities of the Welshman are to be found in him'.[2] Even S. R. Gardiner was not immune to such conjecture, wondering whether this 'Welsh strain' showed itself in the 'fervid idealism lighting up the stern practical sense of the warrior and statesman'.[3] More often than not (perhaps thankfully given this kind of speculation) most commentators have been inclined to dismiss Cromwell's Welsh blood as of no consequence. The most vociferous was Thomas Carlyle, who observed 'Facts, even trifling facts, when indisputable may have significance; but Welsh pedigrees... are highly unsatisfactory to the ingenuous mind!'[4] His dismissal of pedigree and Cromwell's Welsh roots may have been over-hasty, however, for we shall see that when Cromwell represented himself through the personal-political symbology of seals and shields, his Welsh ancestry took centre stage.

As Sir Geoffrey Elton observed, it was 'by the merest whisker' that England did not have a Lord Protector Williams'.[5] This was because on the spear-side Cromwell was descended from Morgan Williams, a modest freeholder who hailed from Whitchurch near Cardiff in Glamorgan. Morgan married Katherine, sister of Henry VIII's chief minister, Thomas Cromwell, and his son, Richard, adopted a composite surname to emphasise his associations, styling himself 'Richard Williams alias Cromwell'.[6] The family moved to

Putney, Surrey and thence to Hinchingbrooke, Huntingdonshire, where Richard purchased a considerable amount of ex-monastic land. A pedigree commissioned in 1602 by the protector's grandfather traced the family line back through many generations to Gwaethfoed, a key symbolic figure in the history of Glamorgan and Monmouthshire, as well as Gloddian, prince of Powys.[7] The young Cromwell would have seen evidence of the family's Welsh past at his grandfather's imposing house at Hinchingbrooke, where the windows and heraldic masonry incorporated the quarterings of Gloddian as well as those of Mathiaid of Morgannwg (Glamorgan) and Ynyr, king of Gwent (Monmouthshire), whose line reputedly married into that of Gwaethfoed.[8] These were figures from the distant, and often imaginative, Welsh past, which were used as vehicles in Welsh heraldry and genealogy to claim regal blood and the gentle status.[9] Such ancient noble stock was an essential element in the Welsh conception of gentility: *bonedd* or *uchelwriaeth*.[10]

The Huntingdonshire Cromwells maintained a presence in Glamorgan long after their migration east, as Richard Williams had acquired the lands of the dissolved monastery of Neath, which descended to his second son, Francis Cromwell alias Williams of Hemingford Grange. Francis was enclosing land in Cadoxton-juxta-Neath as late as 1582.[11] There were also several other families of Welsh descent in Cromwell's Huntingdonshire who may have served to remind him of his background, including the Williamses of Alconbury, the Herberts of Covington and the Turbervilles of Graffham.[12] Indeed, his uncle Henry was brought before the court of Star Chamber in 1620 for seeking violently to rescue one Simon Aprice (ap Rice) from the custody of the sheriff.[13] The Aprice family may well have come from Wales with the Cromwells, and one is found litigating over property in Hemingford Grey in Elizabeth's reign.[14]

Cromwell was clearly aware of his descent from Welsh stock which claimed some very elevated ancestry. The intimate presence of this Welsh context in his early life is suggested by the bond ensuring the conveyance of Elizabeth Bourchier's jointure which Cromwell entered into before their marriage in August 1620. Here he is described as 'Oliv. Cromwell alias Williams, of Huntingdon'.[15] Similarly, in a deed of October 1631 in which Henry Cromwell of Ramsey granted him the reversion of the manor of Upwood, the future protector was described as 'Oliver Williams, al[ias] Cromwell of Huntingdon', although he signed his name as simply 'Oliver Cromwell'.[16] His acknowledgement of his status as a Williams as well as a Cromwell is also reflected in a letter of 1 September 1647 to John Williams, archbishop of York, regarding the army's 'uttermost' endeavours to 'settle the affairs of north Wales'. A response to a lost letter from Williams, Cromwell assures the archbishop that he will provide a welcome for the individual mentioned in the earlier missive and 'study to serve him for kindred's sake'.[17] Carlyle saw his claim of kinship as a piece of facetious jesting.[18] There is nothing in the letter to suggest this, however, and we should be moved to take this assertion of association as a Williams a little more seriously. Contemporaries were certainly aware of Cromwell's Welsh ancestry. One panegyric written shortly after his death recalled that he was 'descended from the ancient and illustrious family of the Williams's of the county of Glamorgan'.[19] The royalist Richard Symonds observed that 'Cromwell alias Williams his name is', although we might perhaps be rather more wary of Symonds' claim that he used this descent to trace his lineage back to the royal impersonator and would-be usurper, Perkin Warbeck.[20]

The intersection of Cromwell's Welsh background and his political persona is most clearly evident in the symbolism with which he surrounded himself as protector. The Williams coat of arms, *sable a lion rampant argent*, was integrated prominently into the iconography of the protectorate. The protectoral arms incorporated a shield with quarterings of flags representing England, Scotland and Ireland (Wales, having no distinct constitutional identity, could not be represented in this way), but at its centre—the escutcheon-of-pretence—was the silver lion, coat of Caredig, lord of Powys.[21] It is also worth noting that the protectoral arms possessed the crowned lion and dragon supporters of the Welsh Tudor dynasty, and we might recall here that William ap Evan, father of the man who married into the Cromwells, was a servant of Jasper Tudor, lord of Glamorgan and Abergavenny (Monmouthshire), and uncle of Henry VII.[22] The iconographic face of the Cromwellian protectorate, then, was one which recalled Welsh associations and Cromwell's ties with the ancient ruling houses of Wales. Cromwell's heraldic symbols were much in evidence at his lying-in-state and funeral (organised by a Glamorgan man, Colonel Philip Jones). The funeral procession which worked its way through the capital on 23 November 1658 possessed an imposing array of heraldic and political iconography on the escutcheons, banners and flags accompanying the hearse. Significantly, these included the standards of Ynyr (king of Gwentland), Iestyn ap Gwrgant (last native ruler of Glamorgan), the red dragon of Cadwalladr (introduced

into monarchical iconography by Henry VII) and the Welsh arms
of Cynfrig Sais. Also present were flags recalling the marriage of
Cromwell's Glamorgan ancestor, Morgan ap Howell, with Joan,
daughter of Thomas Button of Dyffryn in the county, and another
commemorating the union of Morgan's son, Evan, with Margaret,
daughter of Jenkin Kemeys of Cefn Mabli, Glamorgan.[23] A contemporary publication included a picture of Cromwell's lying-in-state,
and informed the reader that this was 'Oliver Cromwell...born at
Huntington, of the name Williams of Glamorgan and by K[ing]
H[enry] 8 changed into Cromwell'.[24]

It is possible that Cromwell reached back into the mythologies of
Welsh kings when he assumed the protectorship in order to assert
his regal lineage and capacities for personal rule. It is striking that
only days after he became protector, Cromwell produced a personal seal, the most intimate symbol of his authority and legitimacy,
which reflected this Welsh ancestry, incorporating the quarterings of
Madoc ap Meredith (prince of Powys), Iestyn ap Gwrgant (prince
of Glamorgan), Collwyn ap Tangno (a dark age lord of Eifionydd
and Ardudwy in north Wales) and Caradoc Freichfras (son of Ynyr
and a sixth-century king of Gwent).[25] Although Cromwell is often
presented as eschewing pedigree and birth in favour of the qualities
of piety and godliness, we must remember that his persona, particularly under the protectorate, was closely tied up with the imagery
of descent and the visual presentation of authority through a system of heraldic devices which would have made an impression on
the both the lettered and the illiterate. As Sean Kelsey has observed,
'early modern England's political landscape was mapped by a system
of signs and symbols which represented authority', and the representation of Cromwell's personal power was refracted through symbols
of Welshness.[26] As a man of modest birth, it is intriguing to see
Cromwell reach for the eminence which his Welsh ancestry might
bestow. In his often-quoted speech to the first protectorate parliament
in September 1654, Cromwell acknowledged that his beginnings
were unexceptional, but emphasised 'I was by birth a gentleman',
something which demanded ancestry as well as money, land and
gentle deportment.[27] Many in England would have thought his dubious Welsh connections of little value, which makes it all the more
interesting that Cromwell's personal iconography touched upon these
elements. At some level, it seems, Cromwell thought of himself as
Welsh, and his claim of kinship with Archbishop John Williams was
not as facetious as Carlyle believed.

Cromwell's Welsh background did not go unnoticed in Wales. Perhaps the most arresting discussion came in a publication of 1657/8 by Thomas Pugh: *Brittish and Out-landish Prophecies*. This rather bizarre volume looked to reconfigure the myths of ancient British history which had been used to legitimate the rule of the Tudors and Stuarts by tracing their bloodlines to the rulers of pre-Roman Britain. These myths had been especially important in Wales, whose inhabitants claimed to be the descendants of the original Britons. The prophetic elements of this 'British History' had supported the claim of Henry Tudor to the throne, and, although discredited in many circles, it continued to provide an important rallying point for Welsh allegiance to the Stuarts.[28] The British myths, often based on the writings of Geoffrey of Monmouth in the twelfth century, had foretold that a descendant of these ancient British rulers would return to claim their inheritance. This provided for a good deal of speculation by Welsh bards and poets who singled out various candidates that might fulfil this role—the *mab darogan*, or 'son of prophecy'.[29] Pugh twisted these prophecies to demonstrate that 'by his lineal descent from the ancient princes of Britain', Cromwell was 'the conqueror . . . so long prophesied of'.[30] He focused on Cromwell's descent from the princes of Powis to cast him in the role of the fabled deliverer of the Britons—Powis was to be found at the centre of the protectorate arms.[31]

It is uncertain whether such material had much purchase among the people, let alone with Cromwell himself. In December 1657, the Essex clergyman Ralph Josselin reported that he had seen the publication, but concluded this 'book of prophecies giveth me no satisfaction, but perhaps may set men a gadding to greaten him [Cromwell]'.[32] The Wrexham-based mystic Morgan Llwyd observed in 1655 that 'there hath been an old prophecy of him [Cromwell], that he should proceed to be emperor of the north of Europe: yet he himself doth not over-heed prophecies'.[33] Llwyd's comments, however, remind us that Cromwell's associations with the Welsh tied him to ideas of British history and future British empires which had lost a good deal of their lustre, but certainly had not disappeared by the 1650s.[34]

Quite apart from Pugh's fatidic flights of fancy, there were others in Wales who saw Cromwell's Welsh background as something more concrete and politically significant, perceiving it as a potential means of leverage, a point of access for lobbying. John Lewis of Glasgrug, Cardiganshire, published his *Seasonal and Modest Thoughts* on promoting religion in Wales in 1656, and observed in his dedication to Cromwell that the country could 'lay a British claim unto you'.[35] In July 1657, one of Lewis's correspondents, John Ellis of Dolgellau, Merioneth, discussed a long-cherished scheme for establishing a national college in Wales for training ministers and promoting godliness. He was concerned that Oxford and Cambridge might try to block the plans, but was persuaded that Cromwell would be receptive if the backing of some 'powerful agents' could be secured, and that the protector would bestow a substantial sum on the project, 'he being descended, as they say, from Wales'.[36] Cromwell was indeed fired by advancing the condition of the godly in Wales, but whether this was a product of his Welsh roots must remain conjectural. Nevertheless, it is interesting to observe that both Ellis and Lewis believed his Welshness was an opening that potentially could be exploited for promoting godliness in the country, and it is to Cromwell's involvement in this cause that we now turn.

## II

The puritan interest in Wales before the civil war was small, embattled and restricted largely to enclaves in the north east and south east of the country. The core of Welsh nonconformity was to be found in the first gathered church at Llanfaches, Monmouthshire, under its charismatic leader, William Wroth. Wroth established his separate church according to the 'New England way' around 1638. His associate at Llanfaches was Walter Cradock, a curate at Cardiff who had been suspended for nonconformity in the 1630s. Llanfaches formed the nucleus of a tight-knit group of radicals who faced considerable resistance from the religiously conservative majority in Wales before 1640. The key animating force behind the godly cause in Wales in this period was Sir Robert Harley of Brampton Bryan, Herefordshire. In the 1630s Harley had formed close ties with leading nonconformist figures like Cradock and Morgan Llwyd, providing a protective umbrella for their activities at places like Llanfair Waterdine, and forming what Geoffrey Nuttall has described as the 'Brampton Bryan enclave' in the Welsh marches.[37]

As with the other puritans persecuted and marginalised by Charles I's personal rule, the calling of the Long Parliament presented the small band of Welsh nonconformists with an electrifying opportunity for reform and redress. This compact group sought to keep

Wales's lamentable spiritual condition before the eyes of parliament through a petitioning campaign organised largely by Harley. In December 1640, William Erbery, ex-minister of Cardiff and associate of the Llanfaches congregation, presented a petition to the House of Commons decrying the lamentable spiritual condition of Wales and attacking the corrupt and indolent pastorate there. He called for the Commons to 'give liberty to those who are willing and honest... to preach in any parish where there is want of preaching', and to allow parishioners to hear godly preaching outside their own parishes.[38] In January 1641, the Commons gave authority to a closely associated group of Erbery himself, Walter Cradock, Henry Walter, Ambrose Mostyn and Richard Symonds, to preach throughout Wales. Walter and Symonds hailed from Monmouthshire, while Mostyn was from north Wales, but was associated with Harley, Llwyd, Cradock and Erbery, and thus probably also the Llanfaches church.[39] Keen to keep Welsh religious reform on the agenda and contribute to the momentum of the 'root and branch' campaign, a much larger petition was presented to the Commons on behalf of the Welsh radicals on 16 February 1641.[40] Sponsored by Wroth, Cradock, Erbery, Symonds, Walter, Mostyn and Robert Hart of Moccas, Herefordshire, it rounded on the ecclesiastical hierarchy, lamented at the protection which was being given to papists in places like Monmouthshire, and requested support for encouraging preaching in the principality. It also possessed the subscription of over 300 individuals who appear to have comprehended the Llanfaches congregation, but also included radicals from the England–Wales border area like John Browne of Little Ness, Shropshire, and John James of Leintwaterdine, Herefordshire, both of whom went on to sit in the Barebone's Parliament of 1653.[41]

The lobbying efforts of the Welsh puritans were supported, and perhaps even orchestrated, by the long-time sponsor of religious reform in Wales, Sir Robert Harley. Many of the key figures had ties with Harley, and the copy of the February 1641 petition is to be found among his papers. In June 1641, it was Harley who presented a petition from Walter Cradock and Henry Walter complaining of their molestation by magistrates in south Wales when they had attempted to preach.[42] A letter of July 1641 from Oliver Thomas of West Felton (Shropshire) to Harley requested further efforts in supporting the Welsh cause so that 'Wales's spiritual misery be the object of parliamentary mercy'.[43] However, on 7 February 1642, something rather odd happened. At this point, the member for Cambridge, Oliver

Cromwell, presented a petition to the Commons from individuals in Monmouthshire who were being harassed by the authorities for gadding to sermons.[44] One of those named was Edward Hollister, a subscriber to the Welsh anti-episcopal petition of February 1641. On 29 March Cromwell then presented a certificate from Richard Symonds and 'three other ministers of Monmouthshire' which communicated their fears about the strength of popery in the vicinity of Monmouth town.[45] Although the identity of the 'three other ministers' is not specified, it seems likely that they were Walter Cradock and Henry Walter, who were active in south-east Wales around this time, while the remaining minister was probably William Erbery. Cromwell was again in evidence as Commons spokesman for the puritan cause in Wales on 24 May 1642, when he presented a petition from the godly parishioners of Pennard on the Gower peninsula (Glamorgan) against their vicar, William Edwards.[46] This parish had recently petitioned parliament through Denzil Holles to complain about Edwards' ministry, and to request that Ambrose Mostyn be instituted as a lecturer, which had been ordered.[47]

Why was Cromwell sponsoring the Welsh puritan cause? How had he come into contact with these figures? The evidence is lacking to provide definitive answers, but it is probably significant that Cromwell had been involved with Harley in drafting of the 'root and branch' bill for abolishing episcopacy.[48] It is possible that Harley recommended the Welsh cause to Cromwell, or that he put men like Symonds in touch with the Cambridge member. The fact that Cromwell's godly vision was more radical and thoroughgoing than Harley's and meshed more harmoniously with the rabidly anti-episcopalian stance of the Welsh puritans is also significant. Cromwell revealed in parliament that Richard Symonds' petition regarding the popish threat in Monmouthshire had been directed to himself, Sir Arthur Hesilrige and John Pym, all prominent 'root and branch' supporters whose anti-episcopalian credentials were probably known to the Welsh puritans. The original of Symonds' certificate is endorsed 'sent to Mr Cromwell', which indicates that direct ties had been established between Cromwell and the cadre of Monmouthshire puritans.[49] On 18 February 1642, Pym presented a petition that Richard Symonds be placed as lecturer in Andover, Hampshire.[50] Denzil Holles, who originally introduced the Pennard petition against William Edwards, was also a forthright root and brancher. What appears to be happening here, then, is a shifting of focus by the leaders of the Welsh puritan cause away from the comparatively moderate Harley and towards

more radical spokesmen in the increasingly febrile atmosphere of early
1642. Among these radicals was Cromwell himself, a man who was
already gaining a reputation as a militant puritan activist.[51]

The context of Catholicism in Monmouthshire is important for
understanding Cromwell's involvement in 1642. The Monmouthshire
petitions he introduced were formulated against a backdrop of divisions within the county over the influence of recusants in local
government and a deep anxiety over control of the county magazine by Catholics.[52] It is probably not coincidental that on both
7 February and 29 March, Cromwell's presentation of messages from
the Monmouthshire puritans followed discussion of the county magazine, which was seen to be under the malign influence of the
Catholic earl of Worcester.[53] Cromwell's enthusiasm for discovering and frustrating the designs of Catholics provides an important
motivation for his interventions. An added ingredient to the mix
may have been the role of Philip Herbert, earl of Pembroke, who
had a significant landed presence in Monmouthshire and a history
of opposing Worcester. On the day that Cromwell presented the
petition from Edward Hollister and others concerning their persecution for gadding to sermons, Pembroke's son, Philip Herbert,
delivered another petition requesting the removal of the magazine
from Monmouth, where it was under the influence of Worcester, to
Newport, a Pembroke borough.[54] A degree of co-ordination was also
in evidence on 29 March, when another of Pembroke's sons, William
Herbert, member for Monmouthshire, discussed the recalcitrance of
the Monmouth authorities and submitted a list of papists living near
the town. He was followed immediately by Cromwell, who presented
Symonds' certificate.[55] Pembroke did not share Cromwell's fiery anti-
episcopalianism, but did have a commitment to godly Protestantism,
and these episodes indicate an operational alliance between the two
on the sponsorship of Welsh puritanism and opposition to the earl of
Worcester.

In the early 1640s, Cromwell was one of those fired by the prospect
of creating a principality where the truth of God's Word would
triumph over the profane corruption of a people who seemed half-
reformed, suffering under the twin evils of a negligent pastorate and
widespread Catholic influence. His knowledge of the harsh treatment
meted out to godly ministers like Symonds and the royalist disaffection which swelled out of Worcester's Monmouthshire in 1642,
helped colour his view of the Welsh and the remedial measures they
required in the years to come.

**III**

After 1642, the dreams of the reformers in Wales were shattered by the outbreak of war and the dominant royalism which isolated the principality from parliamentary policy for four years. Stephen Roberts has shown that as the war progressed the model of itinerant preaching in Wales, endorsed by the House of Commons in 1641–1642, became an important principle for the Independent faction of which Cromwell was a key member.[56] There is, then, an important line of continuity from Cromwell's activity on behalf of the Welsh puritans in 1642 down to his support for the commission for the propagation of the gospel in Wales established in 1650. However, Cromwell was not the guiding force behind the commission, it was his close associate, Major-General Thomas Harrison, who sponsored the initiative in the Rump Parliament. The two had worked together previously on Welsh religious matters, having been appointed in May 1649 to a committee considering a petition from the 'well-affected' of Anglesey, who complained about the lack of preaching on the island and the power of malignant gentry and clergy there.[57] Harrison, along with Cromwell's ally, Colonel Philip Jones, were prominent members of the committee established on 20 December 1649 to consider another petition from Independents in north Wales which called for an act to address grievances in the principality—this was the seed which brought forth the propagation commission the following February.[58] Also on this committee was Sir Arthur Hesilrige, another Cromwell ally who had also been involved with the Monmouthshire puritans in 1642, and who was to be the guiding hand behind the commission for propagating the gospel in the four northern counties of England. Hesilrige also had connections with Welsh puritans like John Lewis of Cardiganshire, which stretched back to the mid-1640s.[59] Cromwell was not active in drawing-up the propagation act in early 1650, however, as by this time he was campaigning in Ireland.

Although we possess little direct evidence of Cromwell's involvement with the propagation commission, it is clear that it was one of the initiatives closest to his heart. This can be seen in his reaction to the Rump Parliament's refusal to continue the commission after its term of three years had expired. The hostility towards the scheme among sections of the Rump arose from fears about the commission's infiltration by sectaries and radicals, its inability to replace the ministers it ejected with such enthusiasm and continuing allegations of corruption and peculation levelled against its agents, particularly

Philip Jones. Cromwell viewed the unwillingness of the Rump to support the mission of evangelisation in Wales as a sign that the parliament had lost its way and could no longer be seen as God's agent for reforming the republic. Shortly after expelling the Rump in April 1653, Cromwell wrote to the Welsh propagation commissioners, addressing them as 'my loving friends'. He asked them to 'go on cheerfully in the work as formerly . . . and put in execution the things settled by former acts and ordinances in that behalf'.[60] The commissioners did indeed continue to act on the authority of this letter alone until the establishment of the protectoral 'triers' and 'ejectors' a year later.[61] The letter is eloquent testimony of his support for the propagation scheme and his continuing attention to the plight of further reform in Wales.

Cromwell's gravitating towards figures like Thomas Harrison and the calling of the Barebone's Parliament in the summer of 1653 were impelled in part by the zealous fire of religious enthusiasm lit by the propagators in Wales, and of their abandonment by the Rump. In one passage of his speech at the opening of the Barebone's Parliament, Cromwell provided his most detailed commentary on Wales which throws some informative light on his sense of the importance of the propagation commission, and also of Wales's position in his vision of the spiritual well-being of the commonwealth. Referring to the failures of the Rump and 'trials' such as the 'case of Wales', he confessed that this was a business 'I set myself upon'. He recalled bitterly how the Rump 'threw that business underfoot to the discountenancing of the honest people', and concluded that this was, for himself and other officers, 'as perfect a trial of their spirits, as anything, it being known to many of us that God kindles a seed there, indeed hardly to be paralleled since the primitive time'.[62] Clearly, then, Wales presented a trial of faith and commitment for Cromwell and officers like Harrison. Particularly striking here is Cromwell's commitment to nurturing the imperilled 'seed' of true reformation in such hostile territory. His language recalls that of his closest Welsh clerical associate, Walter Cradock, who had made an impassioned plea to the Commons in 1648 for ministers to be sent into Wales to nurture the 'glorious work' already in train. He informed them that 'the gospel is run over the mountains between Brecknockshire and Monmouthshire as fire in the thatch'.[63]

Some of Cromwell's enthusiasm for the mission to evangelise Wales may have resulted from his visits to south Wales in 1648 and 1649. One commentator before Pembroke Castle in June 1648 recorded that Cromwell considered the 'natives of Wales' to be 'but a seduced ignorant people'.[64] One is reminded here of Cromwell's language when discussing the Irish in 1649–1650, although he evidently viewed the Welsh as wayward brethren to be brought back into the fold while the Irish were treacherous and incorrigible papists requiring much sharper correction. The relationship between Welsh religious ignorance and their political disaffection was plain enough in the explosion of anti-puritan sentiment which energised the large-scale risings in south Wales during the second civil war. Cromwell linked the religious and political disaffection of the Welsh again in 1654 during negotiations over the deployment of the armed forces during the first protectorate parliament. Concerning the garrisoning of Hereford, Cromwell observed that it lay close to north and south Wales, 'those mountainous countries which he feared had not forgot their mountainous qualities, and for religion and other things not so well qualified as would be desired. The countries and people there were not so well affected as he could wish.'[65] Religious and political reform in Wales were different sides of the same coin, and Cromwell's consistent support for the puritan mission there is linked to his awareness of the central role played by south Wales in the royalist mobilisations of 1642 and 1648, and of Wales's potential to destabilise his vision of a new Jerusalem. Wales could be a thorn in the side of any godly republic unless the cause of God was protected and supported there, and this may help explain his willingness to go out on a limb for the propagation commission in 1653.

## IV

Cromwell's connection with Wales, and with the south east especially, had been strengthened in March 1648 when a grateful parliament granted him large tracts of lands from the sequestered estates of the earl of Worcester. These were concentrated in Monmouthshire and the area around Swansea in west Glamorgan.[66] (Map 7.1). In Monmouthshire, Cromwell acquired a fairly compact bloc of estates in the south-east of the county bordering Gloucestershire, incorporating the manors of Chepstow, Magor, Redwick and Barton and Hardwick, along with Chepstow town and the tithes of Magor and Hardwick. The manors were valued at £465 per annum by the Monmouthshire committee in 1648 and the tolls and customs of Chepstow town, which was also granted to him, added £50. Cromwell also leased Rogerstone Grange in St Arvans in the county

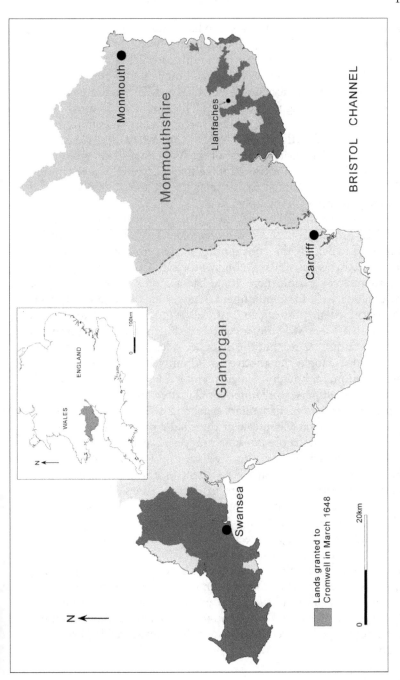

*Map 7.1* **Cromwell's Welsh estates** (this work is based on data provided through EDINA UKBORDERS with the support of the ESRC and JISC and uses Kain and Oliver historic boundary material which is copyright of the AHDS History [University of Essex], Humphrey Southall, Nick Burton and the University of Portsmouth)

for at least one year from 1648, which was valued at £200 per annum.[67] In west Glamorgan, Cromwell effectively seized control over the entirety of the Gower peninsula, acquiring the manors of Gower Anglicana and Gower Wallicana, Lougher, Oystermouth, Pennard (with Kittle, Lunnon and Trewyddfa) and Kilvey, along with the seat of the Gower seignory, Swansea. The Gower lands were valued at £672 per annum in 1648, while a survey Cromwell commissioned in 1650 provided a figure of £480.[68] This means that Cromwell's claim in May 1648 that the total of the Worcester grant was £1680 per annum looks much more plausible than Clement Walker's hostile assertion that it amounted to between £5000 and £6000 a year on account of being 'so favourably rated'.[69]

Whatever the value of the grant, it is clear that throughout the period of propagation and the protectorate Cromwell was a major Welsh landowner. He does not appear to have administered his Gower lands directly, as his chief Welsh counsellor, Colonel Philip Jones, oversaw most operations here. Jones had acquired the stewardship of Gower along with his appointment as governor of Swansea in 1645, and continued in post after Cromwell acquired the estates.[70] It is possible that Jones was also involved in the running of Cromwell's Monmouthshire estates, but the evidence is less conclusive.[71] It is difficult to disentangle the motives of Cromwell and Jones in estate administration, although a later memoir suggests that Cromwell involved himself personally in teneurial matters in Monmouthshire.[72] Moreover, during a parliamentary debate in 1654, Cromwell resisted placing a garrison at Chepstow at the charge of the state 'because it was his own house', a phrase which suggests a personal interest.[73] In any event, Jones toed the Cromwellian line in practically all matters, and we should perhaps view them as a Cromwell–Jones axis working in partnership on estate matters in Wales. The 1648 land grant gave Cromwell a more immediate presence in the principality, and offered him a base from which earlier impulses of puritanisation could be sustained. Indeed, it may be more than coincidence that he acquired these lands from the earl of Worcester, the *bête noire* of Monmouthshire puritans, whose reputation for supporting popery attracted Cromwell's attention in 1642. It is possible that parliament granted him the Worcester property in Monmouthshire and Glamorgan with a view to combating Catholicism and encouraging his acknowledged interest in godliness here through his position as landlord.

There are some suggestions of this in scraps of manorial evidence which indicate that Cromwell (perhaps through Jones) was employing men with a reputation for godliness on his estates; men who had been involved with the propagation commission and even the puritan petitions of 1641–1642. For example, in June 1655 Cromwell's stewards on his manor of Barton, Monmouthshire, were William Blethin of Dinham near Chepstow and Edward Herbert of Moor Grange (Merthyr Geryn), Magor.[74] Both had been propagation commissioners and were dedicated Independents. Herbert was member for the county in the second protectorate parliament and a loyal Cromwellian, who was described after the Restoration as 'Cromwell's right hand, [and] was talked of for a knighthood'.[75] In 1651, Cromwell leased some land in Magor to Herbert, who also purchased the manor of Undy from Colonel Philip Jones, selling him in exchange manors in west Glamorgan which he had acquired in 1648.[76] The other steward, William Blethin, was a long-time opponent of Worcester, an associate of the Llanfaches gathered church and a subscriber to the Welsh anti-episcopal petition of February 1641. He also became a sequestration commissioner in the county and farmed the tithes of Undy—the manor purchased by his fellow steward.[77] The recorder of the manors (and steward on Cromwell's Gloucestershire manor of Tydenham, also acquired from Worcester) was Captain John Nicholas of Trellech, a man who described himself as Cromwell's 'most faithful servant'.[78] Yet another propagation commissioner, Nicholas was also Cromwell's trusted associate in south Wales during the military campaigns of 1648, and was appointed governor of Cromwell's borough of Chepstow, which had rebelled against its master during the second civil war.[79] As a lieutenant-colonel, Nicholas was made deputy major-general to James Berry in 1655, and sat alongside Edward Herbert as member for Monmouthshire in the 1656 parliament.[80] In June 1655, Nicholas and his company offered a declaration of loyalty to Cromwell after the royalist disturbances of the spring.[81] Cromwell leased property in Chepstow to Nicholas in 1657.[82] Nicholas, Blethin and Herbert's names were grouped together at the beginning of the lists of signatories to Walter Cradock's pro-protectorate manifesto, *A Humble Representation and Address*, providing a graphic illustration of the network of reliable associates and ex-propagators which the protector was employing on his Welsh estates.[83]

Some further detail on Cromwell's activities as landlord in Monmouthshire comes from an account published in the eighteenth century which was directed principally against the duke of Beaufort's enclosure schemes in Wentwood Chase. This records that Cromwell's tenants had complained to his 'agents' about the manner in which Worcester's earlier enclosures of Wentwood Forest had violated their ancient privileges. The story ran that Cromwell maintained the enclosure of Chepstow Park but allowed free access to the other parts of his estate. The narrator mentions that the tenants' complaints were communicated to Cromwell by two 'agents' on his Monmouthshire lands, 'Major Blethin' and 'Colonel Rogers'.[84] The first named was Francis Blethin, brother of the aforementioned William, and a man who had been commissioned as captain of foot in the New Model Army.[85] His regiment was placed under Cromwell's command in 1645, so he was possibly acquainted personally with the lord protector. He later served under Colonel Philip Jones in south Wales, and was described by an opponent in 1651 as one of Jones's 'creatures'.[86] Francis Blethin was made lieutenant in the new Monmouthshire militia troop raised in 1656 under the command of John Nicholas.[87] He was also a sequestrator and justice of the peace who assisted Walter Cradock in dealing with Quakers.[88] The other individual was Colonel Wroth Rogers, father of the account's author, Nathan, and a radical Independent of Herefordshire who sat in Barebone's Parliament. Interestingly, Wroth had been a captain alongside Francis Blethin in the same regiment of the New Model. Rogers was a native of Llanfaches, and had witnessed the will of William Wroth, after whom he had probably been named.[89] Like so many of the Cromwellian establishment in south east Wales, then, he also had close links with the first generation of Welsh puritans who had found an early parliamentary sponsor in the future protector during the early months of the Long Parliament. However, he also represents the radicalisation of the Welsh puritan cause from 1642, which saw the godly lobbyists turn to Independent figures like Cromwell rather than their old sponsor, Sir Robert Harley. The events of the late 1640s had seen radicals like Rogers oust the Presbyterian Harley in Herefordshire politics.[90] Unlike Harleian moderates, Rogers supported the Independents' project of propagation, and, as with William Blethin, Edward Herbert and John Nicholas, had himself been a propagation commissioner.

These were clearly members of a compact group in south east Wales which supported the commonwealth and protectorate regimes. Crucially, they all remained vitally concerned with the religious complexion of the area, and, apart from Rogers, were named as commissioners for ejecting scandalous ministers in Monmouthshire in

August 1654.[91] In many respects, then, the propagators so cherished by Cromwell continued to be the state's religious police in protectorate Monmouthshire. From this snapshot, it seems that Cromwell's manorial officers in Monmouthshire were chosen because they shared his vision of radical godly reform in this dark corner of the land. It does not seem to be stretching the evidence too far to suggest that Cromwell envisioned his Welsh estates as providing another method of supporting the saints, acting as a godly core for assisting the righteous and eradicating the notorious poison of popery from places such as Monmouthshire, an objective of his which had been evident as early as 1642.

Cromwell's holding of manors on Gower is also suggestive of some continuities reaching back to 1642, when he had acted as spokesman for the puritans of Pennard against their minister. Pennard was a Worcester possession, placing the parishioners and their landlord at opposite ends of the religious spectrum. Pennard was also one of those manors granted to Cromwell in 1648.[92] One of the Pennard petitioners in 1642 was Rowland Dawkins, who became an ally of Cromwell, brother-in-law to Philip Jones, and John Nicholas' co-deputy-major-general in 1655. Philip Jones himself was a native of Llangyfelach, near Swansea, and entertained Cromwell at his home as the lord general moved to reduce Pembroke in May 1648. On account of his association with parliamentarian Independents and his intimacy with Cromwell, Jones's influence in this area became enormous in the 1650s. It was later observed that Jones was 'the chief' in managing the affairs of the deanery of Gower, with Dawkins and John Bowen of Swansea under him, and a collection of 'understrappers' supervising everyday business such as the collection of tithes.[93] John Bowen was Cromwell's steward on his manor of Gower Anglicana by 1657.[94] Another member of this closely knit group, Evan Lewis of Neath, also acted as one of Cromwell's estate officers in Gower.[95] A lieutenant in Philip Jones's regiment, Lewis married into the family of the religious radical, John Price of Gellihir, becoming Philip Jones's brother-in-law. Lewis was appointed as one of the ejectors of south Wales in 1654, and sat for Breconshire in the 1656 parliament, a return engineered by Jones.[96] As in Monmouthshire, Cromwell relied heavily on propagation personnel to administer his estates, as Bowen had acted as treasurer for the propagation commissioners in south Wales.[97] Stephen Roberts has argued that through channels such as Bowen, Lewis, Dawkins and Jones, Gower became an exemplar

of a diverse Cromwellian religious establishment, incorporating the
Baptists of Ilston alongside 'violent' Presbyterians like Moore Pye.[98]

Perhaps because of ancestral associations and his early connections
with the cradle of Welsh nonconformity, however, it seems that Monmouthshire was the area of Wales which principally held Cromwell's
attention. There are indications of this in his public offices. Cromwell
appeared on the commission of the peace for Monmouthshire in
1649, a time when the only other jurisdiction for which he stood
as JP was the Isle of Ely.[99] He was appointed *custos rotulorum* between
1650 and 1653 in only four jurisdictions, the Isle of Ely, Huntingdonshire, Buckinghamshire and Monmouthshire. His son Richard
was elected to parliament for Monmouthshire in 1654 (although he
chose to sit for Hampshire). Monmouthshire's parliamentary representation in the interregnum parliaments also reflects Cromwellian
interests there. In addition to his son, the county elected his main
Welsh counsellor, Philip Jones twice (although he was also elected for
Glamorgan in 1654 and sat for this county), his local stewards, John
Nicholas (who also sat for the county in 1659) and Edward Herbert, and the steward (and later master) of the protectoral household,
Nathaniel Waterhouse, who also represented Monmouth boroughs in
Richard Cromwell's parliament.

## V

It was in Monmouthshire that the image of the reformed Welshman
was being refashioned in the period after the end of civil war, and
particularly important in this regard was Walter Cradock, the man
who assumed the leadership of the Llanfaches community after the
death of William Wroth in 1641, and who was almost certainly one
of the harassed ministers presented to the House of Commons by
Cromwell in February 1642. Cradock became one of Cromwell's
chaplains and preached before the protector in 1654 and 1655.[100]
He shared Cromwell's antiformalist views in religion, stating that
'Presbytery and Independency are not two religions but one religion to a godly heart; it is only a little rustling at the fringe'.[101] In
1652, Cradock could address Cromwell in effusive terms, requesting offices for two associates, one of whom was his son-in-law and
intimate of Thomas Harrison, Richard Creed.[102] Five months after
this, Cromwell himself nominated Cradock to a lectureship in New-
land, a few miles outside of Monmouth, and put him forward for the
lectureship of Monmouth itself in 1657.[103] The first-named itinerant
minister in the propagation act, Cradock did not share the millennial

excesses of men like Vavasor Powell, the Fifth Monarchist firebrand whose role in the propagation commission helped saddle it with a reputation for sectarian radicalism. Cradock was much more supportive of a state-funded ministry and became the fulcrum for Cromwellian religious policy in south Wales. He was only one of two Welshman (the other was Jenkin Griffiths) to be appointed as commissioners for the approbation of public preachers in March 1654, and was named one of the 'ejectors' in Monmouthshire (along with Henry Walter) and in south Wales later in the year.[104] In an account of Quaker sufferings published in 1659, Francis Gawler referred to Cradock as the 'chiefest priest in south Wales'.[105] His status as the main bulwark of the Cromwellian settlement in Wales was exemplified by his organisation of the *Humble Representation* which he presented personally to Cromwell in February 1656.[106] In this answer to Vavasor Powell's bitter personal attack on Cromwell, *A Word for God*, Cradock rallied an impressive roll-call of loyal Cromwellians to assure the protector that the 'poor saints of Wales who were so much your joy' had not 'degenerated' from their former allegiance like Powell's Fifth Monarchist radicals.[107] Of the Welsh saints, Cradock probably best embodied Cromwell's policy of seeking a radical advancement of the godly cause which did not shade into millennial immoderation, alongside a commitment to a state-funded national ministry.

In terms of religious policy in Wales, Cradock appears to have been a likely man to whom Cromwell turned for advice. His central figure of counsel and advice on Welsh matters more generally during the 1650s, however, was Colonel Philip Jones. Jones's leading role in the sequestration of large amounts of tithe money as a prominent propagator, and his rapid accumulation of wealth from very modest beginnings, led to charges of embezzlement and peculation which appear to have had solid foundations. One hostile commentator wondered whether Jones ought to be made 'chief alchemist of these nations, since he can get an estate out of nothing'.[108] As well as cash and estates, Jones also amassed offices and influence in south Wales. This advancement in the provinces was accompanied by, and was in many ways dependent upon, his elevation at the centre, with Cromwell appointing him to the protectoral council in 1653, the Other House in 1657 and the comptrollership of his household the same year. Jones's pre-eminence produced resentment in Wales, and he was vilified in 1659 as 'the chief and only man to recommend and bring in person to all places of authority, profit or trust, ecclesiastical, military or civil in south Wales [having] . . . the chief governance and superintendency of all public affairs in south Wales'.[109]

Such local power brings into relief the question of how far Lord Protector Cromwell viewed Wales through spectacles provided by Jones, Cradock and their allies. This was a complaint raised by contemporaries. The ejected minister Alexander Griffiths complained to Cromwell in 1654 that he needed to inform him of the misdeeds of the propagators in order to represent Wales's 'sad spiritual condition before your Christian eyes, who (perhaps) have not had as yet a full discovery thereof'.[110] John Lewis, a Cardiganshire Presbyterian, informs us in 1656 that he had tried to present a critique of the propagators to Cromwell, but that some 'eminent countrymen' around the protector, almost certainly Jones, had prevented him.[111] The small constituency of republicans and puritans in royalist Wales meant that the interregnum regimes here rested on a thin substratum of support. Cromwell's reliance on counsellors like Jones and Cradock partly explains how he winked at the excesses of the propagation commission. It helps us understand how the questionable basis of Jones's wealth and power in Wales never led to his fall from Cromwell's inner circle. These were the instruments of God's work in that benighted country, but because of them, Cromwell himself saw Wales through a glass darkly.

## VI

Cromwell did not have a specific policy for Wales over and above his consistent concern to cherish the cause of godliness in the land of his fathers. When Cromwell thought of Wales, he thought of the Welsh saints, 'the poor people of God' as he called them, and of a long-cherished project for evangelising this dark country through a core of believers centred in the south east.[112] Although neither the originator nor principal patron of the radical schemes for reshaping the religious landscape of the principality in the 1640s and 1650s, he was an important supporter of the cause throughout his public life. In no small measure because of his efforts, nonconformity made huge strides in mid-seventeenth century Wales, especially in the south where enduring cells of dissent were established in areas which previously had little in the way of a puritan tradition. Historians have not appreciated Cromwell's consistent interest in the godly cause in Wales, a cause which may have connections with his ancestral association with the crucible of Welsh nonconformity in the south east of the country. The campaign of evangelisation in Wales during the 1650s faced huge obstacles, not least because of the resentment and alienation caused by the zeal of the propagators and the meagre abilities of some itinerants. That the rule of the protector in Wales continued to rest on the shoulders of former propagation personnel, as exemplified by his own manorial officers in Monmouthshire and on the Gower, was a serious obstacle to reconciling traditional communities with his rule.[113] In moderate and Anglican circles, Cromwell was always linked with mechanic itinerant preachers, the indiscriminate ejection of worthy ministers and the military oppression of men like Philip Jones. Although some puritans like John Lewis and John Ellis had looked to trade on Cromwell's Welsh background to advance their own causes in the principality, for a large section of the population in this religiously conservative corner of Britain, 'Usurper Cromwell' was no true Welshman. For them the legitimising blood of the Welsh ran in the veins of the Stuarts, and it was Charles II who 'brought the bones of Cadwalladr home' in 1660.[114]

## Notes

1. An exception is S. Roberts, *Oliver Cromwell, Englishman and Welshman: His Image among His Contemporaries* (University of Birmingham Institute for Advanced Research in the Humanities, Occasional Paper no. 13, 1995).
2. C. V. Wedgewood, *Oliver Cromwell* (1939), 16.
3. S. R. Gardiner, *Oliver Cromwell* (1900), 2; cf. A. Fraser, *Cromwell Our Chief of Men* (1973), 8; Abbott, i. 39.
4. T. Carlyle, *Oliver Cromwell's Letters and Speeches* (3rd edn. 1849), i. 26.
5. G. R. Elton, *Studies in Tudor and Stuart Politics and Government, IV* (Cambridge, 1992), 90.
6. S. T. Bindoff (ed.), *The History of Parliament: House of Commons, 1509–1558* (1982), i. 734–5.
7. BL, Harl. MS 1174, fo. 152v; M. Noble, *Memoirs of the Protectoral House of Cromwell* (Birmingham, 1787), i. 1–2; cf. J. A. Bradney (ed.), *Llyfr Baglan . . . compiled between . . . 1600 and 1607 by John Williams* (1910), 125–8; G. T. Clark, *Limbus Patrum, Morganiae et Glamorganiae* (1886), 4–5; 'Dryasdust', 'The ancestry of Cromwell', *Notes and Queries*, 2nd series, 11 (1861), 184–5.
8. Noble, *Memoirs*, i. 245–8.
9. On this, see M. P. Siddons, *The Development of Welsh Heraldry* (Aberystwyth, 4 vols., 1999–2007); F. Jones, 'An Approach to Welsh Genealogy', *Transactions of the Honourable Society of Cymmrodorion* (1949 for 1948), 303–466.

10. J. Gwynfor Jones, *Concepts of Order and Gentility in Wales, 1540–1640* (Llandysul, 1992).
11. TNA, STAC 5/C3/37; STAC 5/C61/16; TNA, C3/31/31; C3/186/6; C3/196/8; West Glamorgan Archive Service, NAS D1/2/11, 13, 18.
12. H. Ellis (ed.), *The Visitation of the County of Huntingdon... 1613* (Camden Soc., 43, 1849), 17, 20, 57.
13. TNA, STAC 8/101/11.
14. W. Page, G. Proby and S. Inskipp Ladds (eds), *The Victoria County History of the County of Huntingdonshire* (3 vols., 1926–36), ii. 312–13.
15. Noble, *Memoirs*, i. 124.
16. BL, Add. Charter 53668.
17. Abbott, i. 501.
18. Carlyle, *Letters and Speeches*, i. 256.
19. S. Carrington, *The History of the Life... of... Oliver, Late Lord Protector* (1659), 3.
20. F. Madden, 'Cromwelliana', *Notes and Queries*, 2nd ser., 7 (1859), 141.
21. For an illustration, see the reproduction of the reverse of the protectorate great seal in G. Vertue, *Medals, Coins, Great Seals, and Other Works of Thomas Simon* (1780), plate XVIII.
22. Bradney, *Llyfr Baglan*, 128.
23. Noble, *Memoirs*, i. 281–3; Bradney, *Llyfr Baglan*, 127; H. M. Vaughan, 'Oliver Cromwell in South Wales, 1648–9, A Retrospect', *Transactions of the Honourable Society of Cymmrodorion* (1937 for 1936), 44 and plate facing.
24. *Some Farther Intelligence of the Affairs of England. The Death of the Renowned Oliver, Lord Protector of England, Scotland, and Ireland* (1659), plate facing 9.
25. Fraser, *Cromwell*, 457.
26. S. Kelsey, *Inventing a Republic* (Manchester, 1997), 86.
27. Abbott, iii. 452.
28. S. T. Bindoff, 'The Stuarts and Their Style', *EHR*, 60 (1945), 192–216; L. Bowen, *The Politics of the Principality: Wales, c.1603–1642* (Cardiff, 2007), 70–3, 235–61.
29. G. Williams, 'Prophecy, Poetry and Politics in Medieval and Tudor Wales', in his *Religion, Language and Nationality in Wales* (Cardiff, 1979), 71–86.
30. T. Pugh, *Brittish and Out-landish Prophecies* (1658), title page.
31. Ibid., 152–3.
32. A. MacFarlane (ed.), *The Diary of Ralph Josselin, 1616–1683* (1976), 412.
33. J. H. Davies and T. E. Ellis (eds), *Gweithiau Morgan Llwyd* (2 vols., Bangor, 1899–1908), ii. 221.

34. G. A. Williams, 'Welsh Wizard and British Empire: Dr John Dee and a Welsh Identity', in his *The Welsh in their History* (1982), 13–30; D. Armitage, 'The Cromwellian Protectorate and the Languages of Empire', *HJ*, 35 (1992), 531–55.

35. J. Lewis, *Some Seasonable and Modest Thoughts* (1656), epistle dedicatory.

36. G. F. Nuttall, 'The Correspondence of John Lewis, Glasgrug, with Richard Baxter and with Dr John Ellis, Dolgelley', *Journal of the Merioneth Historical and Record Society*, 2 (1953–6), 132.

37. G. F. Nuttall, *The Welsh Saints, 1640–1660* (Cardiff, 1957).

38. BL, Harl. MS 4,931, fo. 90.

39. See entries for Walter and Symonds in the *ODNB*. For Mostyn see L. Bowen, 'Wales and Religious Reform in the Long Parliament, 1640–42', *Transactions of the Honourable Society of Cymmrodorion*, new series, 12 (2006), 43, and H. Jessey, *The Exceeding Riches of Grace Advanced* (7th edn. 1658), 8.

40. BL, Add. MS 70, 109, no. 69.

41. Bowen, 'Wales and Religious Reform', 45–50.

42. *CJ*, ii. 189; BL, Harl. MS 163, fo. 354v; Harl. MS 479, fo. 1v.

43. BL, Add. MS 70, 106, fo. 155.

44. *PJ*, ii. 302–3; *CJ*, ii. 419.

45. *PJ*, ii. 104.

46. *PJ*, ii. 368; *CJ*, ii. 586.

47. *PJ*, ii. 253; *CJ*, ii. 551; Parliamentary Archives, HL/PO/JO/10/1/120 (30 April 1642).

48. J. S. A. Adamson, 'Oliver Cromwell and the Long Parliament', in J. Morrill (ed.), *Oliver Cromwell and the English Revolution* (Harlow, 1990), 53.

49. Bodl., MS Dep. C.168, no. 175.

50. *PJ*, i. 411; *CJ*, ii. 440.

51. Cromwell was also associated with a group of godly peers which included Robert Greville, Lord Brooke, who bemoaned the lack of adequate ministers in Wales in 1641: Lord Brooke, *A Discourse Opening the Nature of Episcopacy* (1641), 112.

52. L. Bowen, 'Wales in British Politics, *c*.1603–42' (University of Cardiff, Ph.D. thesis, 2000), 492–504.

53. *CJ*, ii. 415; *PJ*, i. 294.

54. *PJ*, i. 294; *CJ*, ii. 415.

55. *PJ*, ii. 103–4. The list of recusants can be found in Parliamentary Archives, HL/PO/JO/10/1/75.

56. S. Roberts, 'Propagating the Gospel in Wales: The Making of the 1650 Act', *Transactions of the Honourable Society of Cymmrodorion*, new series, 10 (2004 for 2003), 57–75.

57. *CJ*, vi. 220; NLW, Llanfair Brynodol MS P505; J. G. Ballinger (ed.), *Calendar of Wynn (of Gwydir) Papers* (Cardiff, 1926), 312–13.

58. *Severall Proceedings in Parliament*, no. 12 (14–21 December 1649), 149; *CJ*, vi. 336.

59. J. Lewis, *Some Seasonable and Modest Thoughts* (2nd edn. 1659), epistle dedicatory.

60. Abbott, iii. 13.

61. *The Distressed Oppressed Condition of the Inhabitants of South Wales* (?1659), 2.

62. I. Roots (ed.), *Speeches of Oliver Cromwell* (1989), 15–16.

63. W. Cradock, *Glad Tydings from Heaven, To the Worst Sinners on Earth* (1648), 50.

64. W. S., *Exceeding Good News from Wales* (1648), 3.

65. *Burton Diary*, i. xcii.

66. *LJ*, x. 100, 104–5; Gloucestershire Archives, D2700/QA5/1/3, 5, 8; TNA, SP23/118/973; D. Farr, 'Oliver Cromwell and a 1647 case in Chancery', *Hist. Res.*, 71 (1998), 342.

67. TNA, SP23/118/971–4.

68. J. A. Bradney (ed.), *A History of Monmouthshire* (4 vols., 1904–33), ii. 21; C. Baker and G. G. Francis (eds), *Surveys of Gower and Kilvey* (1870), 94.

69. Abbott, i. 587–8; C. Walker, *Walker's Anarchia Anglicana, or, The History of Independency* (1648), 83; S. Roberts, 'The Wealth of Oliver Cromwell', in Peter Gaunt (ed.), *Cromwell 400* (Brentwood, 1999), 87.

70. *CJ*, iv. 347.

71. One tract notes that he was only 'steward of *some* of the protector's lands in Wales': *The Mystery of the Good Old Cause Briefly Unfolded* (1660), 16.

72. N. Rogers, *Memoirs of Monmoth-shire* (1708), 104–5. See also an estreat of a small grant on the manor of Magor in January 1652 which Cromwell signed personally: NLW, Tredegar Park 59/7.

73. *Burton Diary*, i. xcii.

74. NLW, Badminton Manorial MS 2482.

75. *CSPD 1661–2*, 141.

76. Abbott. ii. 479–81; Bodl., Rawl. MS B238, fo. 21; A. G. Veysey, 'Colonel Philip Jones (1618–74)', *Transactions of the Honourable Society of Cymmrodorion* (1966), 336.

77. Bodl., MS Walker c.13, fo. 43; *CCC*, i. 727.

78. *TSP*, iii. 252; NLW, Badminton Manorial MSS 2531–2.

79. N. Key and J. Ward, 'Metropolitan Puritans and the Varieties of Godly Reform in Interregnum Monmouth', *Welsh History Review*, 22 (2004–5), 657; Abbott, iii. 614–16.

80. *CSPD 1655–6*, 102.

81. Bodl., Rawl. MS A27, fo. 684.

82. Cambridgeshire RO (Huntingdon), Bush MS 731/30.

83. *A Humble Representation and Address* (1656), 6. For Nicholas, Blethin and Herbert working together, see also F. Gawler, *A Record of Some Persecutions . . . South Wales* (1659), 6, 9, 13.

84. Rogers, *Memoirs of Monmoth-shire*, 104–5. See also TNA, C22/481/47 and C22/478/25 for references to Cromwell's administration of Chepstow lordship by his 'officers and agents'.

85. Bradney, *History of Monmouthshire*, iv. 151; R. K. G. Temple, 'The Original Officer List of the New Model Army', *Bulletin of the Institute of Historical Research*, 59 (1986), 61.

86. TNA, E121/3/5; *CCC*, i. 512.

87. TNA, SP25/77, p. 895.

88. Gawler, *A Record*, 24–6.

89. NLW, LL1641/40.

90. D. Underdown, *Pride's Purge* (Oxford, 1971), 179–80, 308, 311–12, 314–15, 353.

91. *A&O*, ii. 973.

92. His west Glamorgan estates comprised part of the jointure settlement of Elizabeth Russell at her marriage to Cromwell's son, Henry, in 1653. Henry administered the land after his father's death: Cambridgeshire RO (Huntingdon), Bush MSS 731/24–5, 29.

93. P. Jenkins (ed.), ' "The Sufferings of the Clergy": The Church in Glamorgan during the Interregnum. Part Three: The Account of Edward Mansell', *Journal of Welsh Ecclesiastical History*, 5 (1988), 76.

94. NLW, Badminton Manorial MS 2743, fos. 1, 5. He was described as an 'officer of the Lord General Cromwell' in Swansea in 1650, where he was made an alderman under the charter Cromwell granted in 1656: Baker and Francis, *Surveys of Gower*, 20; G. G. Francis, *Charters Granted to Swansea* (1867), 33. Cf. NLW, Penlle'r-gaer MSS B, 3/1, 13/10, 18/9.

95. TNA, PRO31/17/33, p. 71. I am very grateful to Patrick Little for this reference.

96. *A&O*, ii. 976.

97. TNA, E113/3; Bodl., MS Walker c.13, fos. 15–18.

98. S. Roberts, 'The Curious Case of Henry Bowen: or, the Gower Ghost of 1655 Exorcised'. I am very grateful to Dr Roberts for allowing me to read this important unpublished article.

99. TNA, C231/5, p. 304; J. R. S. Phillips, *The Justices of the Peace in Wales and Monmouthshire, 1541–1689* (Cardiff, 1975), 359.

100. Abbott, iii. 228, 668.

101. W. Cradock, *Gospel Libertie* (1648), 135.

102. J. Nickolls (ed.), *Original Letters and Papers of State* (1743), 85–6.

103. Key and Ward, 'Metropolitan Puritans', 658, 666.

104. *A&O*, ii. 856, 981, 984.

105. Gawler, *A Record*, 26.

106. *TSP*, iv. 531.

107. *Humble Representation*, 2.

108. *Fourty-Four Queries to the Life of Queen Dick* (1659), 5.

109. *Articles of Impeachment of Transcendent Crimes, Injuries, Misdemeanours, Oppressions and High Breach of Trust Committed by Col. Philip Jones, Exhibited by Mr Bledry Morgan* (1659), 3.

110. A. G[riffith], *A True and Perfect Relation...Concerning the Petition of the Six Counties of South Wales* (1654), sig. A2v.

111. Lewis, *Some Seasonable and Modest Thoughts*, sig. A2v.

112. Roots, *Speeches of Oliver Cromwell*, 15.

113. L. Bowen, 'Wales and the Protectorate', in P. Little (ed.), *The Cromwellian Protectorate* (Woodbridge, 2007), 144–64.

114. E. D. Jones, 'The Brogyntyn Welsh Manuscripts', *National Library of Wales Journal*, 8 (1953), 9.

# 8

# The Lord Protector and his Court

Andrew Barclay

Oliver Cromwell, Britain's archetypal republican, presided over a distinctly regal court. The tone for what would follow was set by his first inauguration as lord protector. On 16 December 1653, Cromwell went in procession by coach from the ex-royal palace of Whitehall to Westminster Hall, a building indelibly associated with royal ritual, the revered traditions of English law and, of course, the deposition of kings. In the preceding days, it had been agreed that, under the new Instrument of Government, 'the supreme legislative authority' was to 'reside in one person', the lord protector.[1] Cromwell was now to assume that office. In the court of chancery at the southern end of the hall, he listened as the Instrument was read out and then took his oath of office. 'His highness' was then invited to sit on a chair of state. The commissioners of the great seal presented him with that seal, while the lord mayor of London offered up to him the pearl sword of the city and the cap of maintenance.[2] This was not exactly a coronation, but, even so, there were some who did detect in it some obvious continuities. The Venetian secretary in England, Lorenzo Paulucci, who would have known a thing or two about republican styles of public ceremonial, thought that the homage was performed with 'the obsequious and respectful form observed towards the late kings'.[3] These monarchical overtones would be even more obvious at Cromwell's second inauguration. In the spring of 1657 parliament had attempted to persuade Cromwell to become king. While Cromwell had refused the title of king, he had given way to parliament's wish that he exercise the full powers of that position. This political compromise was now reflected in the enhanced ritual on 26 June 1657 for his re-inauguration. Once again the ceremony took place in Westminster Hall and, as before, the central act was the taking of the oath. But other elements in the ceremony reminded those present just how close Cromwell had come to being elevated to the kingship. He sat throughout on Edward I's coronation chair, he was invested with a robe of purple velvet and ermine, 'being the habit anciently used at the solemn investiture of princes', and he received his symbols of office, a Bible, a sword and a gold sceptre. Only a crown was missing.[4]

Grand public ceremonies on special occasions were one thing. What was just as telling was the manner in which Cromwell and his family lived after 1653. His court as lord protector—to some extent before 1657 but more especially thereafter—would display this same envious, begrudging respect for the traditions of the English monarchy. Paulucci was thus equally impressed by the more routine ceremonies of the protectoral court. After his first formal audience with the new lord protector in January 1654, he reported that Cromwell 'may be said to assume additional state and majesty daily, and lacks nothing of royalty but the name, which he is generally expected to assume when he wants to'.[5] After the Restoration attempts would be made to suggest that Cromwell's court had been a poor imitation of the real thing.[6] He was to be accused of improperly regal ambitions, while, at the same time, lacking the style needed to carry them off. The implied contrast was with Charles II, who was assumed, rather optimistically, to have the innate flair of one born to that role.[7] This however had not seemed quite so obvious while Cromwell had still ruled the three kingdoms.

This apparent paradox of Cromwell the republican monarch continues to intrigue historians as much it perplexed and offended some of his contemporaries. The case that Protector Cromwell was indeed 'king in all but name' has been set out in greatest detail by Roy Sherwood in his two substantial monographs of 1977 and 1997.[8] Sherwood showed that much of the public face of the protectorate between 1653 and 1659 was consciously modelled on those of the Cromwells' Tudor and Stuart predecessors. The protectoral household was structured along similar lines to those of a royal household of an English monarch and public ceremonies under the Cromwells were often carefully based on royal precedents. Laura Knoppers has taken a rather different view. She has argued that Cromwell himself showed little interest in projecting a specifically regal image.[9] It is true that official portraiture is the one form of court culture that the protectorate undoubtedly did neglect. However, the more recent trend has been for historians to expand on Sherwood's conclusions. Paul Hunneyball's major essay on Cromwell's architectural patronage has revealed the extent to which Whitehall and Hampton Court were maintained in a very grand style. Spending on these two palaces was at least equal to what it had been on all the royal palaces under Charles I.[10] Work by Patrick Little on Cromwellian music, horse-breeding and humour is challenging other complacent assumptions about court culture under the protectors.[11] The Cromwellian court is beginning to look much less 'puritanical' and even more traditional than it did before.

# I

The key decision had been that Cromwell should live at the royal palaces of Whitehall and Hampton Court. In April 1654 Cromwell moved into the king's apartments at Whitehall. For the remaining four years of his life, he would live in exactly the same rooms Charles I had done before 1642.[12] The refurbishments undertaken for him there restored at least some of the former splendours.[13] A number of the paintings from Charles I's art collection, albeit only a fraction of what had once hung there, were probably kept back to furnish those rooms.[14] At Hampton Court, Cromwell instead used the queen's apartments, perhaps because he preferred their east-facing aspect. The most impressive feature of those rooms would have been Henrietta Maria's state bed, which still stood in the state bedchamber.[15] That Cromwell used these two palaces was not inevitable. He could just have continued to live in the Cockpit at Whitehall, as he had done since 1650. His wife and his mother apparently would have preferred to stay where they were anyway.[16] Modesty was an option. But in presenting the remaining royal palaces to Cromwell, the protectoral council surely intended that he would use them as official residences. And occupying Whitehall and Hampton Court necessarily implied a certain minimum level of protectoral grandeur. Buildings of that size, built to house entire royal households, could not be run with only a handful of servants. Cromwell had to have a big household to staff what were very big royal palaces.

The form of those palaces did much to determine the structure of the protectoral household. Documenting this in detail is, however, extremely difficult. For all the attempts by Charles II's government to

hold the spending officers of the 1650s to account after the Restoration, many of the documents were lost, deliberately and accidentally,
after 1660 (or, perhaps, 1659?).[17] We know how much the senior
financial official of Cromwell's household, John Maidstone, received
to cover his expenditure (£70,000, later rising after October 1657 to
£100,000 *per annum*), but have little idea of how exactly Maidstone
spent that money.[18] The names of most of Cromwell's household
servants remain a mystery and many of the others can be identified
only because they appear on the famous list of those who took part
in Cromwell's funeral procession on 23 November 1658.[19] None of
the household servants left a substantial surviving collection of official papers. The anonymous printed account of Cromwell's death
by one of the bedchamber servants is the nearest thing to a memoir by someone of their time in the protector's service.[20] Comments
by visitors are rare. Visual evidence is almost non-existent. Given all
this, it will never be possible to reconstruct the day-to-day activities
of Cromwell's household in anything like the same detail historians
have reconstructed those of the Stuart royal households. Yet the broad
outlines of how it was organised are clear.

At the heart of any British royal palace of the early-modern period
were the apartments of the monarch. These consisted of a sequence
of public and private rooms in which almost all the daily activities of the monarch's life took place. By the seventeenth century
that sequence had evolved into a standard arrangement, although, as
was true at Hampton Court and more especially at Whitehall, additional rooms could make that arrangement even more complicated.
The outer rooms—the guard chamber, the presence chamber and the
privy chamber—provided settings for public ceremonies, such as formal audiences. That the rooms were arranged consecutively allowed
visitors to be filtered out according to rank, with only the most high-
ranking individuals being able to get as far as the semi-private privy
chamber. Each room had its own staff of gentlemen, ushers, grooms
and pages to do this. In the guard chamber and the presence chamber, those servants were joined by the royal bodyguards, the yeomen
of the guard and the gentlemen pensioners.[21]

While little is known about how these rooms were used under
Cromwell, the likelihood is that they functioned in much the same
way. Most of these rooms certainly retained their old names, a point
confirmed by the list of mourning hangings ordered for Whitehall in
September 1658.[22] There would have been no question of these public rooms being left unmanned. In 1657 Samuel Pepys was impressed

by 'the strictness used for stopping that free passage of strangers through Whitehall, and the ceremony used in passing the presence chamber'.[23] Security considerations alone demanded that access be controlled. Cromwell had as much reason as the Stuarts to worry about his own safety and repeated attempts were made on his life throughout his reign. In the case of the attempt by the plotter, Miles Sindercombe, who was arrested while trying to set fire to the Chapel Royal in January 1657, it was Whitehall Palace itself that was targeted. Decorum also mattered. In 1654 Cromwell's cousin, Colonel Richard Ingoldsby, was sent to the Tower after brawling in the public rooms at Whitehall with an Aylesbury innkeeper who had opposed his election as one of the Buckinghamshire MPs. This punishment was interpreted at the time as a sign from Cromwell that he disapproved of army influence in the recent elections.[24] But it was probably just as much an indication that the rules of public behaviour in the royal palaces were being enforced with the same rigour as ever. All these rooms came under the jurisdiction of the lord chamberlain.

Beyond these rooms were the bedchamber and the privy apartments. Like James I and Charles I, Cromwell had separate bedchamber servants to wait on him in these, the most private of his rooms. Cromwell, however, employed just four servants, variously described as gentlemen or grooms, for that purpose. This suggests that he was better able than the Stuarts in resisting the temptation to inflate the number of bedchamber positions. Employing more bedchamber servants was always an easy way of rewarding ambitious courtiers keen to have close contact with their ruler.

Below stairs in a royal palace was another world. As in a modern luxury hotel or cruise liner, there was much that had to be kept hidden from view. This was most obviously the case with the palace kitchens. English kings had always been expected to feed, clothe and house their servants. Of these, feeding them had been by far the most onerous responsibility. Most royal servants had received diet of two meals each day.[25] As Cromwell had a household kitchen, in addition to a privy kitchen for his own use, and as the senior servants are known to have had their own tables, the protectoral household seems to have done likewise.[26] While it would be claimed by one hostile observer that the supper provided for the servants consisted only of broth, that implies that their dinners were somewhat more substantial.[27] There are also hints that guests, including some MPs, were sometimes invited to dine at those tables.[28] All this would have been very expensive. Those meals must have taken up much of the household's budget. A royal household had a lord steward and a committee of senior courtiers, the board of greencloth, to administer the vast number of kitchen servants needed to cook so many meals. Until December 1657 Cromwell instead employed two stewards, John Maidstone and Nathaniel Waterhouse. But after a reshuffle in 1657, he had his own board of greencloth, consisting of a comptroller (Philip Jones), a cofferer (Maidstone), a master (Waterhouse), a clerk and a clerk comptroller. The echo of the more traditional royal structure could only have been deliberate.

Other practical needs required other departments and sub-departments. The protector and his servants attended religious services in the existing chapels royal.[29] The sermons they heard there were delivered by a rota of prominent preachers, including Peter Sterry and Hugh Peter. Travel arrangements by land were handled by the stables, headed by the master of the horse and based in the Mews at Charing Cross. The team of bargemen provided transport by water. While Cromwell as lord protector did not go on progresses and almost never left the immediate vicinity of London, he did travel regularly between Whitehall and Hampton Court.[30] For him to have made that journey without a large escort would have been unthinkable. At least two would-be assassins, John Gerard and Miles Sindercombe, considered attacking him between the two palaces. Other essential servants included suppliers, tailors, huntsmen, workmen and gardeners. In other words, just about every aspect of the personal lives of the Cromwells now required teams of specialists to undertake them. This, of course, was simply the norm for any great household of the early-modern period.

## II

What really makes Cromwell's household so remarkable is that so much of it was created from scratch. By 1653 Cromwell had long since ceased to be the ordinary provincial gentleman he had once been. Yet his private household still seems to have been no more than was appropriate for a successful general and prominent politician. His wife, Elizabeth Cromwell, would later be accused of not having entertained enough during those years. Her critics would present her as a grasping freeloader, who, in her ingratitude, had failed to reciprocate with her own hospitality in the manner expected of great men and their spouses.[31] Such claims were doubtless exaggerated. But in the early 1650s the Cromwells quite possibly did maintain a smaller household than they might have done.[32] What is not in doubt is that their lifestyles changed dramatically once Cromwell became lord protector. The size of their household must have expanded very rapidly almost overnight. Admittedly, some of their new servants were simply those who had already been employed under the republic to maintain the ex-royal palaces. The republican government since 1649 had been unable to avoid at least some of the features of a court.[33] But the servants appointed to the new court positions probably outnumbered those with existing jobs. In any case, the result was that suddenly Cromwell found himself with vast amounts of court patronage at his disposal. The circumstances were ones almost without parallel in English history. Earlier rulers who had seized power, such as Henry IV, Edward IV or Henry VII, had had their own aristocratic affinities with which to fill their new royal households.[34] Cromwell did not. He was no feudal magnate. How then did he use this patronage windfall?

One group who benefited most conspicuously were members of Cromwell's own family. This might seem an obvious move. These were men he could trust and this was his best chance to reward his relatives with a share of the spoils of office. Some measure of nepotism was taken for granted in this period, especially when there were well-paid and well-placed government jobs to give away. Yet, in royal terms, this practice always had its limits. English monarchs usually did not appoint members of the royal family to household offices, for such appointments would have been regarded as being beneath them. Only royal relatives outside the monarch's immediate family circle might be considered. Henry VIII had employed several of his in-laws, such as Charles Brandon, 1st duke of Suffolk, for whom the position of lord great master of the household had been created, and William Parr, 1st marquis of Northampton, his last lord great chamberlain. More tenuously, the 2nd marquis of Hamilton, his son, the 1st duke of Hamilton, and the duke of Lennox and Richmond had held major court offices under the early Stuarts in part because they were distant cousins of James I and Charles I.

What would have been unprecedented was for a king to appoint his own son-in-law as his master of the horse. Yet this is precisely what Cromwell now did with his one of his sons-in-law, John Claypole. As that office had often been held by major figures who aspired to or who had already achieved military distinction, there would have been no shortage of close colleagues from the army whom Cromwell might have appointed. (The idea that this job was particularly appropriate for a soldier was one reason why George Monck would ask for it in 1660.) Overlooking those army grandees was therefore a risk, especially when Claypole's own claims to so illustrious a position were so slight. It really was the case that Claypole was appointed only because he was married to Cromwell's daughter, Elizabeth. Lucy Hutchinson (herself the wife of one prominent ex-army officer) thought that Claypole and his brother-in-law, Henry Cromwell, were 'two debauched ungodly Cavaliers'.[35] Others seem to have viewed Claypole as a bit of a lightweight.[36] This might well have been irrelevant, for, quite possibly, the lord protector simply enjoyed his son-in-law's company. Cromwell does seem to have had a deep interest in horses and, as lord protector, he attempted to improve the English bloodstock.[37] He also made full use of the opportunities for stag hunting and hawking at Hampton Court.[38] Claypole likewise enjoyed hunting.[39] Those interests may well have been the strongest bond between the two men. (The same might have been true for one of the gentlemen of the bedchamber, Sir Thomas Billingsley, an 'old formal courtier' who had been master of the horse to the elector palatine, Charles Louis, and who was considered 'the best horseman in England'.)[40]

The appointment of John Barrington as one of Cromwell's gentlemen of the bedchamber in August 1655 is an example of a more obscure relative being favoured.[41] A younger son of one of the Essex Barringtons, John was Cromwell's cousin once removed.[42] Sir Thomas Barrington, Cromwell's close ally in the early 1640s, was John's uncle. John would in time become perhaps Cromwell's most trusted servant.[43] It was a mark of his closeness to his late master that he rode with the effigy in the funeral procession to Westminster Abbey.[44] Another of the other bedchamber gentlemen, Edward Rolt, was described as 'a near kinsman'.[45] He was another cousin once removed, for his mother was one of the daughters of Sir Oliver Cromwell.[46] In 1655 he was given the honour of carrying the ratified copy of the treaty with Sweden to Stockholm. Barrington and Rolt were young men, both probably only in their early twenties when first appointed. Cromwell presumably gave them these places at court in order to give them useful head starts in their careers. Rolt probably relished the opportunity. His subsequent friendship with Pepys suggests that he became a sociable man about town, keen on drinking, music and the theatre.[47] Claypole, Barrington and Rolt were not the only relatives. The joint steward and later master of the household was Nathaniel Waterhouse. He was a cousin of Cromwell's wife, as their mothers had been sisters.[48] It is likely that William Russell, the eldest son of Sir Francis Russell, was appointed as the cornet of the lifeguards, the protectoral equivalent of the gentlemen pensioners, mainly because his sister, Elizabeth, was married to Henry Cromwell. When Russell died in late 1656, after only about six months in this job, the lifeguards escorted the funeral cortege to the Russell family seat at Chippenham in Cambridgeshire.[49]

Kinship with Cromwell was sometimes enough. Other relatives, however, were appointed for more complex reasons. Cromwell's first cousin, Sir Oliver Fleming, served as the master of ceremonies. But Fleming had held that position since 1643, having first been appointed to it by parliament.[50] He was retained in post after 1653 as much for his professional expertise as for his kinship with Cromwell. His job, which involved overseeing diplomatic protocol, was far too delicate to be left to an amateur. Then there was Richard Beke. It could not have been a coincidence that Beke was named as captain of the lifeguards in 1656 shortly after marrying Cromwell's niece, Levina Whetstone. His appointment followed a purge and reorganisation of the guards intended to ensure that only the most reliable of soldiers were employed to protect the protector.[51] Employing a relative in that role had obvious advantages. But, until the previous year, Beke had been serving as the lifeguards' lieutenant captain, so his promotion cannot be said have come as a complete surprise.[52]

Beke had been the lieutenant captain since 1651. In other words, he was a professional soldier who happened to find his troop seconded to the protector's household. The same is true for his predecessor as captain, Charles Howard, who had also first been appointed to the lifeguards in 1651.[53] That appointment completed Howard's extraordinary transformation from a Roman Catholic royalist into an Independent parliamentarian. It may seem natural to assume that military service was what had brought other protectoral servants into Cromwell's circle. Yet this was not so. The lifeguards and its sister troop, the household guards, seem to have been special cases. They were essentially just elite regiments who had been given military duties at court. As such, they should be thought of as precursors of the post-1660 household division. There were, it is true, one or two other army officers within the household. One was the knight marshal, Colonel John Biscoe. He had started off as a captain in what had originally been John Hampden's regiment and he had since served under those future Cromwellian loyalists, Edward Montagu and John Barkstead. By 1655 he had his own regiment of foot.[54] The knight marshal was another office concerned with the security of the palaces, so appointing a military man to it had some logic. Similarly, the senior serjeant-at-arms, Edward Dendy, was another servant with army experience. He had previously served as a captain under the earl of Manchester and in the New Model Army. But he had also been one of the serjeants-at-arms since 1645 and he was appointed in the first place partly because his father had held the same job in the royal household.[55]

These were the major exceptions. The rest of the protectoral household was overwhelmingly staffed by civilians. This absence of soldiers in court positions perhaps worked both ways. The army officers quite possibly did regard Cromwell's court with disdain, even moral disapproval, while Cromwell may have hoped to use his court appointments to distance himself from the army. Charles Fleetwood and John Disbrowe, the two closest Cromwell relatives who were still serving in the army, were conspicuously not appointed to court offices. It was not even as if the army officers had a monopoly over appointments to the two troops of household bodyguards. The captain of the household guards, Walter Strickland, had no military experience at all. What he did have was a knowledge of European diplomacy as great as that of anyone in government circles. Strickland had spent the years between 1642 and 1650 in the Netherlands as parliament's envoy to the United Provinces. He was now a leading figure on the protectoral council and, as such, worked closely with Fleming in liaising with those foreign diplomats resident in London.[56] That he was appointed to command the household guards underlines that the guards' role was as much a ceremonial one as anything else. It also confirms the bias towards civilian appointments. Tensions between the army and the civilian politicians were never far from the surface in the factional intrigues around the lord protector. Cromwell's household was very much a stronghold for civilian influence.

Also strikingly absent from his household are many servants with whom Cromwell had been acquainted in the period before the civil war. A sense of his network of friends in Cambridgeshire in the 1630s and early 1640s is now beginning to emerge into view.[57] There were a number of individuals from Cambridge and from the surrounding area in that earlier period with whom he can be linked. Those bonds of friendship had often been strong and they had done much to shape Cambridge local politics during the mid-1640s. Yet none of those men seem to have remained close to Cromwell in the 1650s. When the chance for him to reward them came, they were overlooked. Even Thomas French, the mayor of Cambridge at the time of Cromwell's election to the Short Parliament, failed to regain his old role as a court supplier. Indeed, the only one of Cromwell's old friends from Cambridge who can be said to have benefited from the protectoral gravy train was John Lowry, the other Cambridge MP in the Long Parliament. He was appointed as one of the comptrollers of the great and small customs of London.[58] Cromwellian cronyism did not come much more blatant than that. Henry Lawrence also benefited. As president of the council, Lawrence counts as a courtier without a household position. He had been Cromwell's landlord in St Ives in the 1630s.[59]

In the protectoral household itself, only some of the medical appointments can confidently be said to have gone to old acquaintances from Cambridgeshire or Huntingdonshire. John Symcotts, a physician who was based in Huntingdon, had treated Cromwell 'for many years' when his patient was still an obscure country gentleman.[60] Symcotts was not forgotten and he walked in the funeral procession along with the lord protector's more prominent London-based physicians. There was also whichever of the Stane brothers—either Richard or his younger brother, William—who served as another of the physicians.[61] (William certainly treated Elizabeth Claypole.)[62] Richard Stane had known Cromwell at Ely as early as 1644 and by 1651 Cromwell's sister, Elizabeth, was living in Stane's house there.[63] The 'Mr Underwood' who served in the bed-chamber may have been one of the Underwoods of Whittlesey. The leading member of that family, Lieutenant-Colonel Francis Underwood, had certainly known Cromwell at Ely in the mid-1640s.[64] Also worth noting are the two Bacon brothers, Nathaniel and Francis, who became the masters of requests, the two law officers attached to the household to assist those wishing to petition the protector. Nathaniel, a successful barrister who was also the recorder of Ipswich, had got to know Cromwell very well during the war when he had been the chairman of the Eastern Association committee at Cambridge.[65]

The impression nevertheless remains that Cromwell's friends from before the mid-1640s are strangely missing. That reflects a wider feature of Cromwell's later life. By the 1650s his links with his East Anglian heartland were fading fast. It was almost as if he had lost all interest in where he had come from. He pointedly never went back. It could be said that he had no real reason to do so. The bulk of his estates were now elsewhere. His children were being married off to families from other parts of the country. Richard, his heir, was based in Hampshire. It was John Thurloe, his ever-dependable secretary of state, who was now emerging as the figure of consequence in the Isle of Ely and it may even be that Cromwell was deliberately standing back to allow his protégé to succeed to his interests there.[66] In 1631, when he had sold up in Huntingdon, and again in 1640, when he had given up the Ely leases, Cromwell had shown himself more than willing to move on. Now, as lord protector, he was finally free from his provincial roots. The final re-invention was complete.

## III

Yet it was not quite the case that none of Cromwell's previous connections beyond his own family counted for much when he was making his court appointments. Some existing links do stand out. It does seem significant that several of the servants were from Essex. John Barrington has already been mentioned. There was also Abraham Barrington, who began as Cromwell's auditor and who ended up as the clerk of the greencloth. It would be very tempting to suppose that, like John Barrington, Abraham was a scion of the Barringtons of Hatfield Broad Oak. His father, Henry Barrington, who was probably a brewer by trade, was the leading figure on the Colchester corporation in this period and had been one of the Essex MPs in the 1653 Barebone's Parliament.[67] But evidence that these two Essex Barrington families were related has never been discovered and, if there was a connection, it could only have been a very remote one.[68] In any case, that was not the reason Abraham had got his job in Cromwell's household. The connection that had mattered was with his boss, the steward and cofferer, John Maidstone. Both of them had been sequestration commissioners in Essex from 1650 and so were already very well known to each other.[69] Maidstone simply turned to his faithful friend now that he needed someone to assist him in administering the household below stairs. The favour was soon repaid. In July 1654 Henry Barrington helped get Maidstone elected as MP for Colchester. These excellent contacts at court were also one reason for the protectoral council to come down on the side of Henry Barrington and his friends in the vicious factional disputes within the Colchester corporation during the mid-1650s.

What is more difficult to explain is why Maidstone had got his job. The roles of steward and cofferer were ones of particular importance. As has been mentioned, the sizable sums of money for the household all passed through his hands, so the rewards to be gained from it, whether legitimate or corrupt, are likely to have been considerable.

Cromwell must have had good reason to favour him. Yet Maidstone remains a mysterious figure. His substantial pen portrait of Cromwell in his letter to his distant relative, John Winthrop junior, the governor of Connecticut, has often been quoted.[70] That however reveals little about Maidstone's own career. And, given that it was written on the eve of the Restoration, what it does say may well be carefully mis-leading. The only sure facts about Maidstone's early career are that he was the eldest son of a minor gentry family from Boxted in Essex and that he had been a captain in the Essex county militia. His service as a sequestration commissioner confirms this impression of him as some-one who until 1653 had been no more than a purely local figure.[71] If he did have some previous link with Cromwell, it is one that will therefore almost certainly be found in and around northern Essex. Did he know the Barringtons? Or Thurloe? Or the Mashams? Only one lead seems remotely significant. Someone close to Cromwell who did know Maidstone was the aforementioned Nathaniel Bacon, for Bacon's first wife, Elizabeth Maidstone of Boxted, had been Maidstone's cousin. There are a few hints that Bacon and Maidstone had remained close. In 1656 Thomas Bushell, who had once been a protégé of Bacon's late uncle, Francis Bacon, approached both Nathaniel Bacon and Maidstone in his attempt to gain government support for his mining schemes in the west country.[72] In 1657 Bacon and his brother authorised Maidstone to collect their official salaries for them in 1657.[73] But then that may simply have been because their former kinsman was so well placed to do so. Most telling of all, perhaps, is that Maidstone witnessed Nathaniel's will three years later.[74] So the possibility that Bacon had recommended Maidstone to Cromwell cannot be ruled out and indeed, to date, this remains the only plausible explanation.

Before the creation of the new board of greencloth in 1657, Maidstone acted as steward in conjunction with Nathaniel Water-house. Even then the two men were probably dividing their roles into distinct spheres of responsibility: Maidstone concentrated on the household finances, while Waterhouse, who was sometimes described as the steward of Cromwell's lands, probably oversaw his estates. Waterhouse also managed Henry Cromwell's financial affairs in England during his absence in Ireland.[75] Waterhouse's duties may therefore not have been so very different from what he had been doing before 1653. He first appears in association with the future lord protector in January 1651, when he entered into a bond to expedite payments to Thurloe of rents due from some of Cromwell's

Monmouthshire estates.[76] Moreover, at about the same time he and Thurloe acted as the trustees for Cromwell's daughter, Bridget Ireton, and her children.[77] He also received some of the payments made to Cromwell during the Scottish campaign.[78] All this confirms that Waterhouse was being employed by his kinsman well before the advent of the protectorate. He was not alone. Charles Harvey, who went on to become one of the bedchamber servants, may well have been the man who, along with Waterhouse, witnessed the deed for a land purchase by Cromwell in Rutland in early 1653.[79] Thurloe himself was another. At this stage, the careers of Waterhouse and the future secretary of state had strong similarities. How Thurloe had come to know Cromwell is easy enough to explain. In the 1630s Thurloe had progressed from the service of one Cromwell kinsman, Sir William Masham, into that of another, Masham's son-in-law, Oliver St John. The backing of St John then became the crucial factor in Thurloe's advancement.[80] But by the late 1640s, Thurloe was, like Waterhouse, also handling legal business arising from Cromwell's rapidly expanding collection of landed estates.[81]

This group of trusted aides also included Philip Jones. As Lloyd Bowen has pointed out in the previous chapter, Jones became linked to Cromwell in 1648 in his capacity as steward of his new Welsh estates in Glamorgan. As a result, the two men became effective political allies and close friends. In December 1657 Jones was rewarded with one of the most senior of the court offices, the comptrollership of the household. He now presided over the new board of green-cloth and oversaw the administration of the household below stairs. He was Maidstone's and Waterhouse's immediate superior. Of the other courtiers, only the lord chamberlain could be considered to outrank him. Jones's advancement therefore further underlines the importance of this earlier group. Cromwell's landholdings had dramatically increased during the late 1640s, most obviously as a result of parliament's grant to him of the Welsh lands. One less obvious consequence had been that, more than ever before and, indeed, perhaps for the first time, Cromwell needed a network of agents to assist him in managing his estates. Jones, Waterhouse, Thurloe and the others supplied that need. In a sense, they were still doing so. Having already proved their dependability in the management of Cromwell's financial affairs, these men of business prospered more than most under the protectorate. Those to whom Cromwell evidently felt most obliged were not those who had served alongside him on the battlefield, but those who had instead been looking after his money.

Jones however was never just a Cromwellian client. Locally, he had become a man of real power in his own right in south Wales. Nationally, in parliament and on the council, he was a political heavyweight.[82] That was why he was such a credible candidate for so important a court office. The same was true for his counterpart above stairs, the lord chamberlain, Sir Gilbert Pickering.[83] The paths of Pickering and Cromwell had probably first crossed many years earlier, if only because Pickering's father-in-law, Sir Sidney Montagu, had been the man who had bought Hinchingbrooke from the senior branch of the Cromwells in 1627. As the local knight of the shire, Pickering had been one of the more important Northamptonshire parliamentarians during the civil war, but it was only under the Rump that he can be considered to have become a politician of real substance at Westminster. He had been a particularly strong supporter of the new republic. That was why it could be said of him that he had been 'a great stickler in the change of the government from kingly to that of a commonwealth'.[84] Under the Rump he was regularly elected to the council of state, making him one of the few men to have been a member of that body continuously between 1649 and 1653. Now, under the protectorate, he was an equally obvious person for Cromwell to include on the protectoral council. The new lord protector needed such powerful figures around him. Of course, if Cromwell was no feudal magnate, neither were Jones and Pickering. This was not a case of overmighty subjects being bought off with court office so that their local influence would not be used against the regime. Rather they were smart, experienced operators whose skills could now be put to good use in parliament, on the council and at court. Cromwell would have been foolish not to have given the most responsible and most valuable household offices to such men.

Yet any court was always more than just its household servants. St John remained close to Cromwell, although, as he was now lord chief justice of common bench, any influence by him had to be exercised with some discretion. Other friends and relatives, such as Sir Francis Russell, Lord Broghill, Edward Montagu, Sir Charles Wolseley and William Pierrepont, were as much courtiers as Claypole and Jones. Whitelocke claimed that he and Cromwell would regularly meet in private with Broghill, Pierrepont, Wolseley and Thurloe to smoke and to chat at length about politics.[85] Broghill, Montagu and Wolseley, like Claypole, Howard and Beke, were the next generation, all at least twenty years younger than Cromwell and so closer in age to the Cromwell sons. These were the men to perpetuate the rule of the

Cromwells after Cromwell himself was dead. It must also be remembered that networks of female friendship must have existed around Cromwell's mother, wife and daughters, although these sadly remain largely obscure. All these relatives, friends and associates played their part in shaping the increasingly courtly character of the protectoral entourage.

Throughout his reign Cromwell ruled in tandem with his protectoral council. It was his councillors, not the household servants, who seem to have done most to shape his policy decisions.[86] However, three household servants—Pickering, Jones and Strickland—were also councillors. This, in itself, was not too surprising. The departmental heads in a royal household, such as the lord steward and the lord chamberlain, had routinely been included on the privy council and, as has already been suggested, Pickering, Jones and Strickland were major figures anyway, even without their household offices. All three of them were also summoned to sit in the Other House, as were Claypole and Charles Howard (recently created Viscount Howard). The council's deliberations carried great weight. It was there that the army grandees were able to ensure that the army continued to influence policy.[87] It was there too that the courtier-councillors had to count. At times it might have seemed as if the soldiers in the army were at odds with civilians at court and that the council was the most convenient forum in which they could argue out their disagreements. But things were rarely quite that simple. Pickering, for example, was a friend and political ally of Fleetwood and, perhaps as a consequence, he had a tendency to side with the army.[88] In July 1657, following the second inauguration, he had qualms about taking the oath of loyalty to Cromwell.[89] Yet as the reign progressed, and as the protectoral household became ever more like a royal household, the civilians did become more prominent. Their great gamble was to promote the offer of the kingship. As it happened, its rejection turned out to make no difference. John Lambert, the grandest of the army grandees, still refused to serve and so was dismissed. Thurloe, far from being weakened, joined the council as a councillor for the first time. Whitelocke, Broghill, Wolseley and Thurloe remained the protector's regular dining companions, when, in Whitelocke's word, they still indulged in 'some frolics of diversion'.[90] Cromwell did not need to be king to have a court and, even without the formal title of king, he could still rule like one.

By 1658 it was all beginning to work. Whitehall once more felt like a real court. The protector's servants had found their style, albeit one mostly plagiarised from the monarchy. If nothing else, reviving traditions which it had rejected in 1649 meant that what was being created afresh had the appearance of being that little bit more permanent. Most important of all, those around Cromwell had started to act like courtiers. They had come to believe in both the concept and the reality of a Cromwellian court. It was not to last. In 1659, without Cromwell to guide them and under the harsh intensity of the short-lived republican revival, their confidence faltered. The protectoral court then evaporated like the morning dew. Its disappearance would be as rapid as its creation. Even so, one hesitates to conclude that the experiment had failed. It was more that it could not continue without the man around whom it had always revolved.

## Notes

1. *A&O*, ii. 813.
2. *Perfect Diurnall*, no. 210 (12–19 December 1653), sig. [10B4]; *Severall Proceedings of State Affaires*, no. 221 (15–22 December 1653), sig. 19Kv–19K2v; *Mercurius Politicus*, no. 184 (16–22 December 1653), 3052–3; Sir Frederic Madden, 'Cromwelliana', *Notes and Queries*, 2nd series, vii. (1859), 141.
3. *CSPV 1653–4*, 164.
4. *Mercurius Politicus*, no. 369 (25 June–2 July 1657), sig. [32Y3]–[32Y4v]; *CSPV 1657–9*, 82; *Prestwich's Respublica* (1787), 3–21.
5. *CSPV 1653–4*, 177.
6. Most famously in *The Court & Kitchen of Elizabeth, Commonly Called Joan Cromwel, the Wife of the Late Usurper* (1664).
7. In reality, Charles II's attempts to revive a traditional court would run into trouble almost immediately. Andrew Barclay, 'Charles II's Failed Restoration: Administrative Reform Below Stairs, 1660–4', in E. Cruickshanks (ed.), *The Stuart Courts* (Stroud, 2000).
8. R. Sherwood, *The Court of Oliver Cromwell* (1977, reprinted 1989); *Oliver Cromwell, King in All but Name, 1653–1658* (1997).
9. L. L. Knoppers, *Constructing Cromwell: Ceremony, Portrait and Print 1645–1661* (Cambridge, 2000).
10. P. M. Hunneyball, 'Cromwellian Style: The Architectural Trappings of the Protectorate Regime', in P. Little (ed.), *The Cromwellian Protectorate* (Woodbridge, 2007).
11. P. Little, 'Music at the Court of King Oliver', *The Court Historian*, 12 (2007); P. Little, 'Uncovering a Cromwellian Stud: Horses and Horse-Breeding at the Court of Oliver Cromwell, 1653–8', *Hist. Res.* (forthcoming, 2008); P. Little, 'Oliver Cromwell's Sense of Humour', *Cromwelliana* 2nd ser., no. 4 (2007).

12. S. Thurley, *Whitehall Palace: An Architectural History of the Royal Apartments, 1240–1698* (New Haven and London, 1999), 98.
13. Hunneyball, 'Cromwellian Style', 67–9.
14. J. Brotton, *The Sale of the Late King's Goods: Charles I and His Art Collection* (2006), 276–82. But, as the late Sir Oliver Millar pointed out in his important review of Brotton's book, it is not entirely clear why these paintings were withdrawn from the sale. *The Court Historian*, 12 (2007), 77.
15. TNA, SP 18/203, fos. 68–81; Simon Thurley, *Hampton Court: A Social and Architectural History* (New Haven and London, 2003), 126–8.
16. *Ludlow Memoirs*, i. 379.
17. G. E. Aylmer, *The State's Servants: The Civil Service of the English Republic 1649–1660* (1973), 75.
18. *CSPD 1653–4*, 457; *CSPD 1654*, 254, 396, 403, 444, 446, 447, 450, 452, 453, 457, 458; *HMC Laing*, i. 298; *Fifth Report of the Deputy Keeper of the Public Records*, appendix II, 248, 250, 258, 563, 564, 570; *CSPD 1655*, 76, 100, 139; BL, Add. MS 4196, fos. 9, 86, 154, 160, 195, 271, 280, 295, 343, 349; *CSPD 1656–7*, 98, 140, 149, 168, 193, 237, 262, 304, 331, 362, 427; *CSPD 1657–8*, 33, 51, 83, 94, 100, 128, 130, 132; BL, MS Add. 4197, fos. 31, 46, 80, 95, 103; Sherwood, *Court of Oliver Cromwell*, 36–41.
19. *Burton Diary*, ii. 516–29.
20. *A Collection of Several Passages Concerning His Late Highnesse Oliver Cromwell, In the Time of His Sickness* (1659); *An Account of the Last Houres of the Late Renowned Oliver Lord Protector* (1659).
21. The best introductions to royal use of these rooms are D. Starkey (ed.), *The English Court from the Wars of the Roses to the Civil War* (1987) and R. O. Bucholz, 'Going to Court in 1700: a Visitor's Guide', *The Court Historian*, 5 (2000). See also J. Adamson, 'The Tudor and Stuart Courts 1509–1714', in J. Adamson (ed.), *The Princely Courts of Europe: Ritual, Politics and Culture Under the Ancien Régime 1500–1750* (1999); B. Weiser, *Charles II and the Politics of Access* (Woodbridge, 2003), esp. 24–53.
22. Longleat House, Warminster, MS 67A, pp. 19–20 (consulted on microfilm at the History of Parliament Trust).
23. Guy de la Bédoyère (ed.), *The Letters of Samuel Pepys 1656–1703* (Woodbridge, 2006), 23. See also *Clarke Papers*, iii. 129.
24. *HMC Egmont*, i. 545; *A Second Narrative of the Late Parliament* (1658), 12; *Clarke Papers*, v. 191–2.
25. G. E. Aylmer, *The King's Servants: The Civil Service of Charles I, 1625–1642* (1961), 168–71, and, more generally, F. Heal, *Hospitality in Early Modern England* (Oxford, 1990).
26. *Burton Diary*, ii. 519, 520, 521; TNA, SP 18/203, fos. 72v, 79–80; *Court & Kitchen*, 42.

27. *Court & Kitchen*, 43.
28. *Burton Diary*, i. 321.
29. S. Thurley, 'The Stuart Kings, Oliver Cromwell and the Chapel Royal 1618–1685', *Architectural History*, 45 (2002), 253–5.
30. P. Gaunt, *The Cromwellian Gazetteer* (Stroud, 1987), 227; M. Roberts (ed.), *Swedish Diplomats at Cromwell's Court, 1655–1656: The Missions of Peter Julius Coyet and Christer Bonde* (Camden Society, 4th series, xxxvi. 1988), 107.
31. *Court & Kitchen*, 1–24.
32. At the time of Cromwell's death, 38 of his servants were listed as his 'private family'. TNA, SP 18/182, fo. 157.
33. S. Kelsey, *Inventing a Republic: The Political Culture of the English Commonwealth, 1649–1653* (Manchester, 1997).
34. C. Given-Wilson, *The Royal Household and the King's Affinity: Service, Politics and Finance in England 1360–1413* (New Haven and London, 1986), 190–3; D. A. L. Morgan, 'The King's Affinity in the Polity of Yorkist England', *Transactions of the Royal Historical Society*, 5th series, 23 (1973); S. B. Chrimes, *Henry VII* (1972), 53–7.
35. L. Hutchinson, *Memoirs of the Life of Colonel Hutchinson*, ed. J. Sutherland (Oxford, 1973), 209.
36. *A Second Narrative of the Late Parliament (So Called)* (2nd edition. 1659), 21.
37. See P. Little, 'Uncovering a Cromwellian Stud'.
38. *Swedish Diplomats at Cromwell's Court*, 120n, 299; *Whitelocke Diary*, 412; John Aubrey, *Brief Lives and Other Selected Writings*, ed. Anthony Powell (1949), 381.
39. F. P. Verney and M. M. Verney, *Memoirs of the Verney Family* (2nd edn. 1907), ii. 2.
40. *Clarke Papers*, iii. 47; Madden, 'Cromwelliana', 142; Aubrey, *Brief Lives*, 379.
41. *Clarke Papers*, iii. 47.
42. P. Morant, *The History and Antiquities of the County of Essex* (1768), ii. 342; A. Barclay, 'John Barrington', draft biography, 1640–1660 Section, History of Parliament.
43. *TSP*, vii. 364.
44. TNA, SP 18/183, fos. 190v, 193.
45. *Swedish Diplomats at Cromwell's Court*, 78.
46. F. A. Blaydes (ed.), *The Visitation of Bedfordshire, Annis Domini 1566, 1582, and 1634* (Harleian Society, xix. 1884), 135; J. H. Round, 'Sir Thomas Rolt, "President of India"', *The Genealogist*, new series, 17 (1901), 145–9.
47. R. Latham and W. Matthews (eds), *The Diary of Samuel Pepys* (1971–83), ii. 108, 121, vi. 320–1, 323, vii. 2, 100, viii. 28, 29, 51, 172–3, 323–4, 575, ix. 166, 175, 203, 219.

48. Bodl., MS Ashmole 1137, fo. 55v; C. H. Josten (ed.), *Elias Ashmole (1617–1692)* (Oxford, 1966), ii. 740. I would like to thank Vivienne Larminie for kindly checking the first of these references.

49. BL, Lansdowne MS 821, fo. 144v; Bodl., MS Carte 73, fo. 56.

50. *LJ*, vi. 291a, 292a, 293a; *CJ*, iii. 299a.

51. Thomas Carte (ed.), *A Collection of Original Letters and Papers Concerning the Affairs of England* (1739), ii. 81–2; *CCSP*, iii. 415.

52. C. H. Firth and G. Davies, *The Regimental History of Cromwell's Army* (Oxford, 1940), i. 52.

53. Firth and Davies, *Regimental History*, i. 52–3.

54. A. Barclay, 'John Biscoe', draft biography, 1640–1660 Section.

55. Ibid., 'Edward Dendy', draft biography, 1640–1660 Section.

56. D. Scott, 'Walter Strickland', draft biography, 1640–1660 Section.

57. This will be the subject of my forthcoming book, *Oliver Cromwell: The Unknown Politician*.

58. Bodl., MS Rawl. A 328, p. 81; *CJ*, vii. 786b.

59. C. Clifford and A. Akeroyd, *Risen from Obscurity? Oliver Cromwell and Huntingdonshire* (Huntingdonshire Local History Society, 2002), 32–3.

60. Sir Philip Warwick, *Memoires of the reigne of King Charles I* (1701), 249; F. N. L. Poynter and W. J. Bishop, *A Seventeenth Century Doctor and His Patients: John Symcotts, 1592?–1662* (Bedfordshire Historical Record Society, xxxi. 1951), 76.

61. TNA, SP 18/182, fo. 161 (list of mourning approved by the council, 7 September 1658). Which of them is listed here along with the other physicians is uncertain. Neither walked in the funeral procession as a physician, but William Stane did so as commissary general of musters.

62. BL, Lansdowne MS 821, fo. 58.

63. Abbott, i. 282, 324; ibid, ii. 507–8.

64. Abbott, i. 268, 353–4.

65. A. Barclay, 'Nathaniel Bacon', draft biography, 1640–1660 Section.

66. P. Aubrey, *Mr Secretary Thurloe: Cromwell's Secretary of State, 1652–1660* (1990), 190–3.

67. A. Barclay, 'Henry Barrington', draft biography, 1640–1660 Section. His civic career is discussed in detail in the classic study of the Colchester corporation in the 1650s. J. H. Round, 'Colchester during the Commonwealth', *EHR*, 15 (1900), 641–64.

68. A. Woolrych, *Commonwealth to Protectorate* (Oxford, 1982), 176n.

69. *CCC*, 171, 173, 201, 204, 396, 504, 514, 519, 565, 636, 703, 728, 740.

70. *TSP*, i. 763–8; 'Letter of John Maidstone to John Winthrop', *Collections of the Massachusetts Historical Society*, 3rd series i. (1825), 185–98.

71. A. Barclay, 'John Maidstone', draft biography, 1640–1660 Section.

72. *Publick Intelligencer*, no. 40 (7–14 July 1656), 681–3.

73. BL, Add. MS 4196, fo. 245.

74. TNA, PROB 11/305, fo. 22.

75. BL, Lansdowne MS 821, fos. 56, 87; ibid, MS 822, f. 204.

76. *CCC*, 393, 603; Roland Thorne, 'Nathaniel Waterhouse', draft biography, 1640–1660 Section.

77. *CCC*, 658.

78. *CSPD 1651*, 571.

79. Abbott, ii. 609 and n.

80. A. Barclay, 'John Thurloe' draft biography, 1640–1660 Section.

81. D. Farr, 'Oliver Cromwell and a 1647 Case in Chancery', *Hist. Res.*, 71 (1998), 341–6; Cambridgeshire County Record Office, Huntingdon, Hunts. RO, Cromwell-Bush 731/27. He may also be the unnamed lawyer mentioned in Abbott, i. 592.

82. S. Roberts, 'Philip Jones', draft biography, 1640–1660 Section.

83. S. Jones, 'Sir Gilbert Pickering', draft biography, 1640–1660 Section.

84. *Second Narrative of the Late Parliament*, 16.

85. *Whitelocke Diary*, 464, 477.

86. P. Gaunt, ' "The Single Person's Confidants and Dependants"? Oliver Cromwell and His Protectoral Councillors', *HJ*, 32 (1989), 537–60; B. Worden, 'Oliver Cromwell and the Council', 82–104, in Little, *Cromwellian Protectorate*.

87. Worden, 'Oliver Cromwell and the Council', 82–104.

88. *TSP*, vi. 37; Worden, 'Oliver Cromwell and the Council', 102; P. Little and D. L. Smith, *Parliaments and Politics during the Cromwellian Protectorate* (Cambridge, 2007), 109–10.

89. TNA, SP 78/113, fo. 261.

90. *Whitelocke Diary*, 477.

# 9

# John Thurloe and the Offer of the Crown to Oliver Cromwell

Patrick Little

---

> If his highness can be moved to accept of it [the crown], the services
> he hath done the nations have abundantly deserved it; but if he who
> hath so much merited it do judge it fit to continue his refusal of
> it, the contempt of a crown—which can not proceed but from an
> extraordinary virtue—will render him, in the esteem of all whose
> opinion is to be valued, more honourable than any that wear it.[1]

When the ambassador to France, Sir William Lockhart, wrote this
in April 1657, it had been nearly two months since the question of
making Oliver Cromwell king had first been raised in the House of
Commons, and the people of all three nations were waiting anxiously
for the lord protector to make up his mind. Would he choose to
become King Oliver or not?

The offer of the crown in the spring of 1657 marked the end of a
long series of rumours, backed up by indiscreet comments by those
around the protector, that he would soon assume the crown of the
three kingdoms of England, Scotland and Ireland, which had been in
abeyance since the execution of Charles I in 1649. Cromwell's position since the founding of the protectorate in the closing weeks of
1653 was already quasi-regal. As protector, he was head of state, and
enjoyed many of the familiar trappings of power—he lived in the former royal palaces, he held sway over his own court, and he was the
dominant figure not only in the government but also in parliament.
There were certain restraints: he had to govern in accordance with

the written constitution—the Instrument of Government, which had come into force on 16 December 1653; he had to rule with the consent of a council; and (apart from the early months of the protectorate) he could only legislate through parliament. There was also a fourth, and equally important, limit to the protector's power: the army. The importance of the army in drawing up the Instrument of Government and the presence of senior officers on the council reinforced Cromwell's dependence on the military for security reasons, and this dependence was the Achilles heel of the protectorate. Military rule was expensive and unpopular, and condemned the regime to receive support from only a minority of the people. Nowhere was this more apparent than in the hostile reaction received by the major-generals, who ruled the counties of England and Wales from the autumn of 1655. To secure the 'healing and settling' of the nations, and provide permanent solutions to the problems raised and exacerbated by a decade of civil war, a more broadly based, civilian government was needed. It was this that prompted the initial offer of the crown to Cromwell, under a new constitution known as the Remonstrance, presented to parliament on 23 February 1657. Parliament debated the proposals long and hard, and after substantial modification, the renamed Humble Petition and Advice was formally submitted for Cromwell's approval on 31 March. After a long period of deliberation and prayer, on 8 May Cromwell rejected the crown, while accepting the main tenets of the new, civilian, constitution.

Most historians agree that the rejection of the crown was Cromwell's finest hour. Like Sir William Lockhart, they see his decision to refuse the top job as a touchstone of his greatness, the benchmark of his 'extraordinary virtue'. In recent years, historical explanations for Cromwell's refusal of the crown have shifted. Sir Charles Firth, writing over a century ago, emphasised Cromwell's prudence in not antagonising the army, whose officers had grown suspicious of the protector's worldly ambitions, which they saw as a betrayal of all that they had fought for during the civil wars. Taking the crown would be a step too far, and Cromwell knew it.[2] More recent historians, while accepting the importance of the army in the protectorate, see Cromwell's motives as religious, rather than political. The delay in Cromwell making up his mind over the crown was caused by a kind of spiritual paralysis. Although tempted by the fruits of a return to traditional forms of government, Cromwell was acutely aware of God's judgement on him and his actions. While the godly New Model Army continued to be victorious, it was clear that

Providence was on his side; but recent military reverses, especially the disastrous 'Western Design' to take the island of Hispaniola in the West Indies from the Spanish in 1655, had raised doubts in his mind. The religious radicals (including many in the army) were insistent that the ambitious Cromwell risked incurring God's anger. The crown had been destroyed forever with the execution of Charles I, and to resurrect the title would be dangerous—even suicidal. Like the biblical Achan, whose greed had brought a curse on the people of Israel after the capture of Jericho, the crowning of Cromwell would bring God's wrath not only against himself, but also against the entire commonwealth.[3] It was this, we are told, that caused Cromwell to reject the crown, and he made direct reference to it when addressing a parliamentary committee in April:

> Truly the Providence of God has laid this title aside providentially... I would not seek to set up that that Providence hath destroyed and laid in the dust, and I would not build Jericho again.[4]

In the historical accounts of the period, Cromwell's dramatic refusal of kingship has naturally taken centre stage. In this chapter, however, it is intended to approach Cromwell and the crown from the beginning rather than from the end, by asking three questions. How did the initial offer of the crown come about? How did the supporters of kingship prepare the ground for the presentation of the Remonstrance that began the 'kingship debates' in parliament? And what does this process reveal of Cromwell's own attitudes to the crown before his well-publicised, and apparently altruistic, decision to turn it down?

## I

Historians have tended to follow a well-trodden path when trying to explain the sequence of events that led to the introduction of the Remonstrance on 23 February 1657. The territory was first mapped out by Firth, who saw the origins of the offer of the crown as lying in the debates on the 'hereditary succession' that briefly flared up in November 1656. But these early discussions were sporadic, and inconclusive; and from early December 'very little was heard of it, until [Sir Christopher Packe] brought in his Remonstrance of 23 February'. This was apparently because the supporters of a new civilian settlement were concerned 'that they had gone a little too fast' and were in danger of provoking known opponents of the scheme within the army without being sure that 'the public mind'—and still less, that of the protector—was in favour of the idea. In the meantime, 'other questions came before parliament', especially the case of the notorious Quaker, James Naylor, and the militia bill that would decide the future of the unpopular major-generals. As a result, 'the great question was pushed into the background'.[5] Firth's chronology has been modified by later historians, who have seen such matters as the Naylor debate and the militia bill as part of a steady progress towards kingship. Most famously, perhaps, Hugh Trevor-Roper outlined the political programme forced through by the 'kingship party' led by the Irish peer, Lord Broghill, which manipulated the House of Commons almost like an automaton. In the winter of 1656, Broghill and his clients 'set methodically to work. The government of the major-generals was abolished; the kingship . . . was proposed'.[6] While historians have baulked at Trevor-Roper's view of this well-organised political bloc carrying all before it, they have nevertheless accepted his basic chronology. Carol Egloff, for example, while attacking Trevor-Roper over the notion of a unified 'kingship party', states that the debate on the militia bill 'provided the direct stimulus for the preparation of the new monarchical constitution and its presentation to the House in February'.[7] For John Morrill, 'the timing of the offer of the crown, just after the Naylor affair and the debates on the major-generals, is indicative' of the aims of the sponsors of kingship in the Commons.[8] While there is much to commend this chain of events—and the militia bill, in particular, was undoubtedly the essential precursor of the kingship debates—there is a danger that the chronology of kingship encourages over-simplification, with important events missed out. Furthermore, it does not explain the gap in the sequence: the awkward pause between the voting down of the militia bill on 29 January and the presentation of the Remonstrance on 23 February while (in Firth's words) the plans for kingship were 'secretly maturing'.[9] Why the delay? It will be argued here that this hiatus was more apparent than real, and that what happened in those few weeks is in fact vital to understanding the origins of the Remonstrance and the formal offer of the crown to Cromwell. Indeed, the 'missing link' is not hard to find: it is the plot against Cromwell's life, led by a disgruntled former soldier, Miles Sindercombe, and its aftermath.

The Sindercombe plot was the last in a series of abortive attempts made since the previous September. At first, the conspirators had intended to shoot Cromwell, either by lying in wait for his coach in suitable houses along his route from Whitehall to Hampton Court, or by attacking him in Hyde Park. Each time, the opportunity had been missed, and a different approach was adopted in early January. On 8 January the plotters gained access to the chapel at Whitehall, which stood beneath the apartments where Cromwell lived. There they planted a basket of flammable materials with a gunpowder charge, and lit slow-matches, intending the whole device to explode and set fire to the palace shortly after midnight. Once all was set, one of the conspirators, having second thoughts, went to the authorities, and the incendiary bomb was found. In the hours that followed, the ringleaders, including Sindercombe, were arrested.[10]

Sindercombe's plot has never been taken seriously by historians. The hare-brained nature of the scheme; the ridiculously small number of conspirators and the apparent weakness of their links with the court in exile; above all, its complete failure: aspects of the plot are mentioned in histories of the interregnum, but have warranted little detailed discussion.[11] Instead, Sindercombe's plot is seen as a sad indicator of how hopeless the cause of Oliver's enemies had become, and it pales into insignificance beside the major issues of the early months of 1657: Naylor's case, the militia bill and the kingship debates.[12] Most biographers of Cromwell ignore it altogether.[13] With hindsight, it is easy to underestimate the effect of Sindercombe's plot. But contemporaries were acutely aware that the protectorate, and the peace and stability that it had brought to the three nations, was dependent on the life of one man. The protectorate was built around the protector, and his death would cause its collapse. Those around Cromwell also recognised the potential of the plot to determine the future of the country, but in a more positive way. This was just the excuse they had been seeking to re-introduce the question of 'settlement', and to push for a civilian constitution. On 19 January the secretary of state, John Thurloe, revealed the details of the plot to an alarmed House of Commons. Thurloe's account was hard-hitting. From the start he emphasised the international conspiracy that lay behind Sindercombe's bungled attack, saying that 'the place where that design was hatched is in Flanders, a place fit for such designs of assassination, at the Spanish court there. Two parties are in it, the old malignant and Levelling party.' Having accused both the royalists and the radicals of involvement, he then proved his point by reading out the confessions of two of the plotters, and revealing that others were being investigated, including 'a considerable person of the late king's party' and another 'suspected to hold close correspondence with Charles Stuart'.[14]

The speech was followed by general discussion, when MPs demonstrated the horror that they felt at this attempt by 'the Levellers and the Cavaliers' to kill the protector and 'overthrow the government', and there followed proposals to hold a 'day of thanksgiving' to acknowledge God's mercy in preventing the atrocity from happening.[15] But they were also alive to the other implications of the plot, as revealed in an emotional outburst by John Ashe, who asked to have

> something else added, which, in my opinion, would tend very much to the preservation of himself and us, and to the quieting of all the designs of our enemies; that his highness would be pleased to take upon him the government according to the ancient constitution; so that the hopes of our enemies' plots would be at an end. Both our liberties and peace, and the preservation and privilege of his highness, would be founded upon an old and sure foundation.[16]

Ashe's proposal was deeply controversial, but its basic premise was not. Supporters of the army did not want a new settlement, but they acknowledged that the security threat was serious. Their solution was to call for the militias and the major-generals to be continued, for the militia bill to be resurrected, as the best hope for protection against enemies.[17] Others supported Ashe, emphasising 'that our enemies took advantage of our unsettlement' and also the need to secure 'the safety of the nation' in the longer term.[18] The debate that followed Ashe's motion has always appeared to be inconclusive, premature and (in the words of one supporter of it) 'only started by way of probation'.[19] This is too hasty a conclusion, however. The parliamentary discussion may have died away without a resolution, but the issue of the new 'settlement' remained very much alive. Indeed, revelations about Sindercombe's plot, and the issues they had raised, may have had an impact on the militia bill, which again took over as the pre-eminent issue at Westminster during the next few days. Its rejection on 29 January marked both a fatal blow to the major-generals and a great victory for those who looked for a civilian constitution to replace the Instrument of Government. The defeat of the bill did not lead to a slackening of the pace, moreover, as in the days that followed MPs bustled about, passing resolutions and arranging the details of a day of thanksgiving for Cromwell's survival of the plot, and, amid all this activity, a crucial decision was taken: to name a committee, 'to prepare a narrative of the grounds and reasons' for it.[20] When this committee reported to the Commons on 31 January, the wording of its declaration echoed (and endorsed) the statement read by Thurloe in parliament in blaming for the plot:

> A sort of discontented spirits [*sic*], called Levellers, plotting to disturb our peace . . . and these have so far degenerated, as to associate themselves with the inveterate enemies of the English nation and Protestant religion, those of Spain; and for malice and hire, to submit themselves to be executioners of their barbarous designs, and against their native country . . . [and] that one Boyes (a principal actor in those designs) did assure them, that when the protector was dispatched, forces were to come from Flanders, in ships to be hired with the king of Spain's money.

The declaration was published on 2 February, and distributed across the three nations.[21] Its intention was plain: to frame the plot as an attack on the people as a whole, led by political radicals linked to the army ('the Levellers'), backed by Catholic Spain, and on behalf of the Stuarts. As Ashe had pointed out, this threat demanded not just security measures, but a change in the constitutional basis of the state. Over the next three weeks, using Sindercombe's case as fuel, the engine of reform did not stall—it was able to continue at full throttle.


## II

Two days after the declaration for the day of thanksgiving was published, the formal legal process against Sindercombe began, with the lord chief justice, John Glynn, presiding. Witnesses were heard the next day and the sentence was passed on 9 February.[22] During this period there were constant reports that the constitutional settlement was about to be changed. On 3 February, Vincent Gookin—an Irish MP with close connections with those who looked for a civilian settlement—predicted that there would soon be 'a reducing of the government to kingship', adding that 'his highness is not averse' to the proposal.[23] On 7 February, one royalist agent told Sir Edward Hyde that Thurloe planned to make Cromwell king, that a royal purse had been made for the great seal and that 'some design is on foot'.[24] Another newsletter, dated the same day, also picked up the gossip: 'many citizens of London have laid several wagers of late that we shall have suddenly an alteration of the present government'.[25] Gookin attributed this to the joy felt by many at the failure of the militia bill,[26] but others were eager to make a connection between settlement and the threat of plots. Once again, Secretary Thurloe was a key figure in stoking up concerns, and pointing to possible solutions. The edition of *Mercurius Politicus*—edited by Marchmont Nedham and effectively controlled by Thurloe—that appeared on or after 4 February, opened with a letter purporting to come from Edinburgh, expressing delight at the failure of the Sindercombe plot. The letter continued with more general comments, which were probably added by those at Whitehall (if, indeed, the whole letter is not a fabrication):

> It seems Charles Stuart will hardly be able to effect any thing upon England, so long as his highness is alive; which should induce us and all the people of these nations, the rather to set our selves to use our utmost endeavours for the preservation of his highness' person, and to come to such a settlement, as may secure him and us.[27]

This explicit connecting of the plot with the need for constitutional change is revealing.

The opening of the proceedings against Sindercombe coincided with an apparent increase in discussion of 'settlement', but its conclusion could not be so easily used for political purposes. 14 February had been set for the day 'it was expected that Sindercombe should have been brought forth to execution' in a very public display of the fate of traitors and plotters;[28] but the main actor in the drama refused to come on stage, instead taking his own life, with the aid of poison smuggled into his cell, the night before. This was little short of a disaster for the government. Although Sindercombe's body was dragged out for burial beneath the gallows at Tower Hill, and transfixed by an iron spike 'as an example of terror to all traitors',[29] this did not have the same impact as the full gory spectacle of hanging, drawing and quartering.[30] Worse still, the suicide raised doubts as the government's role in the whole affair. There had been mutterings for several weeks that 'the whole affair [was] a sham, invented by the court',[31] and now there were questions raised by the manner of Sindercombe's death. As one hostile source alleged later, it was thought by some that Cromwell himself had 'caused him to be smothered'.[32] The government moved quickly to counter such allegations. On 15 February a suicide note was found in Sindercombe's cell, and it was made public when the other government newsbook, *Publick Intelligencer*, was published a day later; but it was only on 19 February that *Politicus* could finish the story, with a detailed account of the suicide, including the post mortem (by five named physicians) and the coroner's verdict.[33] Even then, it was felt necessary to advertise, in the next edition of *Politicus*, a separate publication of 'The whole business of Sinder-combe, from first to last . . . worthy the perusal of all such who remain unsatisfied, as to the manner of his destroying himself.'[34] This pamphlet, apparently published on 16 February, not only retold the story of the plot, the trial and the suicide in detail, but also reprinted the physicians' and coroner's reports and nine pages of depositions by those who were with Sindercombe shortly before his death.[35] Small wonder the French ambassador, also writing on 16 February, thought that 'quelques uns veulent que toute cette histoire ayt esté jouée pour donner couleur aux pretentions du Protecteur' [some of them would have it that the whole story was put about to enhance the claims of the protector].[36]

Sindercombe's premature end might have caused some embarrassment, but it did not affect the celebrations laid on for the thanksgiving day on 20 February. The day's events had been carefully arranged. Sermons were to provide the religious part of the thanksgiving, and these were to take place not only at Westminster but also 'through the three nations'. Copies of the declaration had been sent into the localities in early February, and distributed to the minister of every parish.[37] The day was kept even in the furthest parts of the nation, according to local notions of celebration. In Edinburgh it was more like a fast day. The city council proclaimed the thanksgiving day on 18 February, ordering that the citizens 'keep the said solemn day and repair to the patent churches and forbear the keeping of mercats [markets], and that they keep close their houses, shops and taverns', and the council records show that the holiday was duly observed—by the councillors, at least.[38] In the Cornish town of Bodmin, the day of thanksgiving was celebrated in a more ebullient manner, with the accounts of the mayor listing the cost of wine and cakes, beer and bread, wood for the bonfire, bell-ringers and also private entertainments enjoyed by the 'town council' in private.[39] These provincial celebrations came nowhere close to what took place at Whitehall. On 18 February Cromwell had issued a formal invitation to MPs to dine with him at the Banqueting House.[40] There were immediate rumours as to the nature of the feast, with one newsletter writer claiming that 'the protector . . . hath provided 400 dishes of meat' for the members.[41] Later reports show that the entertainment provided on 20 February more than lived up to expectations. The Venetian ambassador was told that the 'entertainment' was 'the rarest ever seen in England' with the feast being accompanied by 'exquisite music'.[42] The French ambassador was equally impressed, saying that the MPs 'sont bien recognissons de ce bon traictement' [are very grateful for such a good reception].[43] *Mercurius Politicus* reported the day's proceedings with gusto, describing the feast and the entertainments, including 'rare music, both of instruments and voices, till the evening'.[44] The courtly entertainments offered to MPs by the protector appear more like the celebration of a foreign treaty or a special event, rather than a solemn day of thanksgiving for his survival of an assassination plot. This was no coincidence.

In the days leading up to the thanksgiving celebrations, observers had again started to pick up rumours that Cromwell was to be offered the crown, as part of a new 'settlement' of the nations. Unlike those of early February, these rumours were precise, with dates even being suggested for the formal offer of kingship. On 14 February, Sir Archibald Johnston of Wariston heard that 'the great business of the government... comes into the parliament the next Wednesday [18 February]'.[45] On 16 February, Bordeaux reported 'Ill ne se parle présentement que du couronnement de M. le Protecteur, et la voix publique veut que dans trios jours la proposition en doibve estre faict au Parlement' [at the moment he speaks of nothing but the coronation of the protector, and it is said that in three days [19 February] the proposal will certainly be made in parliament].[46] As it turned out, the rumours heard by Wariston and Bordeaux were not accurate, and, for once, the Venetian ambassador proved to be better informed, reporting that the offer of the crown would take place on the day of thanksgiving: 'Many think that on this occasion his highness will be presented with the crown, since the question of the succession was brought up again some days ago and they speak as if it was decided'. He also reported that Payne Fisher, the unofficial laureate, would present verses to celebrate the occasion, and that gold and silver coins had been minted as souvenirs.[47] In the event, the crown was not offered to Cromwell on Friday, 20 February, but as part of the Remonstrance read in parliament on the following Monday, 23 February.[48] Nevertheless, it seems clear that the thanksgiving day had originally been planned as the setting for the great event. The courtly entertainments fitted such an occasion; those around the protector's court were expectant that change was imminent; and, perhaps most compelling of all, the Remonstrance itself was built around the threat to the protector's person, as revealed in the Sindercombe plot. The preamble made the link explicit:

We beseech you likewise give us leave to reflect upon that which lies much upon our hearts, which is the continual danger [which] your life is in from the bloody practices both of the malignants and discontented party, (one whereof, through the goodness of God, you have been lately delivered from), it being a received principle amongst them that (no person being declared to succeed you in the government) nothing is wanting to bring us into blood and confusion and them to their desired ends, but the destruction of your person, and therefore they leave nothing unattempted to effect it.[49]

Once again, the solution to the threat of assassination plots was civilian 'settlement', with Cromwell accepted as monarch, and the succession defined and secured. Such arguments certainly had the desired effect on ordinary MPs, and the majority in favour of giving it a formal reading was a thumping 144 to 54.[50]

## III

As we have seen, the Sindercombe plot was closely linked with the threat from Spain, and the plotters' confessions (or at least the versions of them presented for public consumption in the declaration for the day of thanksgiving) admitted that they had intended 'to unite with the Spaniard' to assassinate Cromwell, 'and when the protector was dispatched, forces would come from Flanders, in ships hired with the king of Spain's money' to put Charles Stuart on the throne.[51] Such revelations were seconded by Thurloe's newsbooks, which printed lurid accounts of preparations for invasion, especially in the early days of February. The edition of *Mercurius Politicus* published on 4 February is particularly worthy of close analysis. It contained a letter from Bruges (of 16 January) relating the mustering of ships off the Flanders coast 'to transport an army, belonging to the Scottish king', and also reporting that Charles Stuart's men had at last been paid, and were now 'enquartered along the sea-towns';[52] and also a further letter from the same (19 January) warning of the arrival of Irish troops, and that the king of Spain had ordered Don John 'to be aiding and helping to him in all what he is able to do'.[53] This issue of *Politicus* also made public further details of the Sindercombe plot, including the alarming revelation that he and his confederates had been 'assured ... of forces out of Flanders, as soon as the protector should be dispatched, which were to be wafted in ships hired at the charge of Spain'.[54] And the whole heady brew was begun by the letter, purporting to be from Edinburgh, which explicitly linked Sindercombe and the risk of invasion, and urged the people to 'come to such a settlement, as may secure him [Cromwell] and us'.[55] The newsbooks issued later in February were dominated by the Sindercombe plot, but they also included news (some of its rather elderly) of the growing foreign menace. The *Publick Intelligencer* of 9 February printed a letter from Brussels (20 January) reporting that 'there are expected 5000 horse and 8000 foot, all which are the emperor's soldiers, for the recruiting and advancing our progress in the war'.[56] *Mercurius Politicus* of 19 February included letters from Madrid (of 30 December) noting the preparations of the Spanish fleet, and from Vienna (15 January) with news that 'the Spanish ambassador hath received great store of moneys for to raise soldiers'.[57] There was a more menacing revelation in *Mercurius Politicus* of 26 February—published three days into the debate on the Remonstrance—which printed a letter from Antwerp (14 February) concerning 'the great designs they give out to have in hand for the re-establishing of them again, which only waits the safe arrival of the king of Spain's plate fleet, to furnish them with money for the putting the same into execution'.[58] Like the reports of the Sindercombe trial and afterwards, the newsbook accounts were written with half an eye on the government's agenda, as determined by the secretary of state, John Thurloe, who controlled both official periodicals, and, as the chief intelligence officer of the state, provided them with their information from abroad. Much of this foreign news was no doubt aimed at MPs, debating the raising of money for the Spanish war; but it was also for wider public consumption, not least by the army.

The army officers had been strongly in favour of the Spanish war before January 1657. The army interest in the Commons had complained at the sidelining of foreign policy during December 1656, with its leaders saying that MPs were 'very unreasonable to vote for a war and leave it unprovided for' and that 'we could not take Spain nor Flanders with a bare vote'.[59] The army and its supporters also made the connection with domestic threats. Major-General William Boteler told Admiral Edward Montagu on 9 January that

we have not all this time raised one penny towards the Spanish war, nor are we like to do after this rate we go till we hear of him upon our border, I think, but instead of hastening that great concernment we have more mind to take away the militia and lessen our army, as though we had the greatest calm of peace that ever yet we saw.[60]

The senior officers still had a strong personal attachment to Cromwell, and they also shared the government's readiness to link foreign war and internal security; but there were soon worrying signs that the defeat of the militia bill had provoked the army interest and shaken its trust in the regime. There were very real fears of an army revolt, not in favour of the Stuarts, but in defence of the 'good old cause': the political and religious aims of the Revolution of 1649. With the army in a state of unrest, any sudden shift towards a civilian constitution might trigger mutiny, if not rebellion.[61]

Apart from the use of newsbooks to heighten background fears of invasion, Thurloe used his personal correspondence with army commanders to issue direct warnings during the period between the formal declaration of the day of thanksgiving on 2 February and the introduction of the Remonstrance on the 23rd. On 3 February, for example, he sent a letter to George Monck in Scotland (which must have been despatched with the orders for the day of thanksgiving) with specific warnings. Thurloe's letter does not survive, but Monck's reply refers to it, 'by which I understood, that Charles Stuart intends to land 5000 men some where about the north'.[62] On 10 February Thurloe sent a letter to the commander of the Irish army, the protector's younger son, Henry Cromwell, giving full details of Sindercombe's trial, and adding, darkly, that 'the common enemy is certainly stirring, and that very vigorously. They threaten an invasion some time in March'.[63] As the thanksgiving day approached, Thurloe's warnings were reinforced by those of Oliver Cromwell himself. On 19 February, letters signed by the protector were sent to all the militia officers in England and Wales, ordering them to be on their guard for both a foreign invasion and a domestic insurrection. These officers were told to work with their regional commanders, the major-generals.[64] Finally, on the evening of 23 February, after the Remonstrance had been read in the Commons, 'the same day his highness sent cautionary letters to all the militia troops, wherein notice was taken of Charles Stuart's preparations abroad, and of his intention to land an army this spring, requiring their readiness and care to oppose them, and promising a reward for their service'.[65]

The various letters warning of invasion and insurrection certainly had an impact on the army officers. On 24 February, for example, Monck told Henry Cromwell of the 'news' he had heard, 'which is, that Charles Stuart intends this summer (if monies doe not fail him) to give some trouble both in Ireland and Scotland', and voiced fears that England would also be attacked.[66] On the same day, the senior officer and councillor, Charles Fleetwood, wrote to Henry from Whitehall, indicating that he, too, was fearful of unrest. He was bitter that the Remonstrance had been introduced in spite of the security threat, 'that when Charles Stuart is in preparation with a considerable army to transport himself into England, men's minds should now again divide about government', and he passed on information affecting Henry directly, 'for it is from very good hands that Charles Stuart intends action very suddenly, and though it is pretended that England is the place intended, yet I cannot think Ireland to be secure'.[67] A very similar reaction was reported from the Yorkshire town of Leeds, where 'none of the army or their friends' supported the new constitution, but they were nevertheless concerned to maintain 'peace and unity, lest our common enemy at this juncture take his advantage'.[68] Monck in Scotland, Fleetwood at Whitehall and the soldiers at Leeds fully accepted that there was a grave threat to the regime, and their reaction was no doubt echoed by Henry Cromwell and others across the three nations. Yet there is compelling evidence to suggest that their fears were unfounded—for the warnings did not reflect a true crisis for the protectorate, but a clever propaganda campaign, masterminded by Thurloe, designed to prevent a mutiny by the army during the critical period from 20 to 23 February, when the new constitution was to be unveiled. There are three reasons for believing this.

First, although there had been alarms throughout the winter of 1656–1657, the likelihood of the royalists being able to mount an invasion was rapidly diminishing even before February 1657, despite the promises and assurances of the Spanish.[69] The public row between Charles and duke of York, at the beginning of January, had thrown the court in exile into disarray, and many feared that it would compromise the possibility of support in England as well as the backing of Spain.[70] The failure of the Sindercombe assassination plot was another reverse,[71] and there seems to have been little hope of mounting an invasion during February. In the meantime, life in Bruges became increasingly uncomfortable. At the end of January, Hyde was pressing for the king's allowance to be paid, complaining that he had to borrow money even to pay messengers to England. A month later, money was so tight that 'they have not £5 for military service or to buy anything the king wants', and Charles was forced to admit that any invasion would have to be put off until the winter.[72] It is uncertain how much of this was known at Whitehall. Since November 1656 Thurloe had been kept well-informed about domestic conspiracies by the double-agent, Sir Richard Willis, and probably picked up intelligence about foreign designs from the same source.[73] In general, reports sent from intelligence agents to Thurloe were mixed.[74] In January, one agent in the Netherlands had said that the money offered to Charles Stuart is 'not enough to cause him to undertake any thing', while those in Flanders stated that any possibility of invasion before the spring had been prevented by the lack of money from Spain, and the refusal of Don John of Austria to provide 4000 troops as promised.[75] The sinking of ships carrying 14,000 muskets and 5000 pistols for the Stuart forces was also seen as significant.[76] At the beginning of February, three reports arrived, two warning of some attempt 'this spring', the third, from Bruges, stated that the Stuarts had no more than 2000 soldiers, and most of those were unarmed.[77] Other reports may also have given some cause for alarm at this time,[78] but by mid-February there was general agreement among the intelligence agents that the Stuart cause was in decline: Charles 'cannot expect much assistance at present' (7 February); there were suspicions that any troops raised would be used in the Spanish campaign against the French in Flanders (12 February); and this was soon confirmed, leaving the royalists 'very much discouraged . . . and that they speak no more at all of that enterprise, as being a thing of no manner of probability (13 February).[79] It was only Ambassador Lockhart at Paris, who was presumably dependent on information from a French government keen to cement its own anti-Spanish alliance with the protectorate, who continued to send regular warnings of imminent invasion.[80] At the very least, the reports received by Thurloe during this period were contradictory, and almost always stressed that any invasion was dependent on Spanish troops, money and ships; and by the middle of February there was increasing agreement among them that the Stuart invasion was a nonstarter. Thurloe must have been well aware of this when Cromwell sent out his letters to the militia officers on 19 February, warning that invasion was imminent.

The second reason for suspecting Thurloe of manipulating the army is the total lack of evidence for an invasion in the records of central government. Admittedly, under the Instrument of Government the council's role in such cases was less than clear. The protector exercised the 'chief magistracy' of the nations with the council's assistance, and he was to 'direct in all things concerning the keeping and holding of a good correspondency with foreign kings, princes and states' with their advice, and 'with the consent of the major part' when it came to 'the power of war and peace'. But, when parliament was sitting, the 'dispose and order of the militia and forces' were to be in the protector's hands 'by the consent of parliament' and without the need to seek the council's advice.[81] In February 1657, according to the council order books and the *Commons' Journals*, the possibility of an invasion was not addressed by either body. Indeed, the first mention of an invasion in the House of Commons (aside from generalisations connected with the Sindercombe business) came only on 23 February, when the preamble to the Remonstrance raised the spectre of assassination leading to 'sedition and civil war ... and therein these nations exposed to be made a prey to foreigners'.[82] Arguments based on lack of evidence are problematic, but in this case the silence is deafening. The third cause for suspicion is much more straightforward. On 24 February, the day after the Remonstrance had been presented to the Commons, Thurloe suddenly announced that the threat of invasion had ended. In his letter to Henry Cromwell of the same date, he reported that 'I hear Charles Stuart's intention of landing forces doth somewhat cool, the Spaniard as yet failing him in his supplies promised'.[83] His letter to Monck repeated the refrain: 'the alarm of Charles Stuart's landing his forces doth somewhat cool, the Spaniard not as yet making good his promised supplies'; but he then let the cat out of the bag, asking the Scottish commander to watch 'the posture of the army with you, because some unquiet spirits or other will take this or any other occasion to put the army into discontent by false reports'.[84]

The constant warnings of foreign invasion in newsbooks or by personal letters; the silence in parliament and the council on the same issue; the rapid move to reduce such fears once the Remonstrance had been introduced to parliament: all suggest that John Thurloe was mounting an elaborate confidence trick, with the army as the main target. And it very nearly worked. As predicted, the army was outspoken in its opposition to the new constitution, but there was no mutiny, and the soldiery limited themselves to grumbling. As Fleetwood's comments on 24 February show, the senior officers were alarmed that the Remonstrance had been brought in at the height of a security scare, and some resolved to prevent a 'divide about government', although the immediate effect of the Remonstrance was indeed a split not only among MPs, but in the protectoral council itself. Yet Fleetwood's trust still lay in the protector: 'the only hopes of honest men, is that the Lord will so manage his highness' heart in this business, who we know hath been a man of great prayer and faith and to whom the Lord hath given much of his counsel in dark cases, and I trust will still own him with a more then ordinary presence of His at this time'.[85] Others were not so sure. In an angry confrontation with Cromwell in the evening of 23 February, 'some of the major-generals . . . complained of the parliament [to] his highness', and were nonplussed when Cromwell 'answered hastily, "what would you have me do, are they not a thing of your own garbling? Did you not admit whom you pleased and keep out whom you pleased? And now do you complain to me? Did I meddle with it?" '.[86] Cromwell might well have been evasive: he spent the same evening writing a letter to the militia captains warning them once more of the threat of invasion and insurrection—a threat that Thurloe (and, almost certainly Cromwell himself) already knew was an illusion.

## IV

Historians have routinely rejected the possibility that Cromwell actively sought the crown. The logic seems to be that as Cromwell eventually rejected the crown, he had not sought to be king at any time. However sorely tempted by the blandishments of the 'kinglings' or the hopes of securing 'healing and settling' across the three nations, he remained, at heart, true to the 'good old cause'. The offer of the crown came from others, and it came as a nasty surprise; even if Cromwell had an inkling of what was afoot, he did not approve of it, nor did he encourage it. Yet, as we have seen, there are good grounds for suspecting that Cromwell's real view, at least in February 1657, was very different. It is suspicious that the original plan was to offer him the crown at a feast hosted by himself; and there can be no doubt that the protector repeatedly endorsed Thurloe's attempts to bring the army into line by playing up fears of insurrection and invasion, either by letter or by face-to-face confrontation with his senior officers. The rancorous meeting of 23 February was matched by another, a few days after the Remonstrance was unveiled, when 100 officers attended Cromwell, demanding 'that his highness would not hearken to the title [of king] because it was not pleasing to his army and was a matter of scandal to the people of God'. Cromwell's reaction is instructive. Instead of calming their fears, he shouted them down. He praised parliament's actions—'if they do good things, I must and will stand by them. They are honest men and have done good things'—and warned that the days of military rule were numbered: 'it is time to come to a settlement, and lay aside arbitrary proceedings so unacceptable to the nation'. When it came to the title itself, he waved it away as a thing of little importance: 'for his part he loved the title, a feather in a hat, as little as they did'. This was presumably meant to reassure them that he did not covet the title, but it was a deeply ambiguous statement, and far from the open renunciation of the title that the officers were looking for.[87] Such enigmatic utterances are not a solid foundation from which to argue that Cromwell 'from early on indicated a willingness to accept everything except the title'.[88]

In the absence of definitive evidence of Cromwell's opinions in the early spring of 1657, the activities of his secretary of state are of great importance. Although scholars have varied in their estimation of Thurloe's abilities, and of his importance to the protectoral government, they do not doubt his closeness to Cromwell. Hugh Trevor-Roper sees Thurloe as 'greatly overrated' adding that 'he seems to have been merely an industrious secretary who echoed his master's sentiments (and errors) with pathetic unoriginality'.[89] By contrast, Blair Worden sees Thurloe as Cromwell's *eminence gris*: 'foreigners and natives alike perceived that the only way of reaching Cromwell was not through the council but through John Thurloe, Cromwell's "intimus" or "factotum" or "right-hand man"'. Furthermore, Worden sees Thurloe's discretion as his crucial ability, for 'Thurloe was too shrewd to jeopardise his position by seeking to manipulate the protector, whose skill in detecting motives he knew'.[90] Thurloe's most recent biographer, Philip Aubrey, concurs: 'Thurloe was not so much an echo of his master's voice as someone who genuinely shared the ideas of the protector on most questions of policy at home and abroad.'[91] Despite differences in emphasis, all these historians agree that Thurloe and Cromwell acted as one, and by the spring of 1657 there had been no major public disagreements between the two. The two men were also intimate friends. Thurloe was Cromwell's companion when the protector overturned his coach in Hyde Park in September 1654; in the winter of 1655–1656 he was reputedly one of the protector's 'cabinet' of chief advisers; and in 1657 he was among those routinely invited by Cromwell 'into a private room together and be there shut up two or three hours discoursing of his great business'.[92] The two belonged to a social circle that was rooted in the Fens, and Thurloe came into Cromwell's service through the protector's friend and cousin, Oliver St John, a man who was said, in February 1657, to have been 'often, but secretly, at Whitehall' to persuade Cromwell to take the crown.[93] Such evidence strengthens the case that Thurloe's actions in January and February 1657 were undertaken with the knowledge, and support, of the protector. Indeed, it beggars belief that Thurloe would go behind his master's back when managing the press, manipulating parliament or misleading the army, or, indeed, when playing up threats of insurrection and invasion. And if this is taken alongside the relatively sparse evidence of the protector's own views at this time, there are strong reasons for believing that Cromwell also saw eye-to-eye with Thurloe on the subject of kingship.

The argument that Cromwell originally sought the crown is supported by what happened later in the kingship debates. It was only at the very end of March, when the monarchical version of the Humble Petition and Advice was presented to Cromwell, that there are signs that he was having second thoughts. Interestingly, his speech to parliament on 31 March did not pour cold water on the idea of kingship—rather he wanted assurance that taking the crown was the right thing to do:

> It would give you very little cause of comfort in such a choice as you have made [of me becoming king] in such a business as this is, because it would savour more to be of the flesh, to proceed from lust, to arise from arguments of self. And if . . . my decision in it should have such motives in me, and such a rise in me, it may prove even a curse to you and to these nations.[94]

An element of doubt was there, but a definite sign that Cromwell had decisively turned against kingship came only on 3 April, when he stated, unequivocally, that 'I have not been able to find it my duty to God and to you to accept the charge under that title'.[95] Significantly, Cromwell's change of mind came close to wrecking his relationship with Thurloe. Thurloe's confidence, so obvious in March,[96] suddenly evaporated in April, when he admitted to Ambassador Lockhart that 'whether his highness, when all this is done, will accept of kingship, I am not able to say'.[97] The situation was not improved by Cromwell's final refusal of the crown on 8 May, which marked the end of efforts by MPs and others to persuade him to change his mind. As the courtier, Sir Francis Russell, told Henry Cromwell on 25 May, 'the little secretary tells me that he seeth now that nothing is so considerable in any business as simplicity'.[98] This remark has been taken as 'gnomic', but there one plausible explanation: despite all his best efforts, all the spinning and weaving, Thurloe had failed to secure the most simple of prerequisites—the protector's own support for the plan. The miscalculation was excusable, and it was one he shared with other leading proponents of kingship. Lord Broghill, John

Glynn and Sir Charles Wolseley absented themselves from the Commons in early April, once Cromwell's opposition became known. His final refusal in early May caused some 'country gentlemen' and Presbyterian supporters of kingship to react with anger, while friends of the protector, including William Pierrepont and Edward Montagu, were in such despair that it was said that they 'will never trust to politics any more'.[99] The blank incomprehension of these men, some of whom, like Thurloe, were very close to the protector, again suggests that Cromwell's decision to reject the crown was very sudden, and very late.

## V

The reintroduction of the Sindercombe plot and its aftermath into the narrative of the 'kingship' debates helps to answer the three questions posed at the beginning of this chapter. The initial offer of the crown had its roots not just in the succession debate of November 1656, the Naylor case of December or the militia bill of January 1657; there was a fourth factor that was as important as the other three: the plot against Cromwell's life, the fall-out from which dominated the political scene for much of February 1657. The management of the trial of Sindercombe and the preparations for the day of thanksgiving, largely conducted by John Thurloe, allowed those who backed a new constitution to present it as essential for the safety of the three nations both in the long and short term. Conversely, the deliberate heightening of fears of foreign invasion helped to prevent a mutiny by the army, which opposed these constitutional changes. Thurloe's importance in this points to an answer to the third question, concerning Cromwell's own attitude to the crown in the spring of 1657. As we have seen, there is no proof that Cromwell was opposed to taking the crown before the beginning of April, and there is sufficient evidence, both direct and indirect, to suggest that he was fully behind the idea when the Remonstrance was introduced in the final week of February. It seems that Cromwell at first supported the offer of the crown, and then changed his mind.

It is evident that the current view of Cromwell's role as protector needs to be re-examined. Far from being aloof from politics, allowing others to conduct a tug-of-war over policy, even when it came to fundamental decisions such as changing the constitution, Cromwell was very much involved in public affairs, if behind the scenes. Cromwell was not a plaster saint; he was a skilled politician whose eye for the main chance had been demonstrated throughout his rise to power. He was also subtle enough to know when not to be in the limelight, and when to disassociate himself from schemes that would prove dangerously controversial, or were about to fail.[100] His rejection of the crown should be seen as another example of this, and it says a great deal for his abilities as a politician that he was able to turn the tables so effectively that men like Ambassador Lockhart, as well as later historians, came to see his refusal as a sign of his 'extraordinary virtue'.

Recognising Cromwell's political skill need not lead us to challenge the idea that religion was at the very heart of all his decisions, or that his speeches claiming to seek only God's glory were a cover for his own lust for power. Cromwell was no hypocrite. He may have sought the crown, but he took very seriously the warnings from other godly people—and from his own conscience—that he should not take it after all. In this way, the traditional view of Cromwell's rejection of the crown needs modification, not rejection. The chronology must be foreshortened, as his rejection of the crown seems to have come over a matter of days rather than weeks, as he realised that by pursuing the best option for the 'settlement' of the three nations, he was in fact on the brink of committing a terrible sin. This, rather than the failure of the 'Western Design' nearly two years before, is surely the proper context for Cromwell's belief that he had nearly brought the wrath of God on the nation. For Achan's sin was not reluctantly to agree, under pressure from others, to take the 'accursed thing'—he went secretly and took it for himself. It was not so much the failure of the army but Cromwell's own failure to resist temptation that troubled his conscience in April 1657, when he finally rejected the crown and refused 'to build Jericho again'.

## Notes

1. TNA, SP78/113, fo. 155r: Sir William Lockhart to Richard Cromwell, 11/21 April 1657.
2. C. H. Firth, 'Cromwell and the Crown [part 2]', *EHR*, 18 (1903), 75–6.
3. This influential argument first appeared in B. Worden, 'Oliver Cromwell and the Sin of Achan', in D. Beales and G. Best (eds), *History, Society and the Churches* (Cambridge, 1985). Other historians have sought a *via media* between Firth and Worden: see, for example, Coward, *Cromwell*, 151–3; Gaunt, *Cromwell*, 196–200.
4. Abbott, iv. 473.

5. C. H. Firth, 'Cromwell and the Crown [part 1]', *EHR*, 17 (1902), 440–2. Firth noted the informal discussion of the constitution in January and February 1657, but did not accord it much significance: see 'Cromwell and the Crown [part 2]', 53–4.

6. H. R. Trevor-Roper, 'Oliver Cromwell and his Parliaments', in Ivan Roots (ed.), *Oliver Cromwell: A Profile* (1973), 128.

7. Carol Egloff, 'Settlement and Kingship: the Army, the Gentry, and the Offer of the Crown to Oliver Cromwell' (Ph.D., Yale University, 1990), 172; see also ibid., 10–12, 531.

8. *ODNB*, 'Oliver Cromwell'.

9. C. H. Firth, *The Last Years of the Protectorate, 1656–1658* (2 vols., 1909), i. 128.

10. This paragraph is based on Firth, *Last Years*, i. 116–19.

11. Firth, *Last Years*, i. 113–21; D. Underdown, *Royalist Conspiracy in England, 1649–1660* (New Haven, 1960), 192–3.

12. Firth, 'Cromwell and the Crown [Part 1]', 422; Firth, *Last Years*, i. 129n.

13. See, for example, Coward, *Cromwell*; Gaunt, *Cromwell*; an honourable exception to this rule is Colin Davis, who has noted the possible implications of a plot which 'underlined the vulnerability of the regime and the desire to get it on to a more stable, inevitably traditional, basis' (Davis, *Cromwell*, 40), but he does not develop the idea further.

14. *Burton Diary*, i. 354–6.

15. Ibid., 356.

16. Ibid., 362–3.

17. Ibid., 363.

18. Ibid., 364–5.

19. Ibid., 365–6.

20. *CJ*, vii. 481a. The committee members nominated were John Thurloe, Bulstrode Whitelocke, Sir William Strickland, Nathaniel Fiennes, John Disbrowe, Sir Charles Wolseley, Lord Broghill and Philip Jones. Of these eight, five (Thurloe, Fiennes, Wolseley, Broghill and Jones) were later to be identified as members of the 'cabal' which championed the Remonstrance in the Commons, and Whitelocke was clearly a fellow-traveller (see P. Little, *Lord Broghill and the Cromwellian Union with Ireland and Scotland* (Woodbridge, 2004), 148).

21. *CJ*, vii. 484a; *A Declaration . . . for a Day of Publique Thanksgiving* (2 February 1657), 1–2, 4.

22. *Mercurius Politicus*, no. 348 (5–12 February 1657), 7588–92; *Publick Intelligencer*, no. 69 (2–9 Febraury 1657), 1180.

23. *TSP*, vi. 37.

24. *CCSP*, iii. 247.

25. *Clarke Papers*, iii. 88.

26. *TSP*, vi. 37.

27. *Mercurius Politicus*, no. 347 (29 January–4 February 1657), 7561–2.
28. *Publick Intelligencer*, no. 70 (9–16 February 1657), 1196.
29. *Mercurius Politicus*, no. 349 (12–19 February 1657), 7608.
30. For the full details of sentence, see *Mercurius Politicus*, no. 348 (5–12 February 1657), 7601; *CSPV 1657–9*, 18.
31. For comments, see *CSPV 1657–9*, 8–9, 11, 14; *TSP*, v. 794.
32. *Killing Noe Murder* (June 1657), [p. 15].
33. *Mercurius Politicus*, no. 349 (12–19 February 1657), 7604–8.
34. Ibid., no. 350 (19–26 February 1657), 7621.
35. *The Whole Business of Sindercombe, from First to Last* (16 February 1657).
36. TNA, PRO 31/3/101, fo. 68r.
37. *CJ*, vii. 481, 484; *CSPD 1656–7*, 258–9; see also C. H. Firth (ed.), *Scotland and the Protectorate* (Edinburgh, 1899), 348–9.
38. Edinburgh City Archives, SL/1/1/19, fo. 188v; M. Wood (ed.), *Extracts from the Records of the Burgh of Edinburgh, 1655–65* (Edinburgh, 1940), 48–50; the day was also held in Dublin: see R. Dunlop (ed.), *Ireland Under the Commonwealth* (2 vols., Manchester, 1913), ii. 653.
39. Cornwall RO, B/BOD/285, unfol. The thanksgiving was also observed by the rival churches of Leeds (see BL, Add. MS 21424, fos. 212r, 218r).
40. *CJ*, vii. 493; *Burton Diary*, i. 377.
41. Bodl., MS Tanner 52, fo. 191r.
42. *CSPV 1657–9*, 21.
43. TNA, PRO 31/3/101, fo. 83r.
44. *Mercurius Politicus*, no. 350 (19–26 February 1657), 7615.
45. J. D. Ogilvie (ed.), *Diary of Sir Archibald Johnston of Wariston, iii, 1655–1660* (Edinburgh, 1940), 61.
46. TNA, PRO 31/3/101, fo. 63r; see also ibid., fo. 67r.
47. *CSPV 1657–9*, 21.
48. *CSPV 1657–9*, 22.
49. P. Little and D. L. Smith, *Parliaments and Politics during the Cromwellian Protectorate* (Cambridge, 2007), appendix 2.
50. *CJ*, vii. 496.
51. *CSPD 1656–7*, 258–9; *A Declaration . . . for a Day of Publique Thanksgiving*, 4.
52. *Mercurius Politicus*, no. 347 (29 January–4 February 1657), 7569.
53. Ibid., 7571.
54. Ibid., 7576.
55. Ibid., 7561–2.
56. *Publick Intelligencer*, no. 69 (2–9 February 1657), 1167.
57. *Mercurius Politicus*, no. 349 (12–19 February 1657), 7593–4.
58. Ibid., no. 350 (19–26 February 1657), 7264.

59. Bodl., MS Carte 228, fo. 81r (*Clarke Papers*, iii. 84n–85n). For the army and foreign policy at this time, see Little and Smith, *Parliaments and Politics*, 253–4.
60. Bodl., MS Carte 73, fo. 18r (*Clarke Papers*, iii. 85n–86n).
61. For the factional position of the army, see Little and Smith, *Parliaments and Politics*, 109–13.
62. *TSP*, vi. 52.
63. *TSP*, vi. 53; see also Thurloe to Lockhart, 19 February, saying the government is alarmed by the malignant party, and preparing measures against them (*CCSP*, iii. 252).
64. Abbott, iv. 408; Lomas-Carlyle, iii. 486; *CSPD 1656–7*, 287.
65. *Clarke Papers*, iii. 92.
66. BL, Lansdowne MS 821, fo. 292r.
67. BL, Lansdowne MS 821, fo. 274r (misdated in MS, but definitely 24 February)
68. BL, Add. MS 21424, fo. 224r; see also ibid., fo. 219r.
69. *CCSP*, iii. 224, 228–9.
70. *CCSP*, iii. 227; *Nicholas Papers*, iv. 1–2.
71. *CCSP*, iii. 234, 236.
72. Ibid., 240, 253–4.
73. Underdown, *Royalist Conspiracy*, 195–6.
74. *TSP*, v. 645, 707, 738.
75. *TSP*, v. 794; ibid., vi. 1–2.
76. *CCSP*, iii. 241.
77. *CJ*, vi. 30–3.
78. See *CCSP*, iii. 242, 244; see also Thurloe's enquiry of truth of rumours, dated 13 February (ibid., 250).
79. *TSP*, vi. 43, 56, 72.
80. Lockhart continued to issue such warnings long after Thurloe had admitted that the threat had evaporated: see *TSP*, vi. 74, 87, 107; cf. T. Venning, *Cromwellian Foreign Policy* (Basingstoke, 1996), 143–4 and Abbott, iv. 408–9.
81. Gardiner, *Constitutional Documents*, 406 (articles 2, 4 and 5).
82. Little and Smith, *Parliaments and Politics*, appx 2.
83. *TSP*, vi. 74.
84. *Clarke Papers*, iii. 89–90.
85. BL, Lansdowne MS 821, fo. 274r.
86. Ibid., fo. 294v.
87. Quoted in Firth, 'Cromwell and the Crown [Part 2]', 60.
88. *ODNB*, 'Oliver Cromwell'.
89. Trevor-Roper, 'Oliver Cromwell and his Parliaments', 132n.
90. B. Worden, 'Oliver Cromwell and the Council', in P. Little (ed.), *The Cromwellian Protectorate* (Woodbridge, 2007), 97.

91. P. Aubrey, *Mr Secretary Thurloe: Cromwell's Secretary of State, 1652–1660* (1990), 36, 50, 214; see also 40, 63, 93, 213.

92. Aubrey, *Thurloe*, 49–51; *CSPD 1655–6*, 80; R. Spalding (ed.), *The Diary of Bulstrode Whitelocke, 1605–1675* (Oxford, 1990), 464, 477.

93. *TSP*, vi. 37; see also *State Papers Collected by Edward, Earl of Clarendon* (3 vols., Oxford, 1757), iii. 423; *Nicholas Papers*, iii. 257.

94. Lomas-Carlyle, iii. 27.

95. Ibid., 32.

96. See, for example, *CSPD 1656–7*, 320; also the editorials of *Mercurius Politicus* from no. 352 (5–12 March 1657) to no. 356 (2–9 April 1657); thereafter the newsbook's open support for kingship was suddenly dropped.

97. *TSP*, vi. 243; see also ibid., 219–20, 243; *CSPD 1656–7*, 335.

98. BL, Lansdowne MS 822, fo. 75r.

99. Cited in Little, *Broghill*, 157–8.

100. See Worden, 'Oliver Cromwell and the Council', 92.

# 10

# 'Fit for Public Services': The Upbringing of Richard Cromwell

Jason Peacey

---

Conventional wisdom suggests that Richard Cromwell was neither fit for public life, nor destined to assume the protectoral mantle. His career during the 1640s and 1650s is often thought to have involved rural retreat, if not crypto-royalism, and this has helped to foster the image of 'the pretended protector', 'the meek knight', 'Queen Dick', and 'tumbledown Dick'.[1] Anthony Wood dismissed him as 'the mushroom prince', while Gilbert Burnet, who considered Oliver Cromwell's sons to be 'weak but honest men', wrote that Richard was 'not at all bred for business, nor indeed capable of it'.[2] George Bate, meanwhile, claimed that 'his genius was so far from affecting rule', and that 'he would have been content rather to have led a private life in peace, free from hatred and danger'.[3] J. H. Jesse claimed that Richard's ultimate failure as protector could be explained largely by the fact that he was 'unacquainted with the arts of government and the intrigues consequent on power', and that he was 'without even the impulse of ambition'; while François Guizot concluded that Richard was 'a man of timid vacillating and undecided character, with no religious or political convictions or passions'.[4] Such views almost certainly contain a kernel of truth, at least in terms of Richard's lack of personal ambition, and they clearly find some support in contemporary sources. One Scottish visitor to London in 1657 described

Richard as being 'morose' and 'reserved', while the author of *A Game at Piquet* could think of little more for him to say than 'I will play my game in the country'.[5] More importantly, Oliver Cromwell's own comments appear to suggest at best fatherly resignation regarding Richard's lack of zeal for public service, and at worst a kind of desperation regarding his laziness. And of course Richard certainly lacked the military prowess and administrative flair displayed by his younger brother, Henry, sometime lord lieutenant of Ireland during the protectorate.[6]

Nevertheless, Richard's short political career is long overdue reappraisal.[7] It is necessary, for example, to recognise the nature and extent of his talents, which were appreciated by those who met him, even if not by the public at large, and to acknowledge his unfair treatment at the hands of those who brought about the collapse of the protectorate in 1659. The aim of this chapter, however, is to challenge standard accounts by reconsidering his upbringing and reassessing his life before 1658. As with so much else in Richard's career, the key to an accurate understanding of this period lies in resisting the temptation to read history 'backwards', and to judge earlier periods on the basis of what happened later. Far too often Richard's early life is analysed in the light of his fall from power in the spring of 1659, rather than read 'forwards' on the basis of the historical record. This reappraisal will involve three closely related tasks: drawing attention to neglected information regarding Richard's activity in both local and national politics and administration; teasing out of such evidence his political and religious views; and contextualising Richard's career in terms of his family's fortunes, and political circumstances, during the 1640s and 1650. Ultimately, it will be possible to suggest not only that Oliver's comments regarding Richard have been misinterpreted, but also that his plans for his son changed in entirely logical and understandable ways during this period. Ultimately, Oliver was perfectly happy to prepare Richard for a life on the highest public stage.

# I

It is of course true that Richard Cromwell took little part in the civil wars during the 1640s, and that he was not always destined to rule the land, but both of these facts are true in ways that are not always widely appreciated or acknowledged. Firstly, at his birth in October 1626, Richard was the third son of a provincial squire of dubious wealth, and as such his education was exactly what one ought to expect: godly but modest. He was apparently educated at Felsted School, under the eye of his maternal grandfather, Sir James Bourchier, and under the tutelage of Martin Holbeach, but thereafter he did not attend university.[8] Secondly, Richard had not yet reached maturity by the time that Charles I surrendered Oxford in May 1646, and as such his lack of military experience can hardly be considered noteworthy.

What is much more interesting is the fact that Oliver's attitude towards Richard changed dramatically when the latter became his heir. This only occurred in the spring of 1644, following the death of his elder brother, Oliver (another older brother, Robert, having died in 1639).[9] Oliver Cromwell junior had received a university education, and had served in the parliamentarian army after 1642, first as cornet and then as captain, and it was entirely understandable that Richard would remain in brother's shadow until the latter succumbed to smallpox.[10] Thereafter Oliver Cromwell senior quite conventionally looked to the career development of his eldest surviving son, at least once Richard had reached maturity (in October 1647), and once he himself had helped to see off the royalist threat in the second civil war. Most obviously, this new attitude took the shape of complex and protracted negotiations, which eventually led to Richard's marriage to the daughter of Richard Maijor, a prominent Hampshire parliamentarian, in May 1649.[11]

The rich documentation surrounding Richard's marriage suggests more than merely the importance that had come to be placed on securing a suitable bride. It also provides significant, if somewhat problematic, evidence regarding Richard's character, and his relationship with his father. Richard, who was described as being 'civil, free, and open hearted', spent a good deal of time in Hampshire in early 1649, and it was soon clear that the young man respected the godliness of Richard Maijor's family, and regarded Maijor himself 'as a man by whose conversation he might much advantage himself'.[12] In April of the same year, Oliver too noted that his son 'had a great desire' to visit his future wife, and that 'he minds this more than to attend to business here [Westminster]'.[13]

This last comment helps to develop a picture of a serious and godly young man, which is rarely evident in conventional historiography, but it also seems to form part of a body of epistolary evidence which has fostered and perpetuated the impression that Oliver was disappointed by his son's lack of enthusiasm for public life, and frustrated by his character.[14] Oliver pleaded with Maijor, for example, to offer parental guidance to his son. In July 1649, therefore, he wrote:

> I have delivered my son up to you, and I hope you will counsel him: he will need it, and indeed I believe he likes well what you say, and will be advised by you... I wish he may be serious, the times require it.[15]

In August 1649 (as he prepared to sail for Ireland), meanwhile, the lord general wrote:

> I have committed my son to you, pray give him advice. I envy him not his contents, but I fear he should be swallowed up of them... I would have him mind and understand business, read a little history, study the mathematics and cosmography, these are good, with subordination to the things of God. Better than idleness, or mere outward worldly contents.[16]

In July 1650 (shortly before he crossed the Scottish border with the English army), Oliver re-emphasised that his son needed good counsel: 'he is in the dangerous time of his age, and it's a very vain world'.[17] He also wrote to his daughter-in-law, Dorothy, imploring her to seek the Lord, and 'to provoke your husband likewise thereunto'.[18] Finally, in June 1651 (shortly before returning to Scotland with his troops), Oliver expressed dismay that Richard had overspent his allowance:

> I grudge him not laudable recreations, nor an honourable carriage of himself in them... Truly I can find it in my heart to allow him not only a sufficiency but more, for his good. But if pleasure and self-satisfaction be made the business of a man's life, so much cost laid out upon it, so much time spent in it, as rather answers appetite than the will of God, or is comely before his saints, I scruple to feed this humour, and God forbid that his being my son should be his allowance to live not pleasingly to our heavenly father, who hath raised me out of the dust to what I am... I cannot think I do well to feed a voluptuous humour in my son, if he should make pleasure the business of his life, in a time when some precious saints are bleeding, and breathing out their last, for the safety of the rest.[19]

The first problem with such evidence is that it is possible to consider Oliver's comments about Richard as representing the normal, and naturally exaggerated, concerns of a father, particularly one whose military duties were taking him to an uncertain fate. It is probably no coincidence that each of Oliver's letters regarding Richard was written on the eve of major army campaigns, and as such he can be considered to have been not so much berating Richard as expressing how he wanted him to be guided in the event of his own death. More generally, Oliver's familial and friendly letters need to be treated with some caution. For example, his famous characterisation of Richard Norton as 'idle Dick' was clearly inappropriate, and almost certainly ironic. Norton was an extremely active local parliamentarian commander, and a zealous committee man, who became one of the more active members of the Rump Parliament and the republican councils of state, and who remained close to Oliver throughout the 1640s and for much of the 1650s. That Oliver should have used such a nickname was, of course, a reflection of how close the two men were, and the term appears to have been coined during the somewhat testy marriage negotiations between the Cromwell and Maijor families, when Norton was an active intermediary.[20] If appropriate at all, the nickname may have related merely to Oliver's frustration regarding the speed at which such talks were progressing, but it is also possible that he was poking fun at a friend by playing upon some of the wildly inaccurate accusations which had been made about him in previous years, by the royalist press, and by political and military rivals.[21] In the light of such evidence, it is at least possible that Oliver's comments regarding Richard displayed at least some degree of irony and playfulness.[22]

More broadly, the Cromwell-Maijor marriage serves to highlight one of the key themes of this essay, relating to Richard Cromwell's age and family position, and the status of his family. Before the second half of the 1640s, Richard lacked both the age to fight and hold office, as well as the familial status to have been singled out by his father. This situation changed in part with the death of Richard's brother, and Oliver's reaction was to treat his new heir as any gentleman would, by trying to find a suitable and lucrative match, but it had not changed beyond recognition. Exalted though Oliver had obviously become by the late 1640s, there was absolutely no reason to suspect that anyone saw in him a future head of state, let alone that his heir would succeed him in such a position. Oliver Cromwell had as yet no cause to groom Richard for greatness.

## II

A second problem with such comments regarding Richard Cromwell relates, therefore, to the need to assess Oliver's expectations of his heir, and the reality of Richard's life after the mid-1640s. The surviving evidence suggests that, to a very great extent, Richard performed exactly in accordance with his father's wishes, and that this meant being a good deal more active in public service than some commentators have recognised. Although there is a widespread perception among scholars that Richard was insufficiently serious, worldly, and active, the role which Oliver envisaged for him actually bears a remarkable similarity to that which he can be shown to have adopted in the years after 1648. Once again, therefore, it is necessary to treat with caution the claims made by unreliable contemporary witnesses and hostile commentators both at the time and subsequently, and to re-examine the historical evidence.

In June 1655, Oliver explained his attitude regarding Richard to his son-in-law, Charles Fleetwood, by saying that 'my desire was for him and his brother to have lived private lives in the country'.[23] In March 1659, meanwhile, the protectoral chaplain, William Hooke, confirmed that Richard himself 'had thought to have lived as a country gentleman', adding that 'his father had not employed him in such a way as to prepare him for such employment; which he thought, he did designedly'. Hooke took this to mean that Oliver feared 'lest it should have been apprehended he had prepared and appointed him for such a place'.[24] This idea of the 'private' life of a 'country gentleman' is somewhat misleading, however, because Oliver clearly envisaged that his sons should fulfill the duties of godly and active local magistrates. Indeed, when he recommended in July 1649 that Richard should read history, mathematics and cosmography—duly subordinated to 'the things of God'—he expressly added that these were the things that would ensure that his son was 'fit for public services, for which a man is born'.[25] In April 1650, Oliver told Richard that 'it's the lord's mercy to place you where you are', and advised him to 'seek the Lord and His face continually; let this be the business of your life and strength and let all things be subservient and in order to this'. He added: 'take heed of an inactive vain spirit. Recreate yourself with Sir Walter Raleigh's *History*: it's a body of history and will add much to your understanding'.[26]

Historians have been guilty not only of interpreting Oliver's words too literally, but also of misunderstanding Richard's actions. The suggestion has been that Richard withdrew from London to live the life of a country squire, and that he played little or not part in the momentous events of the period. In October 1654, the Venetian ambassador claimed that Richard 'thinks of little but living privately and enjoying the ease and liberty conceded to him by his father', and added that he had not inherited the 'high spirit and deep knowledge' displayed by his father 'in the important affairs of state or war'.[27] Others claimed that he was preoccupied by country pursuits such as hunting.[28] Ultimately, this behaviour is thought to have stemmed from royalist sympathies, and Richard is alleged to have been a Cavalier at heart, who mingled with royalist friends, toasted Charles I, and pleaded with his father to save the king's life.[29] In reality, there is scant evidence with which to substantiate such allegations, although Richard certainly flouted godly convention by sponsoring a horse-racing cup in Hampshire, and interceded on behalf of the family of the royalist rebel, John Penruddock.[30] In fact, it is more likely that Richard's supposed royalism actually represented wishful thinking on the part of contemporaries who recognised differences between him and his father. There is probably some truth, in other words, in Gilbert Burnet's observation that, since Richard 'was innocent of all the ill his father had done', and since 'there was no prejudice lay against him . . . both the royalists and the Presbyterians fancied he favoured them'.[31]

In seeking to establish the justice of such claims, it is vital to examine contemporary evidence more reliable than the comments of ill-informed or hostile witnesses. This certainly indicates that Richard was not a particularly frequent visitor to the capital, and the Whitehall lodgings assigned to him as a member of the protectoral household were apparently vacant for long enough to be reassigned to the admiralty commissioners sometime in 1654.[32] Richard's letters, meanwhile, seem to indicate a parochial and non-political outlook. In November 1655, therefore, he wrote of his 'private condition' in a letter to his brother, Henry, adding that 'writing to my unskillful hand is very irksome'.[33] Indeed, Richard often remarked on his lack of political knowledge, as in March 1658, when he claimed to be 'more in the dark than others' on matters of politics.[34] Other letters contain nothing more exciting than family news and recommendations of individuals for preferment.[35] However, such professions of ignorance and lack of epistolary skill almost certainly represented conventional rhetorical modesty, and Richard probably excluded political comment from his correspondence on the grounds that there were 'so many miscarriages of letters', and since 'it is altogether unsafe for either of us to write anything but what the world may see'.[36] Indeed, certain letters actually indicate that he was developing a fairly sophisticated understanding of events around him, not least in terms of European politics.[37]

More importantly, Richard's life was far from lacking in public responsibilities. In fact, the death of his elder brother can be shown to have provoked not merely a concerted effort to arrange for him a prestigious marriage, but also a series of decisions that indicate a determination to alter his career trajectory. The first involved securing at least some degree of higher education, and in May 1647, Richard was admitted to Lincoln's Inn, with John Thurloe, the future secretary of state, as his manucaptor or surety.[38] That Richard was not subsequently called to the bar is not particularly unusual, and certainly does not justify Mark Noble's comment that he 'took no pains to gain a knowledge of the law'.[39] Of much greater significance, however, was Richard's subsequent introduction to wider political and military life. The curtailment of his legal education may have been related to his service as captain of Viscount Lisle's lifeguard in the spring of 1647, and his appointment as the captain of Sir Thomas Fairfax's lifeguard in the following autumn,[40] and equally fascinating is the possibility that Richard was elected as MP for Portsmouth in the days immediately before Pride's Purge (6 December 1648).[41]

Although Richard made no recorded impact upon proceedings either before or after Pride's Purge, he was clearly not out of political favour with the new regime, and indeed became an active servant of the republic. He was made a commissioner for draining the fens in May 1649, and named to a number of local commissions in the same year, including all of the Hampshire committees, on the latter of which he certainly served.[42] Furthermore, the council also nominated him to consider a number of local matters during the early 1650s, such as the preservation of New Forest timber, the securing of ministers for Hampshire parishes, and petitions regarding particular clergymen.[43] He also played a prominent role in the investigation of civic disputes within his county.[44] In September 1655, moreover, Richard issued a certificate on behalf of inhabitants from the parish of Worting in Hampshire, who sought a charitable collection in the aftermath of a devastating fire.[45]

The event that does most to undermine the conventional image of Richard during this period, however, occurred in the summer of 1654, when he was returned to the first protectoral parliament, as a knight of the shire for Hampshire. Although surviving evidence once again suggests that he did not play a particularly prominent part in proceedings—he is certainly not recorded as having made any speeches—he was nevertheless in attendance from the opening meetings, and was named to a raft of standing committees during the first few weeks. He was appointed, therefore, to the committee for privileges, the committees relating to Scottish and Irish affairs, and the committee to consider the state of the army and navy, as well as to committees relating to legal matters and state finances.[46] His local experience and personal interests probably explain his nomination to committees relating to fen drainage schemes and Cambridge University, and his familial relationship with the protector may have prompted his interest in the committee regarding the bill for taking away purveyance.[47] His most significant contribution to national affairs, however, came during debates on the constitutional settlement, when he sought to defend the Instrument of Government by acting as a teller alongside the councillor, Sir Anthony Ashley Cooper, against a successful motion that called for a return to electoral franchise to 40 shillings of freehold land, as it had been before December 1653.[48]

Richard Cromwell may have led a kind of life very different from that of his father, but great care needs to be used when describing it as 'private' or as taking place primarily 'in the country'. Whatever Oliver had once thought that such words might mean, he almost certainly envisaged that his son would become a godly local magistrate, and this Richard certainly did. But during the early 1650s, Oliver's totemic status within both military and civilian regimes probably ensured that his views changed somewhat, and evidence of Richard's earlier military career, his reliability as a local agent for the commonwealth regimes, and his election to parliament, indicates that he was now required to act like a member of the gentry elite, and on a national as well as a local stage. In this, Richard arguably played his part to perfection.

### III

If the late 1640s and early 1650s saw Richard gradually emerge from the ranks of the squirearchy, it is also apparent that things changed dramatically once again in the aftermath of the 1654 parliament. He immediately began to play a much more visible public role, indicating beyond doubt that Oliver wanted to introduce him to a wider world of public life, and once again this change in the protector's attitude towards his son represented a response to new political circumstances. Oliver appears to have been reacting, therefore, to the debate that took place in October 1654 over article 32 of the Instrument of Government, regarding the future form of the protectorate. Although MPs ultimately decided that future protectors should be elected, rather than hereditary, prominent Cromwellians clearly objected to such ideas, and constitutional logic suggested that in practice the identity of a new ruler was likely to be determined by the protector-in-council, rather than by the House of Commons.[49] It was now possible to envisage a situation in which Oliver would play a significant part in the nomination of his successor.

It is surely no coincidence that Richard began to play a much more important role in public affairs after the dissolution of the 1654 parliament, and in the wake of such debates. In part, this meant adopting a more significant position in Hampshire, and he became increasingly assiduous in fulfilling his duties as warden of the New Forest—a post to which he had been appointed in April 1654, and which was of particular importance because of the need to secure supplies of wood for the naval dockyard at Portsmouth.[50] Surviving correspondence in relation to such work not only serves to demonstrate the extent of Richard's involvement in local affairs, but also provides a rare and tantalising glimpse into his political views, which seem to have involved a natural conservatism combined with a willingness to accept that recent innovations could provide new precedents and new models for administrative behaviour. Richard explained that 'it is better to sail in a known way which conducts for safety and easiness (though old) than to find out new rocks and sands, which will hazard the destruction of all'. However, while he confessed that 'the irregular courses of the commissioners of the admiralty in the Long Parliament's time . . . are not to be precedents now', he nevertheless accepted that at least some of the 'actions in this last twenty years' did provide 'new precedents', which were 'more agreeable to the juncture of the times than former orders'.[51]

Richard's increasingly influential position within Hampshire was also reflected in the zealous support that he offered to the regime of the major-generals. When William Goffe arrived in Hampshire as its major-general in November 1655, he immediately held discussions with both Richard Cromwell and Richard Maijor, who advised him who to nominate to local commissions.[52] In May 1656 Goffe reported that Richard was 'very sensible of the wicked spirit of the magistrates' at Southampton, and that he considered it 'absolutely necessary that something be done against them'.[53] Richard's influence was also evident during the elections for the 1656 parliament, apparently motivated by a concern at the power and malign influence of his former friend, Richard Norton, who had supported the creation of the protectorate but had opposed the introduction of the military rule in the localities. Goffe certainly considered Richard to be one of the county's most important power-brokers, and sought to encourage him to settle his differences with Norton, in order that the two men might 'carry it without dispute'.[54] Goffe also indicated that Richard was 'pleased to take great pains on my behalf', helping to ensure his return as one of the MPs for Hampshire.[55] Somewhat panicked by the re-emergence of Levelleresque texts and activism in September 1656, Goffe once again stressed his reliance upon Richard's advice and assistance.[56]

But it was not merely in Hampshire that Richard's political experience and influence grew. Rather, in the aftermath of the 1654 parliament, he genuinely emerged as a political actor on the national stage. In March 1655, for example, Richard joined his brother, Henry, in deputising for the protector in inspecting the London militia,[57] and in the following months reports began to circulate regarding a high-level appointment. In May it was suggested that he would be made deputy in Scotland, and in the following month it was rumoured that he was to be made both lord high admiral and lieutenant of the Tower of London.[58] It is almost certainly no coincidence that such stories emerged at precisely the moment when the constitutional question of hereditary rule resurfaced, in the summer of 1655.[59] And even though such appointments were ultimately not made, Richard was subsequently made chairman of the new committee for trade (November 1655), and added to the committee charged with organising the collection for distressed Protestants in Piedmont (January 1656).[60]

Richard maintained his high public profile by securing election to parliament once again in 1656, opting to sit for Cambridge University (in succession to his brother, Henry, and clearly because of his relationship to the protector), even after topping the list of those returned as knights of the shire for Hampshire, the county where he had made the most noticeable political impact.[61] More significant than his constituency, however, was his activity; once again Richard's parliamentary career focussed on things other than speech-making.[62] Although the bulk of his appointments related to minor matters, local issues, and private legislation, he was named to the committee for privileges and the committee for Scottish affairs, and was also involved in business relating to law reform and the arrears of excise.[63] His experience as warden of the New Forest explains his nomination to committees relating to the preservation of timber, and to bodies appointed to discuss other minor matters relating to Hampshire affairs.[64] He also took an obvious interest in legislation regarding the security of the protector, the issue of his one tellership, and was an obvious choice for a committee to attend the protector regarding the passing of legislation.[65]

More surprising perhaps, given his subsequent reputation, was an evident interest in religious issues: he both helped draft the declaration concerning a public fast, and secured nomination to a committee regarding the bill for the better observation of the Sabbath.[66] Moreover, although he is not recorded as having contributed to debates regarding the case of the notorious Quaker, James Naylor, he was nevertheless reported to have been 'very clear in passing his judgment that Naylor deserves to be hanged'.[67] In so far as they can be discerned, Richard's religious sympathies seem to have lain with the Presbyterians. This would certainly explain his friendship with the Dorsetshire gentleman, John Fitzjames, and the comment made by the French ambassador in January 1657, in which he claimed that Oliver's sons attended Presbyterian churches, even if only in order to render the protector 'agreeable' to them.[68] It may also make sense of his clerical patronage both before and after he became protector, bestowed on a number of Presbyterian ministers, including James Mowbray (sometime fellow of St John's College, Cambridge, and visitor of the university in 1654), John Gipps (chaplain of Magdalen College, Oxford), Zachary Clifton, and Samuel Annesley (sometime chaplain to the earl of Warwick and preacher at St Paul's Cathedral).[69]

That Richard played a less prominent part in proceedings after November 1656 probably says little about either his status or his enthusiasm for parliamentary affairs. He was evidently considered to be one of the 'grandees' by this time, and his absence from the records probably reflects nothing more than the illness which he is known to have suffered during this period, as well as the injuries he sustained on the famous occasion when the staircase collapsed at the Banqueting House, as MPs gathered to hear the protector's speech on 27 January 1657.[70] Moreover, his absence from key Commons debates on the 'Humble Petition and Advice', which offered his father the crown, appears to have been the result of something other than lack of interest. In fact, his views on the issue seem fairly clear from a disparaging comment made in June 1657, regarding those

> whose design hath been for a long time laid to take root for the hindering [of] national advantages, [and] settlement, where it might occasion difficulty to their getting into the saddle, respecting their own ambitious

minds, and advantages before religion, peace, or what else may stand in their way.[71]

In reality, his withdrawal to the country during the kingship debates was the result of his more or less formal exclusion, no doubt on the grounds that he was rather too much of an interested party.[72] In a letter to his brother, written from Whitehall on 7 March, Richard explained: 'there is a bar to my pen in state affairs', adding that 'I know no news being by reasons of some debates in the House shut out for a wrangler'.[73] Moreover, Richard clearly remained busy on the committee of trade, as well as in liaising with the admiralty commissioners in relation to local matters.[74]

Once again, therefore, it is possible to argue that historians have been able to stress Richard's inactivity only by paying insufficient attention to the very real extent to which he became a figure of national standing, with clear areas of personal, political, and religious interest. That this should have been so, and that his career should have entered a new and distinct phase, was entirely natural; as son and heir to the lord protector, there was actually little chance that Richard's life would be unaffected by events in December 1653. What is most remarkable about this period, however, is not that historians have generally failed to appreciate the level of his activity in both national and local politics, but rather the fairly clear correlation between the growing willingness to make the protectorate hereditary, and the more or less conscious enhancement of his status.

## IV

Another of the contributions which Richard made to public life in 1657 was to help organise his father's second inauguration as protector (26 June),[75] and this should be considered particularly appropriate, given that Oliver's attitude towards him changed yet again in the light of his acceptance of the Humble Petition and Advice, albeit without the crown with which it had initially been offered. What had previously been a possibility was now a certainty: that Oliver would be able to 'appoint and declare' the person who would succeed him 'in the government of these nations' (article 1).

Once again, the impact of novel political circumstances upon Oliver's attitude to Richard, and thus upon Richard's public career, has been overlooked by historians, not least because of misleading comments by the likes of the Venetian ambassador. In November

1656, therefore, the ambassador suggested that Oliver was hostile to the idea of making the protectorate hereditary, because he recognised that neither of his sons would be capable of running the country after his death.[76] The ambassador subsequently described the protector's sorrow at not having a successor with sufficient spirit and ability, and at his sons' lack of political vigour, and claimed that Oliver acted 'from fear that the machine may go to ruin with such feeble supports as his two sons, with their slow and heavy wits'.[77] In reality, Richard was clearly recognised by contemporaries as being 'the first peer of the kingdom', even if 'no office or title be as yet bestowed upon him', and the fact that the protector's rejection of the crown was unconnected to concerns regarding the ability of his offspring appears clear from his behaviour after June 1657.[78]

Evidence from Henry Cromwell's correspondence indicates that from the spring of 1657 Richard was once again being considered for high office in Scotland. One newsletter from early March noted that he was to be appointed as general and commander in chief, with the present incumbent, George Monck, as his deputy, and it is likely that it was in expectation of such a change that councillors sympathetic to the protester faction in the Scottish kirk began lobbying Richard. The protesters, who had sought to distance themselves from royalist countrymen after the battle of Dunbar in 1650, and who considered Monck to be an ally, probably sensed that Richard's elevation would further weaken their position with respect to the English government, by promoting the interests of their opponents—the resolutioners—who had found favour with Lord Broghill, the president of the council in Scotland.[79] Writing about the possibility of such an appointment to John Thurloe, Henry Cromwell suggested that, 'if my brother thinks the command in Scotland a bettering of his condition in any sense, I think that motion ought to be pursued', adding that 'there may be much other good in it'.[80] That such plans did not come to fruition was probably a consequence of Richard's riding accident in August 1657, which at one stage was thought likely to result in permanent disability.[81] Indeed, the idea of nominating him to a command in Scotland remained on the political agenda in the months that followed. In January 1658, Richard succeeded to the command of William Goffe's regiment of horse, and in the following March stories once again circulated regarding his likely transfer north of the border, not least as part of plans to undermine Monck.[82]

Richard's riding accident also sheds valuable light upon contemporary perceptions of his status by the summer of 1657. The leading

Scottish protester, Sir Archibald Johnston of Wariston, for example, commented that news of the accident 'was remarked as [being] strangely trysted with his father's design of bringing him forth into the world', while Humphrey Robinson was keen to draw attention to the fact that the accident to 'Prince Richard' occurred in the New Forest, 'that fatal place to the sons of our princes'.[83] At least some people, in other words, thought of Richard as a future head of state, an impression that may only have been confirmed by his appointment— as Oliver's successor—as chancellor of Oxford University, on 20 July 1657.[84]

The chancellorship was more than merely a sinecure, and Richard's duties included supervision of discipline, presiding over elections, approving appointments and granting dispensations, as well as ceremonial duties such as the conferral of degrees and the opening of new buildings. Indeed, Richard had evidently developed a keen interest in educational affairs, not least having been named to a committee relating to the university in January 1657, and he brought both 'zeal' and 'seriousness' to the job, to the surprise of some commentators.[85] Within weeks of his appointment, therefore, he wrote to his brother in order to recommend Robert Whitehall of Merton College, and subsequently solicited Henry's help once again in order to secure the resignation from college fellowships of three men who were serving in the army in Ireland.[86] Richard also dealt personally with a number of petitions from disgruntled and ambitious scholars, but more significantly he also took an active role in some important developments within the university.[87] Not the least of these was helping to deal with factional tension between Independents such as John Owen (the vice-chancellor) and Thomas Goodwin, and Presbyterians such as John Conant, Jonathan Goddard and Richard's uncle, John Wilkins. This religious balance had been created deliberately by Oliver Cromwell, but had caused arguments between those who sought to implement Puritan reforms, such as the alteration of an academic dress-code which was thought to involve popish relics, and those who sought to retain the university's traditions. On these issues, Richard almost certainly sided with the Presbyterians around Wilkins, with whom he is known to have liaised closely in the early phase of his tenure.[88]

Perhaps the most intriguing possibility relating to Richard's role at Oxford is that he helped orchestrate the resignation of Owen as vice-chancellor in October 1657, and his replacement by Conant. Although there is insufficient evidence to demonstrate his decisive involvement, there is every reason to think that he would have been pleased by the outcome. Owen was increasingly critical of the Cromwellian regime, and the drift towards a monarchical constitution, and Richard had been involved in attempts to undermine his ability to implement radical reform of the university, as a member of the parliamentary committee which recommended that the visitation should be brought to an end.[89] Moreover, after Owen's departure, Richard also provided valuable backing for Conant, who sought 'a less ideologically stultifying atmosphere' within Oxford.[90] He helped to promote Conant's drive to protect the practice of civil law within the university, supported the subsequent attempt to block plans for a new university at Durham, and bolstered the position of those who sought to resist change to the process whereby colleges sold fellowships.[91]

Aside from this important and politically sensitive appointment, it is also possible to detect one final stage in Richard's political education after the adoption of the Humble Petition and Advice, which suggests that his father could arguably have done little more to prepare his eldest son for protectoral office. Under the terms of the revised constitution the protector was expected to nominate and summon a second parliamentary chamber, styled the 'Other House', as well as to nominate new councillors to serve life terms (articles 2, 5, 8). It was in accordance with these new discretionary powers that Oliver took the final steps to bring his son onto the highest political stage.

By late November 1657 it was being reported that Richard was living at St James's Palace, 'que les princes avoient coustume d'habiter' [in which princes have traditionally lived], and on 8 December 1657 he was appointed to the protectoral council.[92] After taking his seat on 31 December, Richard proved to be assiduous in its service, in terms not merely of attendance but also of committee appointments and reports, and Thomas Clarges described him as being 'very diligent', and 'much in the esteem of his highness'.[93] On 9 December, moreover, Richard headed the list of those who were to be made Cromwellian peers, and he duly attended every one of their meetings (20 January–4 February 1658).[94] Although he was naturally involved in matters relating to Oxford University during this period, Richard proved active on a much wider range of subjects over the following months, and the protector's ambassador in Paris, Sir William Lockhart, certainly expressed satisfaction at the interest which Richard took in the affairs of both army and council.[95]

Although Richard made a brief recuperative trip to the west country in June 1658, he quickly returned to Whitehall and the council, amid talk of another parliament, within which few could have doubted that he would have played a prominent part.[96] Indeed, as one of the key grandees within the regime, there may have been few who would have felt that he did not deserve the honour granted to him of providing the name for a new addition to the Cromwellian fleet.[97] Some commentators were even prepared to take seriously rumours that the protector had even greater plans for his son. In January 1658, therefore, Samuel Hartlib reported to John Pell that 'the city-statesmen here begin to talk as if my lord Richard ... is to be made king, and that very shortly, his father remaining still lord protector till the government be more and more settled'.[98] Likewise, the royalist, Sir Edward Nicholas, reported that 'Cromwell intends to make his son Richard king, and to be himself protector of both king and kingdom, and general of all forces of England both by sea and land'.[99] Fanciful though such stories may seem, they certainly indicate how far Richard had progressed in the previous decade, and they probably explain why Henry Cromwell already feared a backlash from within the army by the summer of 1658, and why he expressed the hope that Oliver would 'not let such as [John] Disbrowe affront my brother'.[100]

## V

Richard's accession to the protectoral throne on 3 September 1658 was obviously not met with universal approval. Anthony Wood recollected that those who read the official proclamation in Oxford were 'pelted by some junior scholars ... with turnip and carrot tops'.[101] One aspiring poet wrote mockingly that 'Old Oliver's gone, old Oliver's gone, O hone, O hone/ And has left his son Richard/ that pretty young prick-eared/ to govern these nations alone, alone'.[102] More significantly, there was clearly the kind of opposition which Henry Cromwell predicted, from men who 'say they have better deserved to govern there than any of Cromwell's sons', and who felt that 'Henry Cromwell is fitter for that charge than Richard'.[103] Sir Edward Nicholas found it hard to believe that such men would 'tamely submit to the command and government of a young man so far beneath the birth and quality of the one, and the experience and conduct of the other, especially since he is a man whose birth, breeding, and capacity is far unworthy so high a dignity'.[104] Nicholas also argued that Richard would be unable to control a new parliament, since he 'hath neither courage nor conduct to manage it as his father had, and yet you remember that [that] body was too hard for him'.[105]

Although some of these comments may be regarded as intelligent predictions, it would be misleading to suggest that such assessments of Richard's talents and upbringing were universally accepted. Contemporaries who were more supportive took a rather different line. Henry Lawrence, president of the council, wrote that Richard 'hath given such eminent testimony of his faithfulness and great affection to the cause of God, and the public interest of these nations', and Marchamont Nedham suggested that Richard 'in all respects appears the lively image of his father', and was 'the true inheritor of his Christian virtues'. Nedham described the new protector as 'a person who, by his piety, humanity, and other noble inclinations, hath obliged the hearts of all, and thereby filled this people with hopes of much felicity, through God's blessing upon his government'.[106] This chapter has attempted to suggest that, if such propaganda in support of Richard Cromwell needs to be taken with caution, then so too do the comments made by those politically disinclined to support him.

When Richard Cromwell's pre-protectoral career is assessed without the benefit of hindsight, and without retrospective reconstruction, it becomes apparent that many conventional arguments can no longer be upheld. Firstly, there is little meaningful evidence that he was incapable of holding high office, or that he was disinclined to play an active part in public life, particularly if this is taken to represent veiled opposition to the commonwealth, and indeed crypto-royalism. In fact, close consideration of the evidence suggests that Richard was modest, serious and hard-working, and a zealous and godly supporter of both the republic and the protectorate. It is probably true that his natural inclinations led him towards conservatism and moderation in both religious and political affairs, but there is little to suggest that he looked back nostalgically to the period before 1640, or that he rejected all of the innovations of the Long Parliament. He was probably a religious Presbyterian, and almost certainly favoured a more consistent policy of 'healing and settling' than his father ever achieved.

Secondly, it is misleading to suggest that Oliver, recognising Richard's weakness, shielded him from involvement in national affairs, and failed to prepare him for the role of head of state, or that he genuinely felt let down by him. This becomes clear once it is recognised that Richard's public career prior to 3 September 1658 needs to be divided into fairly distinct phases, each of which involved an appreciation of his age, his status within the family, and his family's status, as well as of political and constitutional circumstances. There is little point in examining Richard's early life in order to find evidence of his father's determination to groom him for high office, but it is possible to demonstrate a fairly precise correlation between changes in familial and political circumstances on the one hand, and the roles which Oliver expected his son to perform, and which Richard duly fulfilled, on the other. Oliver's attitude, and Richard's life, changed once he became the eldest son, just as it did when the protectoral constitution raised the possibility that the protector and his courtiers might be able to engineer the succession. A third phase began following the acceptance of the Humble Petition and Advice, when the powers of protector and council altered once again, and when the return to a bicameral constitutional model led to the creation of the Cromwellian peers. Each of these turning points in the history of the Cromwell family and of the commonwealth regimes was marked by a more or less dramatic change in Richard's responsibilities and public profile. Each in turn reveals a rather more subtle picture of Oliver's attitude towards his eldest son, in terms of his willingness to provide him with a political education, and indeed to groom him as a successor. And each in turn also reveals a rather more nuanced picture of Richard's attitudes and abilities in the period before greatness was finally thrust upon him.

### Notes

1. S. Bethel, *A True and Impartial Narrative* (1659), 3; J. H. Jesse, *Memoirs of the Court of England* (4 vols., 1840), iii. 160–1.
2. A. Wood, *The History and Antiquities of the University of Oxford*, ed. J. Gutch (2 vols., Oxford, 1792–6), ii. 694; *Bishop Burnet's History of His Own Time* (6 vols., 1833), i. 150–1.
3. G. Bate, *The History of the Rise and Progress of the Civil Wars in England* (1688), ii. 240–1.
4. Jesse, *Memoirs*, iii. 160; M. Guizot, *History of Richard Cromwell* (2 vols., 1856), i. 6.
5. Aberdeen University Library, MS 2538/1, fo. 34; BL, Stowe 185, fo. 95.
6. *ODNB*, 'Oliver Cromwell', 'Richard Cromwell', 'Henry Cromwell'.
7. For somewhat inadequate existing biographies of Richard, see R. W. Ramsey, *Richard Cromwell* (1935); J. A. Butler, *A Biography of Richard Cromwell* (Lampeter, 1994); J. R. Hammer, *Protector. A Life History of Richard Cromwell* (New York, 1997); E. M. Hause, *Tumbledown Dick: The Fall of the House of Cromwell* (New York, 1972). For recent

re-evaluations of his career, see B. Coward, *The Cromwellian Protectorate* (Manchester, 2002), 94–5; P. Little and D. L. Smith, *Parliaments and Politics during the Cromwellian Protectorate* (Cambridge, 2007), ch. 7; J. Peacey, 'The Protector Humbled: Richard Cromwell and the Constitution', in P. Little (ed.), *The Cromwellian Protectorate* (Woodbridge, 2007), 32–52.

8.  M. Noble, *Memoirs of the Protectoral House of Cromwell* (2 vols., Birmingham, 1787), i. 158; Abbott, i. 50–1, 85.

9.  Abbott, i. 107, 279.

10.  Abbott, i. 49, 194, 216, 279.

11.  Abbott, i. 585, 589–92, ii. 8–9, 12–13, 21, 27–30, 40–1, 46–7, 52, 56–7, 61–2; BL, Add. MS 24861, fos. 17v, 20, 22, 24, 26, 27.

12.  BL, Add. MS 24861, fo. 17.

13.  Abbott, ii. 12–13, 21, 52.

14.  Ibid., 95, 102–4, 159–60, 289, 330.

15.  Ibid., 95.

16.  Ibid., 102–3.

17.  Ibid., 289.

18.  Ibid., 103–4.

19.  Ibid., 425–6.

20.  Abbott, i. 585, 590–2, ii. 8, 236.

21.  *Mercurius Aulicus*, no. 29 (16–22 July 1643), 381; *Mercurius Aulicus*, no. 31 (30 July–5 August 1643), 416; *Mercurius Aulicus*, no. 33 (13–19 August 1643), 441; *Mercurius Aulicus*, no. 33 (13–19 August 1643), 444; J. Peacey, 'Richard Norton', draft biography, 1640–60 section, History of Parliament.

22.  P. Little, 'Oliver Cromwell's Sense of Humour', *Cromwelliana*, Series II, 4 (2007), 73–84.

23.  *TSP*, iii. 572.

24.  *The Winthrop Papers II* (Massachusetts Historical Society, 4th series, 7, 1865), 591.

25.  Abbott, ii. 102–3.

26.  Ibid., 236–7.

27.  *CSPV 1653–4*, 275.

28.  F. P. Verney (ed.), *Memoirs of the Verney Family* (4 vols., 1892), ii. 1–2.

29.  Noble, *Memoirs*, i. 159–60; Jesse, *Memoirs*, iii. 153–4.

30.  For the Winchester Cup see: Hampshire RO, W/E6/2, unfol.; for orders against horse races see: *Perfect Proceedings*, no. 283 (22 February–1 March 1655), 4490; for Penruddock see: Wiltshire RO, 332/265/16, 17, 39, 50.

31.  *Burnet's History*, i. 150.

32.  *CSPD 1654*, 401.

33.  BL, Lansdowne MS 821, fo. 38.

34.  BL, Lansdowne MS 823, fos. 21, 81.

35. BL, Lansdowne MS 821, fos. 64, 58, 109, 160; BL, Lansdowne MS 822, fos. 128, 130, 136, 144, 162; BL, Lansdowne MS 823, fos. 39, 85.
36. BL, Lansdowne MS 822, fo. 140.
37. Ibid., fos. 21, 81.
38. Lincoln's Inn Library, Admission Book 7, fo. 67; for the role of manu-captors, see J. Peacey, 'Led by the Hand: Manucaptors and Patronage at Lincoln's Inn in the Seventeenth Century', *Legal History*, 18 (1997), 26–44.
39. Noble, *Memoirs*, i. 159.
40. *CCAM*, 59; C. H. Firth and G. Davies, *The Regimental History of Cromwell's Army* (2 vols., Oxford, 1940), i. 48; *Cromwelliana* (1810), 36.
41. *CJ*, vi. 80; TNA, C 231/6, p. 128.
42. *A&O*, ii. 130–9; *CJ*, vi. 241a, 367b; BL, Add. MS 24861, fo. 54; TNA, SP 28/306, fos. 430–v.
43. *CSPD 1651*, 151; *CSPD 1653–4*, 217, 296.
44. *CSPD 1653–4*, 287; *CSPD 1655*, 222.
45. *CSPD 1655*, 349–50.
46. *Severall Proceedings*, no. 258 (31 August–7 September 1654), 4087; *CJ*, vii. 366, 368, 370, 371, 374, 387, 419.
47. *CJ*, vii. 380, 407.
48. Ibid., 391.
49. *Burton Diary*, i. li, liii–lviii; *TSP*, ii. 681–2, 684, 685.
50. *CSPD 1655–6*, 544, 548; *CSPD 1656–7*, 392, 521, 557; Bodl. MS Rawl. A.328, p. 33; TNA, ADM 2/1729, fos. 48v, 209; TNA, ADM 2/1730, fos. 51, 56; BL, RP 2573(i).
51. BL, RP 2573(i).
52. *TSP*, iv. 229, 238, 363.
53. *TSP*, iv. 764. See: *TSP*, iv. 582.
54. *TSP*, v. 215.
55. *TSP* , v. 329. See: *TSP*, v. 344; Bodl., MS Rawl. A.41, p. 696.
56. *TSP*, v. 396–7.
57. *Mercurius Politicus*, no. 249 (15–22 March 1655), 5211.
58. M. Roberts (ed.), *Swedish Diplomats at Cromwell's Court, 1655–1656* (Camden Society, 4th series, 36, 1988), 72, 80; *Clarke Papers*, iii. 43; *TSP*, iii. 538.
59. *Weekly Intelligencer*, no. 2 (21–28 August 1655), 6–7.
60. *Swedish Diplomats*, 200; *CSPD 1655–6*, 1, 100; *TSP*, iv. 177; *Mercurius Politicus*, no. 282 (1–8 November 1655), 5738–40. See: BL, Lansdowne MS 821, fos. 64, 72.
61. *TSP*, v. 329. See: *TSP*, v. 344; Bodl., MS Rawl. A.41, p. 696; *CJ*, vii. 432; M. B. Rex, *University Representation in England, 1604–1690* (1954), 88, 184, 187, 189–90.
62. *Burton Diary*, i. 84, 95.

63. *CJ*, vii. 424, 427, 428, 435, 438, 453, 456, 457, 459, 466, 473, 482; *Burton Diary*, i. 215.

64. *CJ*, vii. 429, 444, 457.

65. *CJ*, vii. 429, 437, 459.

66. *CJ*, vii. 426, 493.

67. *Burton Diary*, i. 126.

68. TNA, PRO 31/3/101, fo. 44; for Cromwell and Fitzjames, see Alnwick Castle, Northumberland MS 551, fos. 21v, 22, 27v, 40v, 47v, 65; ibid., MS 552, fo. 14.

69. BL, RP 6455(iii); BL, Add. MS 39531, fos. 39v, 47, 53, 60v, 69v, 70v; *Calamy Revised*, ed. A. G. Matthews (Oxford, 1934), 13–14, 123, 224, 359; *ODNB*.

70. BL, Add. MS 78678, fo. 171; *Burton Diary*, i. 284; *Clarke Papers*, iii. 87; *CSPD 1656–7*, 257; *CSPV 1657–9*, 14; *CCSP*, iii. 245; Bodl. MS Carte 228, fo. 86.

71. BL, Lansdowne MS 822, fo. 100.

72. His last recorded appearance in the Commons was on 18 February 1657: *CJ*, vii. 493.

73. BL, Lansdowne MS 821, fo. 324.

74. TNA, SP 46/118, fo. 22; *CSPD 1656–7*, 232, 308.

75. *Whitelocke Diary*, 471; *Burton Diary*, ii. 513, 515.

76. *CSPV 1655–6*, 284.

77. *CSPV 1655–6*, 312.

78. Aberdeen University Library, MS 2538/1, fo. 34.

79. Bodl. MS Tanner 52, fo. 197v; National Library of Scotland, Wodrow folio MS xxvi, fo. 146. For relations between Whitehall and the Scottish religious parties during this period, see F. Dow, *Cromwellian Scotland* (Edinburgh, 1979), 195–210; P. Little, *Lord Broghill and the Cromwellian Union with Ireland and Scotland* (Woodbridge, 2004), 91–123. I am extremely grateful to Kirsteen Mackenzie for helpful suggestions regarding the Scottish context of Richard's possible appointment.

80. *TSP*, vi. 482.

81. *CSPD 1657–8*, 84; *CSPV 1657–9*, 110.

82. *CSPV 1657–9*, 170, 179; *CCSP*, iv. 17, 32; *CSPD 1657–8*, 335, 338; *Clarke Papers*, iii. 132, 145; BL, Add. MS 78195, fo. 87v.

83. J. D. Ogilvie (ed.), *Diary of Sir Archibald Johnston of Wariston, iii, 1655–1660* (Edinburgh, 1940), 96–7; *CSPD 1657–8*, 87. For other comments regarding Richard's accident see: *TSP*, vi. 455, 493, 496, 516; *Clarke Papers*, iii. 118; *CSPD 1657–8*, 87; *CSPV 1657–9*, 106, 110; BL, Lansdowne MS 822, fos. 174, 176–6.

84. *CSPD 1657–8*, 48; *Publick Intelligencer*, no. 93 (27 July–3 August 1657), 1524–5; *Wariston Diary*, 96–7; *Mercurius Politicus*, no. 373 (23–30 July

1657), 7948. For a detailed account of Richard's installation, see ibid., 7957–6.

85. *CJ*, vii. 482; J. Butler, 'Richard Cromwell and Oxford, 1657–1660', *Cromwelliana* (1982–3), 21.

86. BL, Lansdowne MS 822, fo. 166; BL, Lansdowne MS 823, fo. 85. For a letter to Richard seeking his patronage at Oxford, see *CSPD 1657–8*, 559.

87. *CSPD 1657–8*, 86; Butler, 'Richard Cromwell and Oxford', 214–15.

88. B. Worden, 'Cromwellian Oxford', in N. Tyacke ed. *The History of the University of Oxford. Volume 4: Seventeenth Century Oxford* (Oxford, 1997), 737–8, 747; *CSPD 1657–8*, 215, 349; *Mercurius Politicus*, no. 373 (23–30 July 1657), 7955–6; *CSPD 1658–9*, 352; *Ludlow Memoirs*, ii. 61; J. Conant, *The Life of the Reverend and Venerable John Conant*, ed. W. Staunton (1823), 26.

89. Worden, 'Cromwellian Oxford', 746; Butler, 'Richard Cromwell and Oxford', 21; *Burton Diary*, ii. 63–4; *CJ*, vii. 482.

90. Worden, 'Cromwellian Oxford', 748; Butler, 'Richard Cromwell and Oxford', 21; Conant, *John Conant*, 24–5.

91. *CSPD 1657–8*, 272; Wood, *University of Oxford*, 687–94; Worden, 'Cromwellian Oxford', 747; *CSPD 1657–8*, 260, 278; *CJ*, vii. 476–7, 482; *Burton Diary*, i. 353–4; Conant, *John Conant*, 26–7.

92. TNA, PRO 31/3/101, fos. 437, 496; *CSPD 1657–8*, 206, 208, 210; *Clarke Papers*, iii. 129; *CSPV 1657–9*, 154–5.

93. *CSPD 1657–8*, 239; TNA, SP 25/78, 328, 331; *Clarke Papers*, v. 271.

94. BL, Sloane MS 3246; *TSP*, vi. 668; *Mercurius Politicus*, no. 395 (17–24 December 1657), 192; *HMC House of Lords*, new series, iv. 503–24; *CCSP*, iii. 400.

95. *TSP*, vi. 735; *CSPD 1657–8*, 236–7, 240, 262, 264, 268, 269, 286, 294, 296, 301–2, 324, 329–31, 334, 338, 344, 354, 356, 360, 362–3, 366, 370–1, 374, 376, 377, 379, 381; *CSPD 1658–9*, 3, 8, 22, 27, 30, 35, 39, 41, 45, 47. For Lockhart's comment, see: *CSPD 1657–8*, 266–7.

96. *Mercurius Politicus*, no. 423 (1–8 July 1658), 664–5; BL, Lansdowne MS 823, fos. 75, 81; *Mercurius Politicus*, no. 425 (15–22 July 1658), 686; *CSPD 1658–9*, 98, 99, 101, 102, 112, 113, 118–19, 120.

97. *Mercurius Politicus*, no. 417 (20–27 May 1658), sig. Yyy4v; *CSPV 1657–9*, 209.

98. R. Vaughan, *The Protectorate of Oliver Cromwell* (2 vols., 1838), ii. 436.

99. BL, Add. MS 78195, fo. 77.

100. *TSP*, vii. 56.

101. Wood, *University of Oxford*, 685.

102. *HMC Tenth Report IV*, p. 44.

103. BL, Add. MS 78195, fo. 139.
104. Ibid., 141.
105. Ibid., 145v.
106. Northamptonshire RO, IC 3367; *Publick Intelligencer*, no. 141 (30 August–6 September 1658), 795–6.

# Suggestions for Further Reading

This present book relies on, and responds to, the research and writing of many historians over the past 20 or more years. Most obviously, this work has appeared in biographical form. The best recent scholarly biographies are

> Barry Coward, *Oliver Cromwell* (Harlow, 1991)
> Peter Gaunt, *Oliver Cromwell* (Oxford, 1996)
> J. C. Davis, *Oliver Cromwell* (2001)

To these should be added John Morrill's article for the *Oxford Dictionary of National Biography*, now republished as a separate volume (Oxford, 2007).

Aspects of Cromwell's career are explored in more detail in three collected volumes:

John Morrill (ed.), *Oliver Cromwell and the English Revolution* (Harlow, 1990) has perhaps been the most influential, and it includes such important articles as John Morrill's 'The Making of Oliver Cromwell' and John Adamson's 'Oliver Cromwell and the Long Parliament'.

David L. Smith (ed.), *Cromwell and the Interregnum* (Oxford, 2003) is a collection of key essays, new and old, on various elements of Cromwell's life, including Blair Worden's influential article, 'Oliver Cromwell and the Sin of Achan'.

Patrick Little (ed.), *The Cromwellian Protectorate* (Woodbridge, 2007) presents important new research on Cromwell's later years as head of state, such as Paul Hunneyball's 'Cromwellian Style: The Architectural Trappings of the Protectorate Regime' and Blair Worden's 'Oliver Cromwell and the Council'.

Among the myriad of primary sources for the Cromwellian period, the starting point has to be Cromwell's own words. There are three classic editions:

S. C. Lomas (with elucidations by Thomas Carlyle), *Letters and Speeches of Oliver Cromwell* (3 vols, 1904), which, for all its eccentricities, remains the standard work.

W. C. Abbott, *Writings and Speeches of Oliver Cromwell* (4 vols, Cambridge, Mass., 1937–47) is a vast treasury of Cromwelliana.

A less daunting introduction is provided in Ivan Roots (ed.), *Speeches of Oliver Cromwell* (1989).

As this book has argued, any student of Cromwell must not be content with taking Oliver's own words as gospel. There are several volumes which discuss key documents, such as David L. Smith, *Oliver Cromwell: Politics and Religion in the English revolution, 1640–1658* (Cambridge, 1991), and, for the later period, Barry Coward, *The Cromwellian Protectorate* (Manchester, 2002). Other primary sources can easily be found on the Internet, with British History Online and the Cromwell Association websites (www.british-history.ac.uk and www.olivercromwell.org) as the obvious starting points.

Finally, for a taste of the 'material culture' associated with Cromwell and his family, the collections of the Cromwell Museum, Huntingdon, and the Tangye collection at the Museum of London, are unrivalled.

# Index

CPSIA information can be obtained
at www.ICGtesting.com
Printed in the USA